EXPLORING CITIES AND COUNTRIES OF THE WORLD

VOLUME 2

EXPLORING CITIES AND COUNTRIES OF THE WORLD

Additional books and e-books in this series can be found
on Nova's website under the Series tab.

EXPLORING CITIES AND COUNTRIES OF THE WORLD

VOLUME 2

KATHIE SUMMERS
EDITOR

nova
science publishers
New York

NOTICE TO THE READER

Library of Congress Cataloging-in-Publication Data

ISBN: 978-1-53618-514-0

Published by Nova Science Publishers, Inc. † New York

CONTENTS

Preface   **vii**

Chapter 1   Pakistan: Culture, History and People   **1**
                 Noor Ul Hadi, Assad Mustafa
                 and Shah Jehan Ahmed

Chapter 2   Urban Expansion Pattern and Land-Use Change
                 in a Medium-Sized City in Southern Europe:
                 A Sustainable Trajectory?   **29**
                 Lurdes Barrico, Helena Freitas and Paula Castro

Chapter 3   Street Food in Southern Italy:
                 From the Past to the Future   **55**
                 Maria Neve Ombra, Florinda Fratianni
                 and Filomena Nazzaro

Chapter 4   The Confectionery of Southern Italy:
                 From the Tradition to the Future   **79**
                 Maria Neve Ombra, Florinda Fratianni
                 and Filomena Nazzaro

Chapter 5   Gastronomic Public Policy:
                 Minas Gerais on the Scene   **105**
                 Lelis Maia Brito and Lidiane Nunes da Silveira

Chapter 6   Gastronomy as a Mark of a Tourist Destination   **123**
Lelis Maia Brito and Odemir Vieira Baeta

Chapter 7   Science Research in Singapore   **137**
Sameen Ahmed Khan

Chapter 8   Amphibian Species Discovery Pattern in India:
Past, Present and Future Trends   **187**
*K. P. Dinesh, C. Radhakrishnan
and Nirmal U. Kulkarni*

Index   **199**

PREFACE

Exploring Cities and Countries of the World. Volume 2 first provides a brief overview of Pakistani history, culture and economy, particularly providing insight on the cultural diversity of the country in terms of language, food, religion, arts, gender orientation and family structure. The authors analyse spatial and temporal urban expansion in the medium-sized city of Coimbra in Southern Europe during a ten year period. A better understanding of these dynamics may be a helpful contribution to the planning and organisation of local human activities for sustainable urban development. Street food in Italy, born many centuries ago, is discussed in the context of its cultural implications, along with advice for choosing healthier and more sustainable options. Some typical cakes such as the cassata and the pastiera are described, along with some considerations for bakery products of the future. The authors also analyze and discuss public policies of gastronomy actors focused on local cuisine, highlighting that policies of this nature consider that sustainable tourism can represent a considerable instrument of social strength and economic development. The relationship between gastronomy and destination brands is also examined, expanding these reflections by contextualizing gastronomy in Minas Gerais. Subsequently, the status of science research in Singapore is described, along with the crucial role this has played in making Singapore a model for sustainable development.

Chapter 1 - This chapter provides a brief overview of Pakistani history, culture and economy. Unlike the western perception, there is much more about Pakistan than political and economic instability and issues like terrorism. The country is situated in a region which has been the basis of human cultural development and historically rendered great human civilizations. This provides Pakistan with a dynamically rich history which has gone through an epic evolutionary process spanning over thousands of years. From Indus valley civilization to the current times, region has witnessed major political and social changes. The chapter provides comprehensive in sight in the cultural diversity of the country in terms of language, food, religion, arts, gender orientation, family structure etc. Further, it elaborates the nation brand as a place for economic forces with unlimited opportunities. As a nation Pakistani peopleare focusing on promoting education, export, the CPEC initiative, rejection of extremism, and drive for self-dependency to keep up with the challenges of 21st century. Despite all its problems the country has the potential of becoming the source point of major global economic operations in the upcoming times.

Chapter 2 - Urban spatial expansion will be the largest influence on development in the 21st century. The concentration of people in densely populated urban areas, especially in developing countries, will undoubtedly continue to increase as the majority of the world's population will live in urban settlements. This study analysed the spatial and temporal urban expansion in a medium-sized city in Southern Europe during a 10-year period (2001-2011). Coimbra was chosen as the study area due to its drastic changes in land-use patterns and its demographic dimension to the country scale. The results revealed an urban expansion of almost 42% from 2001 to 2011, mostly at the expense of croplands. There was an obvious enlargement of the city area more directed to the south of the city, reaching an average rate of 244.4 ha/year. This expansion, however, has not been followed by an equally rapid population growth. This physical pattern of low-density expansion in built-up areas has contributed to a less compact city evolution—clearly an indicator of urban sprawl. Urban sprawl contributed mostly to the loss of cropland areas and to a concerning increase of soil sealing, contributing to increasing the probability of natural and human hazards, such as floods, landslides, heat waves, and fires. Therefore, it is important to design and implement suitable strategies that are able to reduce these harmful impacts. A better understanding of the spatial and temporal dynamics of the city's expansion provided by this study may be a helpful contribution to better planning and spatial organisation of local human activities for future sustainable urban development of Coimbra.

Chapter 3 - Street food was born many centuries ago: already the ancient Romans sold it in their kiosks. Essential for travelers that at the time used to eat their meals standing up, quickly, stopping in places overlooking the street. Remains of these structures are in Rome and Pompeii (Southern Italy). In the city destroyed by the eruption of 79, more than 200 have been identified. Street food is an ancient invention still very current. Moreover, street food is one of the easiest ways to know the territory and a tasty, fast and cheap tradition. In a broad sense, street food has often been described as having some elements of the Mediterranean Diet. The famous chefs are well aware of the cultural value and the delicious flavors of these specialties and many of them have chosen to offer, in addition to haute cuisine, their own gourmet version of Southern Italy street food. As for future street food, the advice is to choose healthier and sustainable food options.

Chapter 4 - The confectionery tradition of Southern Italy is as wide as the abundant production of high-quality products: milk, cream, wheat, oil and butter, chocolate, must, fresh and dried fruit. Southern Italy is full of flavors and fragrances. From the sea to the mountains, from ancient Greece to the Middle Ages to contemporary society, many influences have led to the typical desserts we taste today. The cultural background is very rich with traditions that are different from each other, which eventually left their mark in the kitchen. Southern Italy really has a very huge tradition of typical sweets, ranging from poor cuisine to the finesse of Arab pastry. In this chapter, we describe some typical cakes, such as the cassata, the pastiera, etc. making some suggestive considerations on the products of the future. The bakery of the future will look more like an art gallery than a sweet shop: crossing its threshold will involve a multi-sensorial experience. Finally, it should increasingly consider the health aspect and environmental sustainability.

Chapter 5 - Considering the material and immaterial heritage as a reflection of the identity of a community, local gastronomy can be analyzed as an immaterial heritage that involves unique know-how, places and actions that represent local, historical and cultural aspects of a given population. Regarding the relevance of recognizing gastronomy as an intangible heritage, there is a trend towards the rescue of the traditional cook and the revaluation of cultural roots. In this sense, public policies aimed at cultural tourism aim to strengthen the cultural values of a society, since cultural heritage is the expression of people's identity, their territory, their history, tradition and civilization. In this sense, this article proposes to analyze and discuss public policies and actions of gastronomy actors focused on local cuisine. This article highlights that policies of this nature consider that sustainable tourism can represent a considerable instrument of social strength and economic development through employment and income generation, combined with cultural preservation and the increase in tourist and economic activities in general. Thus, for this theoretical essay, the case of Minas Gerais gastronomy, in Brazil, is used as an example, due to the Gastronomy Development Policy created by that State and other mechanisms proposed by public institutions, private institutions and civil society. This theoretical essay concludes that the strengthening of Minas Gerais gastronomy as a public policy enhances the expertise of the region and provides the State, in terms of participation and promotion of public actions, and all sectors involved, conditions to institutionalize gastronomy, not only family farming, but also chefs and, mainly, consumers, as a tourist destination in a specific and competitive market.

Chapter 6 - Destination Marks is a multi and interdisciplinary field of study for addressing various variations and interpretations in terms of place identity. One of these understandings is gastronomic tourism, also known as 'gastrotourism,' or culinary tourism, which has been strengthened based on the appreciation of local cultural and culinary aspects. If gastronomy was considered as a support element for tourism, at that moment, the movement is to consider it as the main attraction, an alternative to present the place, create its identity and attract visitors. With this, this area has become an important brand element capable of promoting tourism and local cultural values. This theoretical article relates destination mark approaches and gastronomy and discusses the role of gastronomy as a destination mark. This aims to discuss, theoretically, the relationship between gastronomy and destination brands. This discussion relates the destination mark elements to gastronomy, aiming to explore the main theoretical approaches in the literature on the subject. The article establishes a connection between the theoretical discussions about destination marks and gastronomy, points out the main researches in the area and expands these reflections by contextualizing Minas Gerais gastronomy in face of the propositions presented.

Chapter 7 - Singapore has made rapid progress in industrial and sustainable development. This would not have been possible without government patronage for science and research. The government agencies responsible for science funding and research policy have played a crucial role in the scientific growth of the nation. Singapore has several premier institutions dedicated to the emerging fields of science and technology. Along with these, Singapore has learned societies and science museums. Singapore has received international recognition in its scientific and environmental endeavours. This Chapter describes the status of science research in Singapore and the crucial role it has played in making Singapore a model for sustainable development.

Chapter 8 - India, a mega diverse country, hosts four biodiversity hotspots harbouring many endemic flora and fauna. Among the fauna, amphibians are the first poikilothermic vertebrates to colonize the land on an evolutionary scale and amphibians are considered as the ecological indicators to define the pristineness of the landscape. To date, India is known to have within its political boundaries, a distribution of 440 species of amphibians; of these, 372 are described exclusively from the country (4.6% of the global amphibian species). Although amphibian discoveries were initiated in the country as early as 1800's, 128 species were discovered during the colonial period. Between the independence and the new millennium, 51 species were discovered and in the new millennium 193 species were discovered. It is interesting to note that more than 50% of the species have been discovered in the past two decades alone. Here we have attempted to (i) show the chronological pattern of species discovery among the amphibians of India (ii) present accumulation curves to understand the saturation of species discoveries among the amphibians of the country. Analyzing the past and present data, the results suggest that there are more chances for discovery of many more new species from the country.

In: Exploring Cities and Countries …   ISBN: 978-1-53618-514-0
Editor: Kathie Summers   © 2020 Nova Science Publishers, Inc.

Chapter 1

PAKISTAN: CULTURE, HISTORY AND PEOPLE

Noor Ul Hadi[1,], Assad Mustafa[2]*
and Shah Jehan Ahmed[2]

[1]Department of Business Administration, Foundation University
Islamabad, Pakistan
[2]Department of Leadership and Management Studies,
National Defence University Islamabad, Pakistan

ABSTRACT

This chapter provides a brief overview of Pakistani history, culture and economy. Unlike the western perception, there is much more about Pakistan than political and economic instability and issues like terrorism. The country is situated in a region which has been the basis of human cultural development and historically rendered great human civilizations. This provides Pakistan with a dynamically rich history which has gone through an epic evolutionary process spanning over thousands of years. From Indus valley civilization to the current times, region has witnessed major political and social changes. The chapter provides comprehensive in sight in the cultural diversity of the country in terms of language, food,

---

[*] Corresponding Author's Email: n_hadi1@yahoo.com.

religion, arts, gender orientation, family structure etc. Further, it elaborates the nation brand as a place for economic forces with unlimited opportunities. As a nation Pakistani peopleare focusing on promoting education, export, the CPEC initiative, rejection of extremism, and drive for self-dependency to keep up with the challenges of 21st century. Despite all its problems the country has the potential of becoming the source point of major global economic operations in the upcoming times.

Keywords: history, culture, economy, nation brand, diversity

INTRODUCTION

A South-Asian nation with approximately over 212 million population, Pakistan is one of the most densely populated countries of the world. It is bordered by China, Afghanistan, India, and Iran and has a vast coastline spanning over 1000 kilometers along the Arabia Sea and the Gulf of Oman. Geographically the country is positioned on the globe offering extremely diverse landscape ranging from Eastern Thar Desert to the Northern mountainous region of Hindu Kush and Pamir. The vast landscape also brings in diversity in the cultural and lingual aspects of the country. A premature democratic governance system is implemented which supports this federal republic whereby the capital Islamabad falls in the federal territory which is linked with four autonomous provinces. The President of Pakistan is the head of state along with the Prime Minister as the head of government. Pakistan has a mixed economic system with a combination of free market activity and government intervention. At global political and economic platform the country is a member of international organizations such as United Nations (UN), Organization of Islamic Cooperation (OIC), The North Atlantic Treaty Organization (NATO), Asian Development Bank (ADB), World Trade Organization (WTO), International Monetary Fund (IMF), and South Asian Association for Regional Cooperation (SAARC), Commonwealth of independent States (CIS) etc (Central Intelligence Agency 2019).

EARLY HISTORY

Pakistan is situated in subcontinent region, which offers rich cultural and social diversity. This is evolved through a broad timeline spanning over thousend of years. These cultural and social patterns are deeply rooted in a rich history and civilization. The known social history dates back to 300,000 years, the known Stone-age hunter-gatherer society of the Potohar plateau and Soan Valley (North Punjab). Archeological research has also provided evidence of the more advanced Bronze Age culture dateing back to 4000 to 2000 BC later known as Indus Valley Civilization. Ruins of the city of Harappa are the signature proof of these early societies' experties in town planning and pictographic writing. External interventions by invadors like Alexander the Great (327 BCE), Mauryans dynasty (323 BCE), later replaced by Afghan Bactrian Greeks and Centeral Asian tribes led way to a social, cultural and economic evolution process in this part of the world. Most significatnt impact on the cultural development was placed by the Arab conquest and British colonoal era shaping the modern social, cultural and economic trends. History also provides a strong foundation to the religious diversity to the region with major influence of Buddhism (under the Mauryans), Hinduism, and Islam (under the Muslims) and so on (Bose, Sugata, and Ayesha Jalal, 2002).

Muslim Influence

Arab conquest of early sixth century was the the base of the Muslim influence in the region. By the arrival of Umayyad General Muhammad Bin Qasim the city of al- Mansurah currently Multan was established. Later Muslim sway become more dominent through invasion from Ghaznarid sultans in the 11th century. Finally, the Moghuls from Central Asia gained control of this part of the world and the Moghul Empire founded. Moghuls ruled the region from 1536 to 1857 (Avari, Burjor 2012). In this era the subcontinental region witnessed fast paced cultural, economic and political development. Resultantly a sophisticated imperial administrative system was established that led to a legacy of diverse culture and infrastructure. This era gave this region architectural identity in form of forts, walled cities, gardens, gateways, mosques, tombs etc. At the same time Muslims brought new dimensions in the cultural aspects including Arts and crafts, language and much more. The cross cultural integration gave way to the present cultural diversity of the region (Losty, Jeremiah P., Malini Roy, and British Library 2012).

European Influence

The Muslim global dominance downfall paved way for the European influence in the subcontinent from early 17th century. Europeans colonial nations like the French, Portuguese, Dutch, etc., initially entered the region as traders. Ultimately the British emerged as the leading force in the subcontinent through East India Company. The British intrusion in the local political affairs resulted in sheer resentment in the public leading to a large-scale revolt in 1857. By then the British indirect involvement in the governance was clearly evident and the revolt was successfully suppressed by the intruders. Consequently, the subcontinent came under the direct control of the British Crown. However, the over ambition of the British to further strengthening its rule by favoring the Hindu majority led to the emergence of a Muslim identity on national level. One of the Muslim leaders at time Sir Syed Ahmed Khan (1817–1889) gave an idea later known to be "The Two Nations theory" (Stepaniants, Marietta 1979). This became the founding stone of the All India Muslim League in 1907. The league was considered to be the only true representative of the Muslim sentiment on the political scene in the British India. Eventually an independent Muslim country emerged on the world map after the demise of the British rule from the subcontinent (Brantlinger, Patrick 2013).

Road to Independence

Early 20th Century (1900-1947) witnessed large scale changes due to major global events like world wars, industrial revolution, economic and political events globally. Technological developments and enhanced communication channels brought the nations ever closer to each other. Increased mutual cooperation among nations led to the economic activities and encouraged new political and social movements to prosper worldwide. Subcontinent was also got directly influenced by the changing global trends which subsequently led to a political Independence movement from the British rule. As the movement progressed it became obvious that the interests of the Muslims and Hindus of the subcontinent were far apart. This ideological gap among the two communities paved way for a strong support for the idea of a separate homeland for Muslims of British India. Between 1920 and 1930, the drive for the separate homeland gained popularity among the Indian Muslims. The movement was directed by the great poet and leader Allama Iqbal and Jinnah - Quaid-E-Azam "the great leader" (Hayat, Sikandar 2015).

Pakistan's Inception

At the dawn of 14th of August 1947 the one and only state was created on the basis of Islamic ideology and was named as Pakistan. Muhammad Ali Jinnah took oath as its first Governor General. The newly formed Muslim state consisted of West and East Pakistan, both separated by a vast Indian territory. After the expulsion of the British and the division of the Indian subcontinent, war broke out between the newly formed Pakistan and India on the Kashmir row. Other social change in the region was the mass migration of Muslims, Hindus and Sikhs communities living in the area. Masses moved for resettlement within the newly formed borders for better life and new opportunities. Resultantly large scale ethnic and religious violence broke out which caused large scale financial and human life loss. The independence from the British and division brought about dramatic impact on the regional religious and ethnic dynamics. Post partition Pakistan predominantly became Muslim society due to the addition of resettled Indian Muslims (Bates, Dr Crispin 2018).

Pakistan after Jinnah

By most western forces and especially India the survival of Pakistan as newly formed country was a long shot. The survival of the newly formed state was seemed inevitable due to the sudden demise of the founder of Pakistan Late Muhammad Ali Jinnah (Quaid-E-Azam) in 1948. Sudden political uncertainty and lack of resources posed immense burden on the governance structure. Power struggle started among the existing feudal political setup due to the absence of a sound political infrastructure. This resulted in large scale political uncertainty and governance related administrative issues. By 1951, Liaquat Ali Khan- the first prime minister of Pakistan was brutally assassinated while addressing a mass gathering at Liaqat Bagh in the city of Rawalpindi. In 1956, Pakistan became federal republic whereby the capital city Karachi was the central point for government operations. Pakistan has been under military rule for extended durations due to the premature democratic and political culture since its inception (Munir, Mohammad 1981).

First Martial Law (1958-1969)

Field Marshal Ayub Khan declared the first martial law and abolished all political parties in 1958. In 1960 through a guided "basic democracy" Ayub Khan became the first president of Pakistan. During his time in power Pakistan's economy flourished through major infrastructural and industrial developmental projects. Mega projects in energy sector, roads, railway communications etc., were successfully completed during this period. During his time in power the capital city of the country was moved from Karachi to newly planned and developed city of Islamabad is considered to be Ayub's biggest achievement. The country was plunged into war with neighboring India in 1965. Ayub's reign was over due to allegations of failure of 1965 Indo-Pak war, nepotism and corruption (Haider, Murtaza 2016). The Awami League of Sheikh Mujibur Rahman form East-Pakistan also showed sheer resentment to Ayub's regime as the Bengali public felt left out of the mainstream governance affairs and lack of representation. The situation turned into a political crisis and Ayub Khan resigned from office in 1969. General Yahiya Khan took over the government affairs (Haider, Murtaza 2016).

First Democratic Electoral Process and 1971 Indo Pak War

Yahiya's regime administered the first national level general elections in December 1970. Sheikh Mujib Ur Rehman's party, the Awami League gained majority and were given electoral mandate based on a demand of more autonomy for East Pakistan. In spite of Mujib's victory, the Awami League was disallowed by the existing setup from contesting for the Prime Minister office and forming government. Instead, newly formed Pakistan People's Party (PPP) led by Zulfikar Ali Bhutto of West Pakistan was favored for the government establishment. This was a biased and racially motivated decision which resulted in sheer resentment within the public in East Pakistan. Mujib and his party issued manifesto for a new constitution and began a movement for independence. The situation got worsens and the movement laid the foundation for the creation of the Bangladesh. This step of Mujeeb followed by the deteriorating law and order situation forced the military intervention by the Pakistani Government in East Pakistan. As a result, in 1971, civil war broke out in East Pakistan. Arch rivals India took this as an opportunity and provided military support to the East Pakistan rebellion. A sheer pressure was created on the Pakistani forces through indirect intervention (By training and supporting the Bengali muktibahni force) in the initial phase of the struggle for independence. Later the Indian military directly intervened which led to the Pakistan forces withdraw from the East Pakistan. In 1972 Bangladesh emerged as an independent country on the global face. Pakistan in 1972 voluntarily gave up its commonwealth status but rejoined in 1989 (Sisson, Richard, and Leo E. Rose 1992).

Post Division Pakistan

After the separation of Dhaka also known as "Sakoot-E-Dhaka" West Pakistan (Now Pakistan) went through large scale constitutional revamp. Mr. Zulfiqar Bhutto became the Prime Minister under the new constitution introduced in 1973. The regime brought about drastic agrarian reforms and promoted nationalization of major industries and banking/financial sector. This led to an urban unrest and in July 1977, due to political unrest the Army chief Late General Zia ul-Haq ordered a military coup. Zia took power by declaring martial law. Bhutto got arrested and got convicted and sentenced to death in April 1977for the charges of conspiring to murder a political opponent through a controversial trial (Quddus, Syed Abdul 1994). General Zia ul-Haq promised general elections within ninety days but extended his rule till his death (17th August 1988) as the sixth President of Pakistan. Zia's regime embarked on a promotion of conservative Islamization and provided strong support to the Afghan struggle against the soviet invasion. In 1985 the Martial law and the ban on political parties and political process was lifted with the return of Benazir Buhtto (Zulfiqar Ali Bhutto's daughter) from exile. Ms. Bhutto popularity increased as the leader of Pakistan People's Party (PPP) known to be the legacy late Zulfiqar Ali Bhutto (Zahid, Masood Akhtar 2011).

The 90's Era 2

After Zia's regime Pakistan's first electoral process was initiated after a decade. The results of general elections shifted the power to PPP who formed a coalition government with the Mohajir Qaumi Movement later changed to Mutatahidda Qaumi Movement (MQM) in November 1988. The alliance was brief and by August 1990, alleged corruption allegations resulted in the demise of Benazir's rule through the executive order of President Ghulam Ishaque Khan. A caretaker leader and setup was installed for organizing the general election in late1990. In this election process Islami Jamhoori Ittehad (IJI) led by Nawaz Sharif became victorious. By October 1990 the rule-making process concluded and Nawaz Sharif took oath as the prime minister of Pakistan. Mr. Sharif pushed for economic reforms and privatization of national institutions and implemented Sharia (Islamic) law. The dawn of 1993 brought bad luck for the political process of the country. President and Prime Minister were forced to resign by the military's indirect intervention. This made way for the fresh elections and Ms. Bhutto came to power with a small majority for a second term in office. The week democratic culture resulted in political unrest and subsequently in late 1996; President Sardar Farooq Khan Leghari used the eighth constitutional amendment and dissolved the National Assembly. Again the alleged corruption charges, financial incompetence, and human rights violations were declared to be the core reason for the collapse of this democratic government. Yet again in February 1997 Pakistani public went to polls resulting in a landslide victory of Pakistan Muslim League (Nawaz) – previously the main component of the Islami Jamhoori Ittehad (IJI) for a second term in power. In these general elections Benazir's PPP managed to only retain 18 seats in the National assembly. By now the political forces joined hands and PML (N) and PPP moved a motion to repeal the eighth amendment in the National Assembly. This was to abolish the President's authority to dissolve the political government. Further, the authority of the appointment of the top judiciary (Supreme Court) and military chiefs was transferred to the Prime Minister's office, previously held by the president. In 1998 tensions between India and Pakistan intensified and prime minister ordered the nuclear blasts in Chagi Mountains of Baluchistan province. This action led to severe economic sanctions by the international community. The uncertain situation worsen with the Kargil war between India and Pakistan. India cashed on the situation by exerting great pressure on the Pakistani political setup through the international community (Noman, Omar 1990).

History Repeated Itself - The Third Martial Law

In October 1999, protected by the new constitutional amendment, Prime Minister Nawaz Sharif practiced his authority and ordered the removal of Army Chief General Pervez Musharraf. Mr. Sharif also refused the permission to land for the commercial aircraft boarding the Army Chief who was returning from an official visit to Sri Lanka. These orders were disregarded by the army, who immediately seized power and declared the third Martial Law. The government- National Assembly was dissolved immediately and the constitution was suspended. Mr. Sharif was detained, charged and convicted of conspiring against the state (Armed forces) and later was exiled to Saudi Arabia under the NRO arrangement. General Parvez Musharraf declared the coup as necessity of time for restoring economy and deteriorating political situation. He was generally conceived as liberal individual who promised the transition of power to a civilian setup after the normalization of political environment of the country. Under Musharraf's administration the National Security Council was formed consisting civilian and military appointees for managing Pakistan's governance for an interim period. In 2001 General Musharraf assumed the presidency and started a dialogue process with neighboring India over the Kashmir dispute. September 11 attacks on world trade center and United States invasion of Afghanistan led to formation of strong ties between the President Bush's administration and the Musharraf regime. The core focus was to end Islamic extremism in Pak- Afghan border region. Musharraf time in power consists of many assassination attempts, constitutional amendments, and agitation with judiciary. Most important highlight of his rule is the assassination of Pakistan People Party Chairperson Benazir Bhutto's in 2007. This led to the collapse of his government. Right after the end of Musharraf's rule general elections were held in 2008. The elections produced a coalition between PML (N) and PPP the two major political forces of Pakistan. After the elections, Musharraf was impeached for severe constitutional violations. Faced with the imminent legal charges, on 18th August 2008 Musharraf resigned from office (Riffat, Fatima 2014).

Road to Democracy – A New Beginning

After the departure of General Parvez Musharraf, first time in history Pakistan has successfully seen two democratic governments complete their tenure. The road to democracy may have brought many hardships, political and economic problems; yet this is a landmark achievement for a resilient nation of 220 million. The PPP Government led the country from 2008-2013 followed by the PML (N) government completing its term from 2013-2018. Despite all the political instability the two democratic terms are the pillars of a much needed stable and sustainable democratic culture. The past decade has brought many positives for the Pakistani Nation. The war on terror and the drive for the eradication of terrorism became stronger than ever. Economic activities such as CPEC, energy projects etc., started and are going strong. The political process itself generated a third political force Pakistan Tehrek-E-Insaaf headed by ex-national cricketer Mr. Imran Khan. Pakistan Tehrek-E-Insaaf won the general elections of 2018 are currently in power with Imran Khan as the Prime Minister. The current government won the elections on popular mandate based on a drive against corruption and improvement in education, health and economic sectors. After all the upheavals of time Pakistan has emerged as a strong, peaceful and united nation thriving to develop and prosper (Waqas, Muhammad 2017). An example to this is the ongoing Kashmir dispute between Pakistan and its neighbor India which has caused prolonged tensions among the neighbours. Recently, Indian air force violated the Pakistani air space and as a defensive measure Pakistani air force shot down two Indian jets. During the ordeal Pakistani government consistently reasserted their stance for peace with showing utter restraint to neutralize the dyre situation. This certainly shows that Pakistan is a responsible and peace-loving democratic nation and its armed forces are fully capable to counter any hostility from its enemies.

CULTURE

The region once home to great Indus Valley civilization dating back to bronze age has seen many cultural developments. Over the historical timeline the area was invaded by Parthians, Kushans, White Huns, Greeks, Persians Arabs, Turks and the British. All these factions played a pivotal role in cultural development of the region. Pakistan has a diverse cultural identity spanning over the centuries. Most prominent cultural forces that influenced and shaped the modern culture of the country are the Muslims and the British. The British infiltrated the indo-Pak Subcontinent as traders through East India Company back in the 18th century. During of imperialism the area witnessed sheer violence and political upheaval in form of Indian uprising against the British oppressors. Consequently, demand for independence and creation of a separate homeland for Muslims of the subcontinent got popular among the masses. Upon the departure of the British, the subcontinent was divided into two parts and a new Muslim state as Pakistan came into being in 1947. For this people of the region bared huge sacrifices through bloodshed and largescale human migration.

Pakistan's culture is very diverse due to a rich history, geography and ethnicity. The national culture is heavily influenced by Indian, Persian, Afghan, Central Asian, South Asian and Western Asian cultures. It is based on somatic features, historical ancestries, customs, clothing, food and music. Approximately the Pakistani society comprises of fifteen ethnic groups classified as Punjabis, Sindhis, Baloch, Pashtuns, Kashmiris, Baltis and many more. The origins of these ethnic elements start from the ancient Indus Valley Civilization to Africa and so on. In spite of the ancient ethnic elements, Islam is the core element that has shaped the culture of Pakistan since its arrival back in 700 AD. Even hardline cast system is absent, but Pakistani society is still divided into segments like Shi'as, Balochis and Pashtuns who are likely to face poverty in contrast to the Sunnis, Punjabis etc. In interior Sindh and Southern parts of Punjab a strong Feudal system is still present. This leads to social injustice and unequal distribution of wealth which also influence the culture. Various aspects related to the Pakistani culture are discussed hereunder:

Languages

The region holds linguistic diversity and a wide range of languages are spoken in Pakistan. Starting with Urdu being the national language of Pakistan, it is developed over the centuries through the cultural integration of the sub-cultures of this region. It is heavily influenced by Sunskirter, Persian, and Arabic. Even though it is articulated like Hindi but is transcribed in a comprehensive Arabic alphabetic format instead of Devanagari. Predominantly the Urdu language is based on the basic elements of Arabic and Persian and not Hindi. Modern times have included English in the main framework of semantics. It is the national language of Pakistan but English is the lingua franca or the bridge language used for most official correspondence by the government institutions and business communities.

At regional level, there are an estimated 73-76 different languages and additional dialects spoken by the population. All this is with one common factor of its origins based on Indo-Iranian language. Officially, at local level there are local languages spoken across Pakistan that groups in certain regions don't speak. Popular languages include Punjabi, Sindhi, Balochi and Pashtu. Other regional languages include Siraiki, Hindko, Brahui, Burushaski, Balti, Khowar and many more. These have been modified over the time due to historic and modern cultural developments in aspects such as literature, folk, academia and religious and spiritual scripts (Gutenberg).

Religious Practices, Cultural Values, Belief System and Festivals

Pakistani society mainly comprises of Muslims including Sunni and Shia sects. This makes Islam as the major religion. Muslim population makes 97 percent further divided into 77 percent Sunnis and 20 percent Shia inhabitants. Remaining 3 percent of inhabitants follow the belief system of Christianity, Hinduism, Sikhism and Ahmadis etc. Islam governs the personal, political, economic and legal aspects of the lives of most Pakistani people. Religious rituals like praying five times on daily basis, and like other

Muslim countries Friday is the Muslim holy day and private sector businesses are mostly closed but Saturdays and Sunday are the official weekend.

Islamic religious activities like fasting during the holy month of Ramadan, Ashura in the Islamic month of Muharram to commemorate the sacrifice of the Prophets Grandson, Eid Ul Fitar, Eid Ul Adha are few notable Islamic festivals celebrated by the masses. Strong religious orientation has created tendency in public to donate for charity on regular basis and its inhabitants heavily give to charities for social and religious cause. Other secular national holidays include Pakistan Day, Labor Day, Independence Day, Defence Day, Muhammad Ali Jinnah Memorial Day, birthday of Muhammad Ali Jinnah and Kashmir Day.

Traditional and religious festivals, arts and crafts show a strong linkage to the religious aspect of "Sufism" which over the centuries has evolved into striking poetry and music. Conventional Islam and Islamic spirituality are both prevailing in the society. This presence also becomes the reason behind sectarian agitation due to the stance of minority of hardline religious clerics of Wahhabi sect. The idea of Sufism is strictly rejected by this religious segment. The tradition of mysticism or Sufism supplements greater magnificence of the existing culture. It adheres to selflessness and utter devotion through the means of dance, poetry, whirling, meditation etc. It gives the Pakistani culture the message of love and peace. There are number of cultural activities associated with the aspect of Sufism including the yearly memorial festivals/Urs of different Sufis and saints. Most notable festivals include yearly Urs of Hazrat Laal Shahbaz Qalandar and that of Hazrat Data Ganj Shaker in Lahore and many more.

To mark the start of spring season, Basant/Kite flying festival is undoubtedly the most famous festival in Pakistan. More recently due to health and safety issues, government has imposed a nationwide ban on the festival. Having said that government sponsored festival is celebrated in confined spaces at occasions. Other cultural festivals include the annual 'Utchal' festival in mid-July to celebrate the Wheat and Barley harvest. In late November "The National Horse and Cattle Show" is held to celebrate the culture of Punjab. The cultural show involves activities like folk singing, dancing, games, and cattle racing and dancing etc., are major attractions for children and adults (https://www.everyculture.com/No-Sa/Pakistan.html Accessed February 16, 2019).

Gender Segregation and Family Structure

Generally, People of Pakistan are friendly but due to overall strong conservative cultural inclination there is religious and tribal influence based gender segregation. This is strongly evident and is deeply rooted in the rural society. Comparatively, in the urban areas intensity is less due to male female integration in academic and professional sectors because of modernization. Women and men are getting education in universities as well as serving private or public-sector firms as coworkers. The male female interaction is mainly confined to the professional and formal boundaries. A conservative national culture unlike west e.g., couples usually do not kiss or hug each other in public as this isn't regarded as a good gesture in Pakistan as it is an Islamic state (Blog 2014).

Traditionally gender roles in Pakistan are clearly defined where women are expected to be home maker and men work. Although women can practice their right to work in any career or even can become an entrepreneur. Nursing and teaching are mainly associated with the female gender. Females are also actively participating in political activities. Notable figure of Benazir Bhutto as the prime minister in 1988 is the prime example. More recently high-profile ministries and government office positions are held by women. Females can practice their right to receive an education and vote as a citizen of the country. New drive for awareness about the gender-based crimes has educated the masses about the women rights. A strict legislation is implemented to eradicate gender discrimination and crime against women. This is aimed at providing women and children security and rights.

The extended family system constitutes the social structure and provides a distinct identity to each family member. A typical family structure comprises of nuclear family, direct relatives, detached relatives etc. Allegiance to the family is the priority over other social relationships and this is even evident in business dealings. Nepotism is dominant factor in professional and personal lives and is thought to be a constructive thing. For example, it is a great source of hiring trustworthy employees. The family structure provides protection to female member against outside threats and influences.

It is considered disrespectful to admire someone's wife or female relatives based on beauty or physical features. Unlike west, Pakistani culture encourages large families. This is to constitute a society based on collectivism shown in robust joint family system. Children are the responsibility of parents for their physical and financial growth throughout their lives. Social rules also stress on looking after the elderly and family includes grandparents, parents, and Uncles aunties and so on. A family unit form strong support system for its members with family. Family structure is heavily influenced by the religion, cultural norms and societal values. Mother is the core of a family system and is the initial source of care, training etc., for the younger generations. The extended family is the second tier for child's social development. Religious and social norms are programed in the young minds from an early age (Cultural Atlas. 2019).

Music, Arts, Crafts and Literature

Pakistani musicians have been exposed to several elegiac forms, styles and literature. Pakistanis love to listen and make music in different genres like Qawwali and Ghazal etc. Pakistani music shows such as Coke studio has won the hearts of millions of international and local music fans. This region has also produced number of legendary singers, poets, writers etc., such as Ustaad Nusrat Fateh Ali Khan, Faiz Ahmed Faiz, and Bano Qudsia etc. Modern musicians have adopted modern styles of playing music and developed fusions in Urdu language of rock, funk, pop, jazz and blues.

Excellent craftsmanship like the world-famous Truck art is one of its kinds. This has been passed from generations to each other which include a wide range of styles, materials and aesthetics. Arabic calligraphy the most prominent arts skill is evident on infrastructure, historical sites and art galleries. Sadqain is a prominent figure in this art. Other crats include skills such as wall hangings, copper work, paintings and carved wood. World renowned blue ceramic work (pottery) is mainly found in Sindh and Multan. Other crafts may include Naqashi, tile work, copper pieces, ornaments, decoration pieces, Glass bangles and Muchmore (Cultural Atlas. 2019).

Food

Pakistani cuisine is diverse and varies greatly depending on geographical area. Halal meat is used as the animal is slaughtered according to the Islamic rituals and the cuisine does not include Pork or Alcohol. Pakistani cuisine includes breakfast, lunch and evening meal which is shared among the family. Few foods items include parathas, lassi, chickpea curry, halwa puri, samosas, biryani, pulao, korma, etc. and wide range of aromatic spices provide it with a unique taste and aroma. Different types of pulses and vegetables are an essential part of the Pakistani cuisine. Just like the lingual diversity, the local food is cooked in different ways aligned with local preferences. With modernization a growing trend of international cuisine and fast food is getting popular among the urban population. Outlets like McDonalds, KFC, Pizza Hut etc., can be seen in all major cities. Pakistan is also the third largest importer of tea in addition to the local harvest. The society is generally considered to be obsessed with tea/chai which is the popular social brew. It is prepared as per individual preference with a variety of flavors on offering to the public. Tea time is regarded so important in the country that people go to five-star restaurants to enjoy it. Dating back to the colonial times tea became an integral part of Pakistani culture (World travel Guide 2019).

Acceptance of Outsiders and Social Attitudes

Society is generally welcoming towards foreigners. Pakistani people are very hospitable towards the visitors. People always welcome domestic and international guests, tourists and visitors with a warm heart. According to statistics Pakistani people are one of the most hospitable, upfront and happy people on the planet. It doesn't matter whether the individual is from rich or poor background, generosity is to be witnessed among all segments of society. Public is always ready for helping foreign visitors in all possible ways as per their individual capacity. The core reason behind the action of giving respect and love to guests is strong cultural and religious identity. This belief system direct Pakistani's behavior by teaching them to show love and respect to guests. Guests are considered as a gift from God and are treated in the best possible way. Pakistanis people who are expressive, colorful and full of emotions. They express their feelings with excitement to show emotions like love, affection and respect for others. People love to celebrate regardless of the occasion, and are considered as a foodie nation. They love sharing presents and organizing parties and share their joys and sorrows with other community members. Large family and friend's gatherings are a common practice among Pakistanis (Cultural Atlas. 2019).

Sports

Hockey is the National sport of Pakistan and over the years country has produced great hockey players. Pakistani hockey team has won many international and regional titles over the past seventy years. Most popular sport is cricket as it is played and watched by the all age groups. Pakistan national cricket team has won the titles such as world champions, ICC champions' trophy and Asia cup and many other. Sports like squash, volley ball, wrestling and badminton etc. also widely played and appreciated. Polo and golf is also played by Pakistan and is most popular among the elites of the country. Pakistan has one of the highest polo grounds in the world. Pakistani society promotes and appreciates sports at all social level. At local and regional levels there are many sport activities like Kabaddi, Gulli danda, etc. are commonly found in the rural Pakistan. This region of the world also holds eight of the world highest mountain peaks. This has introduced new trends in extreme sports like mountain climbing, skiing, rock climbing, para gliding etc. Foreign athletes and adventure lovers find Pakistan a great destination for their extreme sport endeavors (Cultural Atlas. 2019).

Weddings

Weddings events are normally large scale as the preparations start months ahead of the occasion date. Commonly, the celebrations last about three to six days including different events as per local traditions. Celebrations start with the Henna application with musical night and customary sacraments to bless the couple by the family and friends. Later there are diner/lunch parties for two days are thrown by bride and groom's family. Wedding celebrations are symbol of wealth and social status. Different aspects of local traditions can be seen in the event. This occasion is a combination of various colors, embroidered fabrics of silk and chiffon, tasty food, decorated halls, stages, dance and lots of music (Village, Spice 2015).

Pakistan is a developing nation which has suffered from issues like high poverty rate, illiteracy, and political instability, mismanagement of resources, incompetent governance and terrorism in last seventy years. Cultural diversity and deep rooted social history has helped this nation to face and overcome the negative consequences of the mentioned setbacks. Pakistani people are highly motivated and multi-talented individuals and the nation has emerged as more hopeful and united against the evils of the social and economic constraints. Culture is playing a vital role in social development of the masses. Ordinary Pakistanis are hardworking and are resilient to any pressures of the 21st century.

ECONOMY

As per the report by the World Bank, Pakistan's economic growth improved from 5.4 percent in 2017 to 5.8 percent in 2018. This increase is thought to be due to the introduction of major infrastructure projects and low interest rates. According to the ministry of finance the running fiscal year of 2018-19 has seen a sustained progress in exports in last three quarters. It has been increased by 12 percent in contrast to the imports which have slowed down to 16.6 percent. The figure has improved as compare to the start of the fiscal year. Pakistan's economy is still going through developing phase and is listed as one of the 'Next 11'. This means that the country has great potential for transforming into the leading economic power of 21st century. Pakistan is among the top twenty five economies placing it at 143rd place globally as per its gross domestic product (GDP). According to official figures of Ministry of Finance, Government of Pakistan (Pakistan Economic Survey), some important aspects of Pakistani economy are as under;

Growth and Investment

The growth drive remained over 5 percent n 2018, which is a thirteen-year high due to sound performance in agriculture, industry and services sectors. Individually, these economic segments showed a promising growth at 3.81 percent, 5.80 percent and 6.43 percent. Large scale manufacturing industry sector recorded 6.13 percent growth rate. The industrial sector grew by 5.80 percent and the manufacturing sector by 6.24 percent. None the less the services sector performance also showed a steady growth rate of 6.43 percent (Finance Ministry, Pakistan 2018).

Capital Markets, Inflation, Trade and Payments

A poor law and order situation and uncertain political environment resulted in slender capital markets. This was due to a non-favorable economic environment. Yet the situation has shown improvement because of the continuity of democratic process. Over the past decade Pakistan's economy has managed to regain the confidence of external and internal investors. This is directly impacting the capital market as shown by the positive trends in the economic activity within the country. Government has taken investor friendly legislative measures by granting autonomy to Pakistan's top economic regulator, "SECP" to accommodate the reform agenda. Hence, Pakistani markets are in a better position to counter challenges posed by new global economic trends and paved way for a potential rapid growth of the local economy (Finance Ministry, Pakistan 2018).

As per the recent figures ROIs in the capital markets has reached a high point in history of the country. Karachi stock market showed increased trends of new investment. As per the Ministry of Finance report, KSE 100 index closed at its all-time high level at "52,876.46 Index" in May 2017. This was due to an astonishing USD 123.9 million worth of foreign investment denial of securities during July 2017 – March 2018. This resulted in creation of huge prospects for the local investors, businesses and insurance companies. National Savings as always has proved to be the most effective institution to promote the financial inclusion of the females and other weaker financial segments of society. Women make out over 50 percent of National Savings investments shows government drive towards females' inclusion and empowerment in the economic sector (Arifeen, Mohammed 2018).

Ministry also reported that during 2018, CPI fell to 3.2 percent on account of subdued food prices which compensated the effects of the increased petroleum goods prices. The inflation rate was contained at 3.78 percent. Exports recorded a growth of 13.1 percent and imports were up by 15.7 percent in the same year. To contain imports, additional regulatory duty was imposed aimed at minimizing the pressures on country's balance of payments. Imports of capital equipment and fuel and global oil prices recovery was a factor behind increasing import bill. Therefore even the notable export growth and remittances inflows were not enough for overcoming the current account deficit gap. This imposed an immense pressure on State Bank's liquid foreign exchange reserves, which degenerated by US $ 4.5 billion in 2018 (Finance Ministry, Pakistan 2018).

Education Health and Nutrition

A national framework has been devised and implemented at district level for improving the public social service delivery. The current framework is aligned with international practices for achieving drastic improvements in the education system. The federal and provincial governments have generated a strong working relationship with mutual cooperation and coordination. The federal government has offered full scale support for successful implementation of the new framework for quality education for the younger generation of the country. The education expenditure or spending has been set to 699.2 billion rupees showing an increased by 5.4 percent from the previous years.

Further, under 18th constitutional amendment, Provinces have the freedom to navigate their education and health policies. For this purpose long term strategic goals are set for eradication of infectious diseases, disease surveillance, flaws in primary/secondary health care facilities, cultural biases and nutritional gaps. New regulatory measures are in place for improving the pharmaceutical sector for availability of affordable and high quality drugs. Health sector spending for Pakistan has reached 384.57 billion PKR for 2018 and further increase is expected in the coming time (Finance Ministry, Pakistan 2018).

Population, Labor Force and Employment

According to the 6th National Population and Housing Census' provisional results Pakistan's population figures have approximately reached 207.77 million. The findings of the recent census will allow the policy makers to develop effective strategies and resource management. The process of future planning for population control will be accommodated effectively. The data will support government to address problems like unemployment, health and education related issues effectively (Finance Ministry, Pakistan 2018).

Energy

The country has faced severe energy crisis in past two decades which led to dire consequences for economy. The resilient nation is pulling out of this crisis. Government initiatives have pushed for a drive for smart utilization of natural resources in energy sector. Environment friendly solar energy projects, bio gas energy production units, coal, hydro and other renewable energy sources are in development phase. Government's campaign for building new dams has got a united response from the public. Pakistanis consumes approximately 26 million tons of petroleum products each year. Major portion of this need is imported from middle east. Pakistan has a widespread natural gas network to accommodate the requirement of more than 8.9 million local consumers. As per the figures of 2018, average natural gas consumption is about 3,837 million Cubic Feet per day (Finance Ministry, Pakistan 2018).

Climate Change

Climate change is a global issue of which Pakistan is also suffering. Due to global warming this region has also witnessed adverse impacts of the climate change. This may be a major hurdle in the achievement of socio-economic development of the country. Government has introduced wide range of initiatives to address this environmental issue. The strategies have been devised and implemented for climate change adaptation and mitigation. The approach adopted is aligned with the National Policy on the matter. Climate change mitigation strategies are also being implemented at national level in terms of promotion of environment friendly renewable energy, and use of energy efficient appliances. According to Pakistan's Intended National Determined Contributions (INDC) the country's adaptation need is US $7 to US $14 billion per annum. Other initiatives include billion tree tsunami (plantation) project already initiated by the government with full support of the civil society across Pakistan (Finance Ministry, Pakistan 2018).

Social Safety Nets

Pakistan Poverty Alleviation Fund (PPAF) is contributing towards the support of the underprivileged segment of society. The focus is on improving the quality of life for ordinary Pakistanis. Projects like microcredit, water and infrastructure, drought mitigation, education, health and emergency response interventions are few examples of the social safety nets provided by the state to its people. Institutions like Pakistan Bait-ul-Mal (PBM) and Zakat are also supporting the underprivileged. Employees Old Age Benefits (EOBI) is an initiative focused on improving the standards of living for the poor and needy. General masses also indulge themselves in charity and society is mainly based on the mutual cooperation. According to a report Pakistanis people give the most charity (Finance Ministry, Pakistan 2018).

China Pakistan Economic Corridor (CPEC)

CPEC is an initiative which brings in wide range of opportunities for Pakistani economy in terms of infrastructure development, energy self-sufficiency, and eradication of unemployment and so on. The mega project will accommodate superior technology transfer and industrial development. Agriculture sector will be upgraded and the project has already started to show positive results in this sector. CPEC is thought to be the game changer for Pakistan that will open new horizons of development, peace and prosperity for this developing nation. The project has given way to new economic opportunities for a prosperous Pakistan. Studies have declared it as an extensive economic uplift program covering the next three decades for economic development, peace and stability within Pakistan and for the associated region (Hadi, Noor Ul, Saima Batool, and Assad Mustafa 2018).

CONCLUSION

To conclude Pakistan is a diverse nation of passionate and peace-loving people. The country despite all its challenges and pressures of the 21st century is thriving for a better future for its younger generations. Pakistani people have shown resilience against tough circumstances created by the menace of terrorism and are able to eradicate it. The drive for better quality of life through education and health sectors is evident in the strategic approach of the Pakistani government. It is important for the global political and economic forces to realize the importance of Pakistan in world global affairs. The geographical positioning and the military capacity increased Pakistan's importance in the global peace process. Pakistani armed forces have proven time and again that they are one of the best and most professional institutions globally. During the February 2019 Pakistani air force downed two Indian Jets on line of control and Pakistan Navy tracked and repelled the Indian submarine. Pakistan army's efforts and achievements in Operation Zarb-E-Azb portrays a true picture of the Pakistani nation's urge for long lasting peace and stability within the country and in the region. The nation is going through a transitional period and its rich culture has managed to help Pakistan maintain its cultural uniqueness. The progressive nation of over 200 million people welcomes the outsiders with open arms. The country has immense opportunities and potential to grow into a global force to reckon with.

REFERENCES

Arifeen, Mohammed. "*Pakistan's Economic Review 2018.*" Environment. February 17, 2018. Accessed February 9, 2019. http://www.pakistan economist.com/2018/02/19/pakistans-economic-review-2018/.

Avari, Burjor. *Islamic civilization in South Asia: a history of Muslim power and presence in the Indian subcontinent*. Routledge, 2012.

Bates, Dr Crispin. *"History - British History in Depth: The Hidden Story of Partition and Its Legacies."* BBC. March 03, 2011. Accessed February 14, 2019. http://www.bbc.co.uk/history/british/modern/partition 1947_01.shtml.

"Blog." *Gender Segregation in Pakistan.* September 12, 2014. Accessed February 15, 2019. https://gendersegregationinpakistan.weebly.com/.

Brantlinger, Patrick. *Rule of darkness: British literature and imperialism, 1830–1914.* Cornell University Press, 2013.

Central Intelligence Agency. *The World Factbook.* 02 09, 2019. https://www.cia.gov/library/publications/resources/the-world-factbook/ (accessed 02 13, 2019).

Finance Ministry, Pakistan. *"Pakistan Economic Survey."* | Ministry of Finance | Government of Pakistan |. Accessed February 01, 2019. http://www.finance.gov.pk/survey_1718.html.

Gutenberg. *"Languages of Pakistan."* Critical Thinking | Project Gutenberg Self-Publishing - EBooks | Read EBooks Online. Accessed February 28, 2019. http://self.gutenberg.org/articles/Languages_of_Pakistan.

Hadi, Noor Ul, Saima Batool, and Assad Mustafa. "CPEC: An Opportunity for a Prosperous Pakistan or Merely a Mirage of Growth and Development." *Dialogue (Pakistan)* 13, no. 3 (2018).

Haider, Murtaza. *"What They Never Tell Us about Ayub Khan's Regime."* DAWN.COM. November 05, 2016. Accessed February 28, 2019. https://www.dawn.com/news/1293604.

Hayat, Sikandar. *The Charismatic Leader: Quaid-i-Azam Mohammad Ali Jinnah and the Creation of Pakistan.* Karachi, Pakistan: Oxford University Press, 2015.

Losty, Jeremiah P., Malini Roy, and British Library. *Mughal India: art, culture and empire.* London: British Library, 2012.

Munir, Mohammad. *From Jinnah to Zia.* Delhi: Akbar Pub. House, 1981. Accessed February 09, 2019. www.ebooksdownloads.xyz/search/ jinnah-and-the-creation-of-pakistan.

Noman, Omar. *Pakistan: Political and Economic History since 1947.* London: Kegan Paul International, 1990. PDF.

"Pakistan." *Countries and Their Cultures.* Accessed February 16, 2019. https://www.everyculture.com/No-Sa/Pakistan.html.

"Pakistan." *World Travel Guide.* Accessed February 10, 2019. https://www.worldtravelguide.net/guides/asia/pakistan/food-and-drink/.

Pier. "Pakistani Culture - Family." *Cultural Atlas.* Accessed February 12, 2019. https://culturalatlas.sbs.com.au/pakistani-culture/family-c8cd2b 6e-9b45-4399-9d2e-9bd2bff4ba8a.

Quddus, Syed Abdul. *Zulfikar Ali Bhutto, Politics of Charisma.* Lahore: Progressive Publishers, 1994.

Riffat, Fatima. "Controlled Democracy and Political Opposition in Pakistan: A Case Study of Musharraf Era." *Mediterranean Journal of Social Sciences,* 2014. Accessed February 15, 2019. doi:10. 5901/mjss. 2014.v5n14p560.

Sisson, Richard, and Leo E. Rose. *War and Secession: Pakistan, India, and the Creation of Bangladesh.* Karachi: Oxford University Press, 1992.

Stepaniants, Marietta. "Development Of The Concept Of Nationalism: The Case of the Muslims in the Indian Subcontinent." *The Muslim World* 69, no. 1 (1979): 28-41.

Village, Spice. "A Simple Guide to Pakistani Wedding Rituals." *Latest Wedding, Catering & Fine Dinning Trends.* June 18, 2015. Accessed February 11, 2019. http://www.spicevillage.co.uk/blog/a-simple-guide-to-pakistani-wedding-rituals/.

Zahid, Masood Akhtar. "Dictatorship in Pakistan: A Study of the Zia Era (1977-88)." *Pakistan Journal of History and Culture* XXXII, no. 1 (2011): 241-64. doi:10.9737/hist.2018.658.

In: Exploring Cities and Countries ...   ISBN: 978-1-53618-514-0
Editor: Kathie Summers   © 2020 Nova Science Publishers, Inc.

Chapter 2

URBAN EXPANSION PATTERN AND LAND-USE CHANGE IN A MEDIUM-SIZED CITY IN SOUTHERN EUROPE: A SUSTAINABLE TRAJECTORY?

Lurdes Barrico, Helena Freitas and Paula Castro[*]

Centre for Functional Ecology, Department of Life Sciences,
University of Coimbra, Coimbra, Portugal

ABSTRACT

Urban spatial expansion will be the largest influence on development in the 21st century. The concentration of people in densely populated urban areas, especially in developing countries, will undoubtedly continue to increase as the majority of the world's population will live in urban settlements. This study analysed the spatial and temporal urban expansion in a medium-sized city in Southern Europe during a 10-year period (2001-2011). Coimbra was chosen as the study area due to its drastic changes in land-use patterns and its demographic dimension to the country scale. The

[*] Corresponding Author's Email: lurdesbarrico@gmail.com.

results revealed an urban expansion of almost 42% from 2001 to 2011, mostly at the expense of croplands. There was an obvious enlargement of the city area more directed to the south of the city, reaching an average rate of 244.4 ha/year. This expansion, however, has not been followed by an equally rapid population growth. This physical pattern of low-density expansion in built-up areas has contributed to a less compact city evolution—clearly an indicator of urban sprawl. Urban sprawl contributed mostly to the loss of cropland areas and to a concerning increase of soil sealing, contributing to increasing the probability of natural and human hazards, such as floods, landslides, heat waves, and fires. Therefore, it is important to design and implement suitable strategies that are able to reduce these harmful impacts. A better understanding of the spatial and temporal dynamics of the city's expansion provided by this study may be a helpful contribution to better planning and spatial organisation of local human activities for future sustainable urban development of Coimbra.

Keywords: land use change, urban sprawl, urbanisation, sustainable development, European city, South Europe

1. INTRODUCTION

Human activities in urban areas alter the type of land-use and the distribution of resources, affecting population and community dynamics, and ecosystem functions, and thus, being responsible for drastic environmental problems, such as biodiversity loss, ecosystem degradation, landscape fragmentation, and climate change (Alberti 2015; IPCC 2014; Seto et al. 2012). The rapidly growing urbanisation increase the pressure on land availability for urban infrastructures (Zhang 2016). Everyone in the world depends completely on the earth's ecosystems and the services they provide (MEA 2005), so the phenomenon of urbanisation is one of the 21st century's most transforming trends, and European countries seem to follow this pattern as well (Pickett et al. 2011; UN 2015). Since 2007, more inhabitants live in urban areas than in rural ones and the world population has remained predominantly urban (UN 2015). Europe is one of the most urbanised areas in the world. More than 74% of the European population lived in an urban area in 2018 and is expected to be over 77% urban by 2030, in pursuit of a better quality of life (UN 2015, 2018). This unprecedented urbanisation may lead to decline of natural resources and climate change, as well as social and economic challenges (Li et al. 2016; Sato and Zenou 2015; Stone et al. 2010; While and Whitehead 2013). Therefore, it is essential to characterise the spatial and temporal land-use patterns in order to develop a comprehensive understanding of the causes and effects of urbanisation processes.

Since the 1950s, most of European countries have spread their cities and increased their population, with families leaving the city centres and moving to suburban and peri-urban areas. Therefore, cities are being planned as more dispersed, thereby resulting in urban sprawl (EU 2016). In 2006, the European Environment Agency (EEA) published its first report about urban sprawl entitled *"Urban sprawl in Europe- The ignored challenge"* which warned about the scattered expansion of urban areas into the countryside existing on the edge of Europe's urban areas (EEA 2006). Here the concept is described as *"a physical pattern of low-density expansion of urban areas, under market conditions, mainly into the surrounding agricultural space"* (EEA 2006, pp. 6). According to Altieri et al. (2014 pp. 315), urban sprawl results from *"an uncontrolled and inefficient urban dispersion, accompanied by low building and population density, over rural or semi-rural areas, likely to be principally found in peripheral areas ... and occurring when urban planning is not well managed and turns open spaces into built spaces."* As a consequence, urban sprawl leads to negative effects on the environment, transforming the properties of soil, and thus interfering with the performance of its essential functions (EEA 2006). The taking of land for urban development results in soil sealing, i.e., the loss of soil resources due to the covering of permeable land for impervious surfaces, such as housing, roads or other construction types, which is generally irreversible (EC 2012; EEA 2010; Salvati 2014). The increase in impervious surfaces leads to a decrease in infiltration of rainfall to soil and an enhance in surface runoff resulting in an increased flood risk (Chithra et al. 2015; EC 2012). Soil sealing also contributes to the urban heat island effect that increases the temperature of the air inside city relative to the air temperature in surrounding areas (Deilami et al. 2016; Depietri et al. 2012; Scalenghe and Marsan 2009), thereby aggravating the effects of heat waves. The area of Coimbra is, historically, an area with geomorphological and meteorological hazardous events. Of special importance are the recent flood and landslide events that took place in the winter of 2000/2001 and 2006, the heat waves in 2003 and 2005 and the fires in 2005 (Tavares et al. 2010).

It is likely that this physical pattern of low-density expansion will continue in the next years and, as a result, the demand for land around cities is becoming a critical issue in many areas. For this, and since land is a finite resource more effective measures to control urban sprawl are urgently needed (EEA 2016a) as highlighted by the International Year of Soils declared by FAO-UN in 2015 (http://www.fao.org/soils-2015/en/).

Coimbra (Portugal) is an interesting case study as its demographic dimension and drastic changes in land-use patterns during the last half century make it an appropriate site to study the urban expansion pattern of a medium-sized European city. In the 1950s, the centre of urban occupation was surrounded by small outer urban areas and rural areas evidenced the very rural nature of the municipality. Since the 1970s, a large expansion in the artificialisation of the territory has taken place with the construction of important road infrastructures and facilities leading to the definition of new building areas. Thus, urban growth was verified either by the aggregation of existing peri-urban spots, or by expansion to non-occupied areas (CMC 2008; Tavares 2004). All these changes must be considered in order to effectively plan and manage ecologically sustainable cities.

The present work was conducted to analyse the urban spatial expansion and land-use dynamic in the municipality of Coimbra between 2001 and 2011, which may provide useful indications concerning changes in cities' forms and urbanisation patterns on a local scale. We hypothesised that urban expansion has led to changes in land-use patterns. In order to evaluate this hypothesis, we: (1) evaluated the urban development to understand how urban area has expanded and what pattern of expansion has occurred in this municipality and (2) identified and analysed the spatial and temporal land-use changes, outputting land-use maps that are an important tool to assist in problem identification and prioritisation of synergies and compromise solutions to promote environmental sustainability. Given that this kind of analysis has never been done for the municipality of Coimbra before, this study can provide useful information for managers and planners to draw up more effective strategies for land resource management and sustainable urban planning in this region.

2. METHODS

2.1. Study Area

The study was conducted in the municipality of Coimbra located in the central region of Portugal, between latitudes 40°5'N and 40°19'N and longitudes 8°18'W and 8°35'W (Figure 1). The municipality of Coimbra is influenced by a Mediterranean climate, characterised by warm, dry summers and mild, humid winters. The average annual temperature and total annual precipitation is around 15°C and 900 mm, respectively (CMC 2008). INE established the "statistical city," since it defined statistical criteria that allowed it to define territorially the city limits. The statistical city, here referred to as city area (main urban centre), is the territorial unit that corresponds to the adjustment of the urban perimeter, enshrined in the legal instruments of land occupation for the settlement areas with category of city, to the perimeter of the statistical subsections used by INE in the Geographic Basis of Information Reference (BGRI) and that integrate it (www.ine.pt). This municipality occupies about 320 km², and has a resident population of 143,396 inhabitants. More than three-fourths (78%) of these inhabitants live in the city—a worrying fact given that the city area represents only about one-fourth (26%) of the total area of the municipality (INE 2011). Thus, the city of Coimbra is one of the country's main urban centres. Furthermore, due to its singular centrality, demography, and disturbance in land-use patterns, this municipality is an interesting case study. Since the 1970s, an urban expansion has taken place, together with the construction of important road infrastructures and facilities (Tavares 2004).

The municipality of Coimbra is almost fully set within the Mondego river basin. What emerges from the hydrographic basin of Coimbra is the direction from east to west of the Mondego river, with its inflections, and particularly the amplitude of its alluvial plain. The presence of the Mondego river and some of its tributaries, the proximity of the ocean and the weak resistance of lithic units help create a vast alluvial plain—the Mondego Fields (Baixo Mondego), an agricultural area of excellence. Throughout the municipality we may still visualise signs of a recent landscape dominated by agroforestry systems. In today's landscape the country and city are intertwined and the agriculture and forest are diluted in a more urban landscape. The peculiar geomorphology, geographical richness, and diversity of the sites make Coimbra a municipality characterised by distinct landscape unities (CMC 2008).

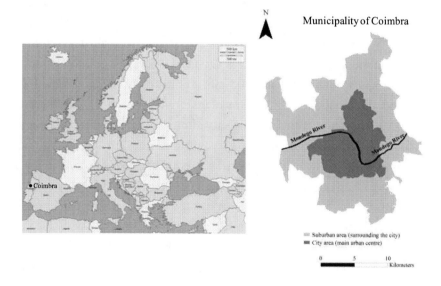

Figure 1. Location of the study area.

2.2. Data Set

The Portuguese Official Administrative Cartography of 2010 (CAOP 2010), a shapefile version with a classification of polygons on a scale of 1:25,000 with administrative boundaries developed by the Portuguese

Geographic Institute (IGP), was used to identify the extent of the municipality of Coimbra.

Digital aerial photographs for the years 1999 and 2010 were used to investigate changes in land-use. Both aerial photographs were ceded by IGP at a scale of 1:15 000 and 1:10 000, respectively, in a raster format. These two years were considered because they were the closest available data set to the study period (2001 and 2011).

The data regarding the inhabitant human population and number of buildings for the years 2001 and 2011 were acquired from the National Institute of Statistics (INE). Cartographic supports, in a shapefile version, containing information on the administrative and statistical delimitation, i.e., the division of the parishes into statistical sections of census and these, in statistical subsections, were also obtained online from the INE (www.ine.pt). Therefore, for the census of 2001 and 2011, the respective cartographic bases of the census were used, i.e., the BGRI2001 and BGRI2011. BGRI was developed according to a hierarchical polygonal structure whose elementary unit of representation is the statistical subsection. Statistical subsection is the maximum level of disaggregation and is characterised by being associated with the code and toponym of the place of which it is part (www.ine.pt).

2.3. Data Analysis

Maps with the resident population and number of buildings for the years 2001 and 2011 were obtained from the two sets of cartographic bases of the census for the city area (main urban centre) as well as for the surrounding areas, here referred to as suburban area. Population density was employed to characterise the population growth pattern. Buildings density was used to reveal the compactness in urban settlements built. They were used as indicators to relate the increase in urban area with population growth and the expansion of built-up area.

The spatial and temporal land-use changes in the study area were evaluated between 1999 and 2010. The 2010 aerial photographs were previously georeferenced by IGP, which helped to georeference the 1999 aerial photographs. The land-use maps for the years 1999 and 2010 were derived from the visual interpretation of these two sets of digital aerial photographs. Land-use classification was adapted from Caetano et al. (2009) and grouped into eight aggregated categories considered adequate for the purposes of this study: built-up land, construction site, cropland, forest, leisure area, inland waters, inland wetlands, and unused land (Table 2.1). Then, land changes was assessed by overlaying the land-use maps of 1999 and 2010. The magnitude and direction of land-use changes in the city were determined based on the transition matrix. For each land-use category in the transition matrix, the land transformation from 1999 to 2010 was calculated based on the equation (1) used by Long et al. (2007):

$$CHi = (pi.-p.i)/p.i \times 100 \tag{1}$$

where:

CHi is the change of land-use in column i relative to the previous compared year;

pi. is the column total of grid cells for category i;

p.i is the row total of grid cells for category i.

The internal conversions between the 8 land-use categories, which took place from 1999 to 2010, was treated as a result of several "loss or gain" conversions. Thus, the area (in hectares) taken or lost by each land-use category in relation to the total loss or gain of the other land-use category was also calculated based on the equations (2 and 3) used by Long et al. (2007):

$$Ploss(i),j = (pj,i - pi.j) / (pi.- p.i) \times 100 \; i \neq j \tag{2}$$

$$Pgain(i),j = (pi,j - pj.i)/(pi.- p.i) \times 100 \; i \neq j \tag{3}$$

where:

Ploss(i),j is the percentage taken by type j in the total "conversion loss" of category column i;

Pgain(i),j is the percentage taken by type j in the total "conversion gain" of category column i;

pi,j and pj.i is the individual entry in a transition matrix.

All maps were projected to the same national coordinate system (PT-TM06/ETRS89) using ArcGIS® version 10.6 (ESRI, Redlands, CA, USA).

Table 2.1. Description of the land-use categories used in this study

Land-use	Description
Built-up land	Land used for urban and rural settlements, industrial and commercial units, road and rail networks, aerodrome, quarries, mining and dumping.
Construction site	Abandoned areas in artificialised territories, potential areas for construction according to the Municipal Master Plan of Coimbra.
Cropland	Areas currently under crop (annual or permanent), orchards and fallow, dry farming land, land under irrigation, cultivated land or land being prepared for raising crop, pasture areas.
Forest	All wooded areas, natural or planted forests, riverine vegetation, shrubs and bushes, sclerophyllous vegetation, transitional woodland-shrub.
Inland waters	Natural watercourses, artificial canals.
Inland wetlands	Inland marshes.
Leisure area	Gardens, parks, sport and leisure facilities, cemeteries.
Unused land	Open spaces with little or no vegetation, bare soils, burnt areas.

3. RESULTS

3.1. Population Growth, Development of Residential Area, and Urban Expansion

The data of the population, buildings, city area and suburban area (around the city) are presented in the Table 3.1 and the maps with its temporal and spatial distribution in the Figure 2, highlighting the dynamic events during the study period. The city's population of Coimbra increased 4.7% and opposite results were found for suburban area, where the population decreased 20.7%. The population density in the city varied between around 1700 persons/km^2 in 2001 and almost 1300 persons/km^2 in 2011. In the suburban area, the population density also decreased. The number of buildings increased 28.4% in the city area, but a slight decrease was verified in the number of buildings existing in the suburban area (-4.1%). The study period witnessed a small drop in the number of buildings per km^2 in the city (-9.4%). The buildings' density in the suburban area always averaged around 60 buildings per km^2 (Table 3.1).

The maps represented in the Figure 2 display the number of population and buildings in the city and suburban area of Coimbra's municipality and are useful to highlight differences in number and spatial distribution of these population and buildings throughout the city and suburban area. The results show that the city, here considered the main urban centre by INE, expanded about 42%, mainly as a result of an expansion to the south of the city, which reached an average rate of 244.4 ha/year (Table 3.1; Figure 2). Although the city occupies a relatively small area of the municipality, around 20%, both the population and buildings are increasingly concentrated in the main urban centre; a scattered occupation in the suburban area, however, may also be observed (Table 3.1; Figure 2).

Table 3.1. Population and buildings in the city area and suburban area of Coimbra's municipality in 2001 and 2011

	City area		Suburban area	
	2001	2011	2001	2011
Population (n°)	101069	105842	47374	37554
Population density	1721.8	1272.1	181.7	159.0
Population (%)	68.1	73.8	31.9	26.2
Buildings (n°)	19144	24580	16738	16058
Buildings/km^2	326.1	295.4	64.2	68.0
Buildings (%)	53.4	60.5	46.6	39.5
Area (km^2)	58.7	83.2	260.7	236.2
Area (%)	18.4	26.0	81.6	74.0

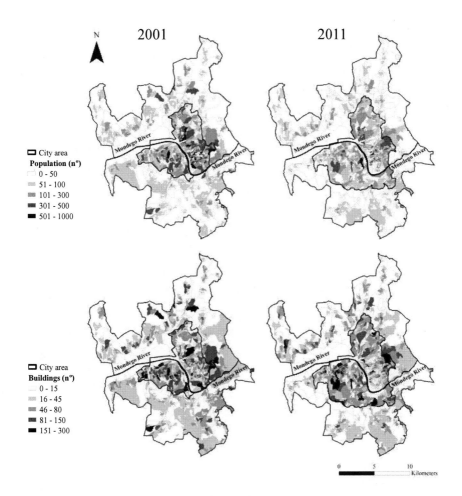

Figure 2. Population and buildings distribution maps along the municipality of Coimbra in 2001 and 2011 (data from INE). The variation in the number and arrangement of the subsections is reflected in the territorial dynamics occurred between 2001 and 2011.

3.2. Land-Use Change

With its economic development, population growth, and urbanisation, the city of Coimbra has experienced a successive increase in its built-up land at the expense of the other land-use categories. The cartographic results for the land-use changes between 1999 and 2010 (Figure 3) and the transition matrix (Table 3.2) illustrate the land-use dynamics in the city area of Coimbra's municipality. The cropland and built-up areas were the two dominant land-use categories in the city, accounting jointly for more than 60% of the total area in both years (Table 3.2). Cropland decreased almost 35%, mostly in the northeast and southwest of the city and along the Mondego River. The built-up land increased around 28%, which occurred over the entire city area and principally close to existing infrastructures (roads, buildings, and leisure facilities) and also close to watercourses. It is worth noting that forested areas also expanded about 28%, mainly in the southwest of the city. The expansion of the leisure area (56%) should also be emphasised. This expansion occurred principally in the centre of the city, close to existing leisure areas, but can also be viewed scattered throughout the city (Figure 3). Overall, around 25.3% of the city of Coimbra experienced land-use changes in the period studied (Table 3.2).

Table 3.2. The conversion matrix of land-use change in the city area of Coimbra´s municipality from 1999 to 2010. As the area of the city has changed, the area corresponding to the recent year (2011) was the one considered

Land use in 1999 (ha)	Land use in 2010 (ha)								
	BL	CS	CL	F	IW	IWL	LA	UL	Total 1999
BL	**2136.6**	16.4	3.7	1.4	0.0	0.0	4.7	4.1	2167.0
CS	221.3	**125.5**	8.8	20.7	0.0	0.0	24.0	23.2	423.6
CL	314.6	183.6	**2159.7**	572.0	1.6	0.0	24.3	141.6	3397.3
F	59.4	79.6	49.7	**1367.3**	2.3	0.0	1.1	104.9	1664.2
IW	0.1	0.1	1.5	9.1	**179.7**	0.0	0.0	0.4	190.8
IWL	0.0	0.0	0.0	0.0	0.0	**1.8**	0.0	0.0	1.8
LA	0.0	0.0	0.0	0.0	0.0	0.0	**110.3**	0.0	110.3
UL	36.3	30.9	0.7	154.7	0.0	0.0	7.7	**132.7**	363.0
Total 2010	2768.4	436.2	2224.1	2125.1	183.5	1.8	172.2	406.8	8318.0
Change	601.4	12.6	-1173.2	460.9	-7.3	0.0	61.8	43.8	

BL - Built-up land, CS - Construction site, CL - Cropland, F - Forest, IW - Inland waters, IWL - Inland wetlands, LA - Leisure area, UL - Unused land. The unchanged area of each land-use category was marked in bold. The rows and columns contain data of 1999 and 2010 respectively.

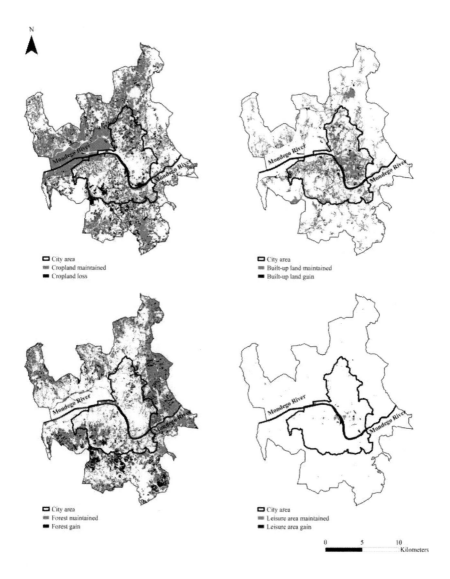

Figure 3. Principal land-use changes in the city area of Coimbra´s municipality from 1999 to 2010. As the area of the city has changed, the area corresponding to the recent year (2011) was the one considered.

The internal conversions between land-use categories in the city area from 1999 to 2010 show that about 80% of the total conversions occurred mainly due to the transformation of cropland into other land uses (Figure 4).

The loss of cropland area contributed to practically all the expansion of the unused land (99.7%), forested area (90.2%) and construction sites (72.4%). Likewise, around half of the built-up land (51.3%) also expanded due to the loss of cropland. It is also worth noting that one-third (33.8%) of the built-up land grew at the expense of construction sites (Figure 4).

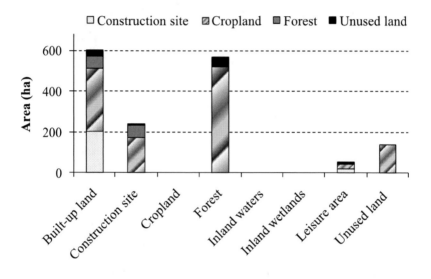

Figure 4. Internal conversions between land-use categories in the city area of Coimbra´s municipality from 1999 to 2010 and the area taken by each corresponding category in loss or gain conversions.

4. DISCUSSION

This research aimed to assess the urban spatial expansion trend in the municipality of Coimbra and provide an overview of the spatial and temporal land-use change patterns between 1999 and 2010 in a medium-sized city in Portugal. The results show that in the past decade the main urban centre has experienced a rapid population growth, a huge spatial expansion and a significant change in land-use. Most of this spatial expansion was due to the artificialisation of the land, especially through the construction of commercial buildings and roads networks. It should be noted that between 2002 and 2006, three big commercial areas were built in the city area. Associated with this commercial development, new road networks, including a new bridge over the Mondego River, were built. The road networks greatly influence the structure and spatial location of urban development which thus assumes a meaningful built-up areas growth along the major roads (Aljoufie et al. 2013; Mundia and Aniya 2005).

From 2001 to 2011 the size of the city increased at a much faster rate than its population. With this expansion the city has become a less compact area (lower population density), which is a clear indicator of urban sprawl. This trend is a common feature observed in Europe, particularly in southern medium-sized cities, such as Porto (EEA 2006), Madrid (López de Lucio 2003), Barcelona (Catalán et al. 2008), Rome (Frondoni et al. 2011) and Milan (Camagni et al. 2002).

Growth of the urban population and even faster urban spatial expansion has resulted in land-use changes in the city of Coimbra. The results show that built-up land was developed mainly at the expense of cropland areas and that the built-up land expansion was the most important process in terms of extent and impact on land composition and patterns. Urban sprawl occurs at the expense of cropland areas since it usually responds to demographic, socioeconomic and policy conditions as observed in other contexts (Barbero-Sierra et al. 2013; Skog and Steinnes 2016). Due to its abandonment or on account of planning decisions, cropland areas are generally available for urban growth, and in most cases, these areas are more suitable for construction than natural areas (mainly forested) as observed by Kasanko et al. (2006). Europe has a recognised tradition of municipal forest ownership also referred as "town forestry" by Randrup et al. (2005), and thus, the forested areas are often considered to be valuable green spaces and used as recreational and leisure areas. Cities have, therefore, been able to protect them from the construction sector (Randrup et al. 2005; Tyrväinen et al. 2005). The construction sector has acted as an investor refuge given the limited options offered by industrial and technological sectors. This has led to a vicious circle of construction development at a high environmental cost (Barbero-Sierra et al. 2013). It should be noted that, once consumed by urban sprawl, the land losses the potential for other uses and the soil is irreversibly degraded (Barbero-Sierra et al. 2013; EEA 2016a). Land take and soil sealing processes affect the production capabilities of the agricultural sector and thus have a negative impact on food security. Europe's intense urbanisation at the expense of agricultural land loss has reduced its capability to produce food (Gardi et al. 2015).

In 2009, the Portuguese legal framework established the criteria and categories of qualification of the rural and urban soil, giving great emphasis "*on combating the indiscriminate expansion of urban perimeters with the consequent disproportionate damage to croplands, forested areas or green spaces*" (Regulatory decree No. 11/2009 of 29 May, pp. 3383). Along these lines, attempts to create conditions for urban expansion to fit into a planned development, and therefore be more efficient and valorise the territory (Regulatory decree No. 11/2009 of 29 May), have been undertaken consistent with the European measures for controlling urban sprawl. Driven by an increasing population and a shift towards greater urbanisation, as verified in the city of Coimbra, more unsealed surfaces are being replaced by impervious surfaces. Built-up lands (housing, road infrastructures, industrial and commercial developments) are therefore being laid down over what was once cropland, forested or unused land. Different uses of soils result in drastic changes to their chemical, physical, and biological characteristics, and thus in the ecosystem services provided by these soils (Setälä et al. 2014).

This study showed that cropland was the area that faced the greatest loss to artificial areas and also to forested areas, in response to a classic model of urban spatial expansion behaviour (Abrantes et al. 2016). In a world strongly urbanised, forest ecosystems are increasingly recognised as fundamental elements for keeping urban inhabitants in contact with nature (DeClercq et al. 2007; Konijnendijk et al. 2005). These unsealed urban soils provide an array of ecosystem services to inhabitants of cities. They serve as habitat for soil organisms and plants, as well as provide key functions such as the degradation of pollutants, storage of carbon and mineral nutrients, and moderation of the hydrologic cycle (Lehmann and Stahr 2007; Pouyat et al. 2010). The expansion of forested areas may also be the outcome of a complex process caused by the regeneration of natural vegetation in abandoned cropland areas, thus demonstrating the natural fitness of Portuguese soil for the forest system (ICNF 2013) as observed by Barrico et al. (2012) for Coimbra. On the other hand, in European countries, this has prompted managers and decision makers to implement strategies to increase the rate of forested areas (DeClercq et al. 2007; Van Herzele et al. 2005). Forested areas have increased partly as a result of the plantation of forests on former croplands as part of the European Common Agricultural Policy (CAP) (http://ec.europa.eu/agriculture/cap) that provides support to a range of forestry measures. One of which was the Regulation (EEC) 2080/92 instituting a Community aid scheme for forestry measures in agriculture (Official Journal of the European Communities 1992). Posterior forestation actions were stipulated by the Council Regulation (EC) No. 1257/1999 (Official Journal of the European Communities 1999) and by the Council Regulation (EC) No. 1698/2005 (Official Journal of the European Union 2005). The major objectives of these forestry measures include the promotion of sustainable forest management and development of forestry, maintenance and improvement of forest resources, extension of woodland areas, enhance the biodiversity, and also protect the value of forests with respect to soil erosion, maintenance of water resources, water quality, and natural hazards (Official Journal of the European Communities 1999; Official Journal of the European Union 2005).

The city of Coimbra also showed an increase in its leisure areas (gardens, parks, sport and leisure facilities). Green spaces in an urban environment have the potential to provide a range of benefits as they may contribute to protect biodiversity and ecosystem processes, help to better adapt to climate change, as well as improving air and soil quality, provide opportunities for recreation and leisure, and increase overall human well-being (Bertram and Rehdanz 2015; EC 2011; EU 2016). Furthermore, the preservation of green spaces will be important to achieve the target n.º 2 of the European Biodiversity Strategy which states

"by 2020, ecosystems and their services are maintained and enhanced by establishing green infrastructure and restoring at least 15% of degraded ecosystems." (EC 2011, pp. 5)

In order to achieve sustainable urbanisation, cities need to develop more smarter plans so as to achieve a balance between environmental, economic and social needs enhancing the city's competitiveness and the quality of life of its citizens (Abu-Ghazalah 2008; Lee et al. 2014). It is important to be aware that the UN-Habitat shares a vision of sustainable cities and human settlements for all adopting a *"New Urban Agenda"* in the Habitat III conference held in Quito in 2016. This New Urban Agenda commits

> "to promote sustainable land use, combining urban extensions with adequate densities and compactness preventing and containing urban sprawl, as well as preventing unnecessary land-use change and the loss of productive land and fragile and important ecosystems." (UN 2016, pp 11)

In recent years, we have become increasingly aware of the huge risks that climate change poses to cities (EEA 2016b; Jabareen 2013). Portugal, a predominantly Mediterranean biogeographical region, located in Southern Europe, is thus more vulnerable to environmental changes, like climate change, with its potential impacts in the decrease of precipitation, increase of forest fires and biodiversity loss (Andrade et al. 2014; Costa et al. 2012; IPCC 2014). Well-managed urban development may give rise to cities that are more economically, socially and environmentally sustainable, and more resilient to climate change and natural disasters (Barrico and Castro 2016; Terakado and Williams 2014). With the increase of environmental hazards, such as heat waves and extreme rainfall, urban strategies are needed to reduce vulnerability, promote health, and building resilience (Stone et al. 2010). Therefore, it is important to design and implement suitable strategies that are able to reduce these harmful impacts. A better understanding of the spatial and temporal dynamics of Coimbra's city expansion provided by this study may be helpful input for better local and regional planning, spatial organisation and decision-making.

CONCLUSION

This study examined the dynamics of urban spatial expansion in the city of Coimbra from 2001 to 2011 and identified the land-use changes that have occurred inside and outside the main urban centre during the period studied. The city area expanded about 42% from 2001 to 2011, at an average rate of 244.4 ha/year, mostly at the expense of cropland areas. The urban sprawl pattern observed in this city threatens its resilience and adaptation to climate change, the services provided by natural resources, as well as the desirable standards of quality of life and well-being for the population. This poses an essential challenge to decision makers and other stakeholders, particularly in the Mediterranean region, as achieving sustainable development will require the adoption of integrative and inclusive actions to lead the legitimate aspirations to further economic and social progress while strengthening environmental protection.

ACKNOWLEDGMENTS

The 1999 and 2010 digital aerial photographs were ceded by the Portuguese Geographic Institute (IGP), under the FIGIEE Program - Support Program for the Supply of Information Geographic for Research, Education and Edition. Corresponding author was supported by an individual research grant (SFRH/BD/69630/2010) from the Portuguese Foundation for Science and Technology.

REFERENCES

Abrantes, P., Fontes, I., Gomes, E. and Rocha, J. (2016). Compliance of land cover changes with municipal land use planning: evidence from the Lisbon metropolitan region (1990-2007). *Land Use Policy*, 51: 120-134.

Abu-Ghazalah, S. (2008). The sustainable city development plan for Aqaba, Jordan. *Journal of Developing Societies*, 24(3): 381-398.

Alberti, M. (2015). Eco-evolutionary dynamics in an urbanizing planet, *Trends in Ecology & Evolution*, 30(2): 114-126.

Aljoufie, M., Zuidgeest, M., Brussel, M. and van Maarseveen, M. (2013). Spatial-temporal analysis of urban growth and transportation in Jeddah City, Saudi Arabia. *Cities*, 31: 57-68.

Altieri, L., Cocchi, D., Pezzi, G., Scott, E. M. and Ventrucci, M. (2014). Urban sprawl scatterplots for urban morphological zones data. *Ecological Indicators*, 36: 315-323.

Andrade, C., Fraga, H. and Santos, J. A. (2014). Climate change multi-model projections for temperature extremes in Portugal. *Atmospheric Science Letters*, 15(2): 149-156.

Barbero-Sierra, C., Marques, M. J. and Ruíz-Pérez, M. (2013). The case of urban sprawl in Spain as an active and irreversible driving force for desertification. *Journal of Arid Environments*, 90: 95-102.

Barrico L. and Castro P. (2016). Urban Biodiversity and Cities' Sustainable Development. In: *Biodiversity and Education for Sustainable Development*. World Sustainability Series, Castro, P., Azeiteiro, U. M., Bacelar-Nicolau, P., Leal Filho, W. and Azul, A. M. (Eds.), Springer International Publishing Switzerland, pp. 29-42.

Barrico, L., Azul, A. M., Morais, M. C., Coutinho, A. P., Freitas, H. and Castro, P. (2012). Biodiversity in urban ecosystems: plants and macromycetes as indicators for conservation planning in the city of Coimbra (Portugal). *Landscape and Urban Planning*, 106(1): 88-102.

Bertram, C. and Rehdanz, K. (2015). The role of urban green space for human well-being. *Ecological Economics,* 120: 139-152.

Caetano, M., Nunes, V. and Nunes, A. (2009). CORINE *Land Cover 2006 for Continental Portugal*. Technical Report, Portuguese Geographic Institute.

Camagni, R., Gibelli, M. C. and Rigamonti, P. (2002). Urban mobility and urban form: the social and environmental costs of different patterns of urban expansion. *Ecological Economics*, 40(2): 199-216.

CAOP (2010). Carta Administrativa Oficial de Portugal. [Official Administrative Charter of Portugal]. http://ftp.igeo.pt/produtos/cadastro /caop/shapes_2010.htm.

Catalán, B., Saurí, D. and Serra, P. (2008). Urban sprawl in the Mediterranean? Patterns of growth and change in the Barcelona Metropolitan Region 1993-2000. *Landscape and Urban Planning*, 85(3-4): 174-184.

Chithra, S. V., Nair, Dr. M. V. H., Amarnath, A. and Anjana, N. S. (2015). Impacts of impervious surfaces on the environment. *International Journal of Engineering Science Invention*, 4(5): 27-31.

CMC (2008). *Plano Diretor Municipal de Coimbra-revisão: estudos de caracterização*. Câmara Municipal de Coimbra, Direção Municipal de Administração do Território, Departamento de Planeamento, Divisão de Ordenamento e Estratégia. [*Coimbra Municipal Master Plan - revision: characterization studies*. Coimbra Municipal Council, Municipal Direction of Territory Administration, Department of Planning, Planning and Strategy Division].

Costa, A. C., Santos, J. A. and Pinto, J. G. (2012). Climate change scenarios for precipitation extremes in Portugal. *Theoretical and Applied Climatology*, 108(1-2): 217-234.

DeClercq, E. M., De Wulf, R. R. and Van Herzele, A. (2007). Relating spatial pattern of forest cover to accessibility. *Landscape and Urban Planning*, 80(1-2): 14-22.

Deilami, K., Kamruzzaman, Md. and Hayes, J. F. (2016). Correlation or causality between land cover patterns and the urban heat island effect? Evidence from Brisbane, Australia. *Remote Sensing*, 8(9): 716, doi:10.3390/rs8090716.

Depietri, Y., Renaud, F. G. and Kallis, G. (2012). Heat waves and floods in urban areas: a policy-oriented review of ecosystem services. *Sustainability Science*, 7(1): 95-107.

EC (2011). *Our life insurance, our natural capital: an EU biodiversity strategy to 2020*. COM (2011) 244 final, Brussels, European Commission.

EC (2012). Science for environment policy. *In-depth report: soil sealing.* *DG Environment News Alert Service*, European Commission. http://ec.europa.eu/environment/archives/soil/pdf/sealing/Soil%20Seali ng%20In-depth%20Report%20March%20version_final.pdf.

EEA (2006). Urban sprawl in Europe: the ignored challenge. *EEA Report No. 10/2006*, Luxembourg, Office for Official Publications of the European Communities, European Environment Agency.

EEA (2010). The European environment: state and outlook 2010 - Land use. *EEA Report.* Luxembourg, Publications Office of the European Union, European Environment Agency.

EEA (2016a). Urban Sprawl in Europe. Joint EEA-FOEN report, *EEA Report No. 11/2016*, Luxembourg, Publications Office of the European Union, European Environment Agency.

EEA (2016b). Urban adaptation to climate change in Europe 2016: transforming cities in a changing climate. *EEA Report No. 12/2016*, Luxembourg, Publications Office of the European Union, European Environment Agency.

EU (2016). *Urban Europe: statistic on cities, towns and suburbs.* ISBN 978-92-79-60139-2, Luxembourg, Publications office of the European Union.

Frondoni, R., Mollo, B. and Capotorti, G. (2011). A landscape analysis of land cover change in the Municipality of Rome (Italy): spatio-temporal characteristics and ecological implications of land cover transitions from 1954 to 2001. *Landscape and Urban Planning*, 100(1-2): 117-128.

Gardi, C., Panagos, P., Van Liedekerke, M., Bosco, C. and De Brogniez, D. (2015). Land take and food security: assessment of land take on the agricultural production in Europe. *Journal of Environmental Planning and Management*, 58(5):898-912.

ICNF (2013). *Áreas dos usos do solo e das espéciesflorestais de Portugal Continental.* Resultadospreliminares, 6º Inventário Florestal Nacional (IFN6), Lisboa, Instituto da Conservação da Natureza e das Florestas. [*Areas of land use and forest species in mainland Portugal.* Preliminary results, 6th National Forest Inventory (IFN6), Lisbon, Institute of Nature Conservation and Forestry].

INE (2011). *Censos 2011*. InstitutoNacional de Estatística. [*Census 2011*. National Institute of Statistics]. http://censos.ine.pt/xportal/xmain?xpid =CENSOS&xpgid=censos2011_apresentacao.

IPCC (2014). Climate Change 2014. Impacts, Adaptation, and Vulnerability. Part A: Global andSectoral Aspects. Contribution of Working Group II to the *Fifth Assessment Report of the Intergovernmental Panel on Climate Change*, Field, C. B., Barros, V. R., Dokken, D. J., Mach, K. J., Mastrandrea, M. D., Bilir, T. E., Chatterjee, M., Ebi, K. L., Estrada, Y. O., Genova, R. C., Girma, B., Kissel, E. S., Levy, A. N., MacCracken, S., Mastrandrea, P. R. and White, L. L. (Eds.), Cambridge University Press, Cambridge, United Kingdom and New York, NY, USA.

Jabareen, Y. (2013). Planning the resilient city: concepts and strategies for coping with climate change and environmental risk. *Cities*, 31: 220-229.

Kasanko, M., Barredo, J. I., Lavalle, C., McCormick, N., Demicheli, L., Sagris, V. and Brezger, A. (2006). Are European cities becoming dispersed? A comparative analysis of 15 European urban areas. *Landscape and Urban Planning*, 77(1-2): 111-130.

Konijnendijk, C. C., Nilsson, K., Randrup, T. B. and Schipperijn, J. (Eds.) (2005). *Urban Forests and Trees*. Springer, Verlag, Berlin, http://doi.org/10.1007/3-540-27684-X.

Lee, J. H., Hancock, M. G. and Hu, M. C. (2014). Towards an effective framework for building smart cities: lessons from Seoul and San Francisco. *Technological Forecasting and Social Change*, 89: 80-99.

Lehmann, A. and Stahr, K. (2007). Nature and significance of anthropogenic urban soils. *Journal of Soils and Sediments*, 7(4): 247-260.

Li, B., Chen, D., Wu, S., Zhou, S., Wang, T. and Chen, H. (2016). Spatio-temporal assessment of urbanization impacts on ecosystem services: case study of Nanjing City, China. *Ecological Indicators*, 71: 416-427.

Long, H., Tang, G., Li, X. and Heilig, G. K. (2007). Socio-economic driving forces of land-use change in Kunshan, the Yangtze River Delta economic area of China. *Journal of environmental management*, 83(3): 351-36.

López de Lucio, R. (2003). Transformaciones territoriales recientes en la región Urbana de Madrid. *Urban*, 8: 124-161. [Recent territorial transformations in the urban region of Madrid. *Urban*, 8: 124-161].

MEA (2005). *Ecosystems and human well-being: synthesis*. Island Press, Washington, DC, Millennium Ecosystem Assessment.

Mundia, C. N. and Aniya, M. (2005). Analysis of land use/cover changes and urban expansion of Nairobi city using remote sensing and GIS. *International Journal of Remote Sensing*, 26(13): 2831-2849.

Official Journal of the European Communities (1992). Council Regulation (EEC) No. 2080/92 of 30 June 1992 instituting a Community aid scheme for forestry measures in agriculture. No. L 215/96-99.

Official Journal of the European Communities (1999). Council Regulation (EC) No. 1257/1999 of 17 May 1999 on support for rural development from the European Agricultural Guidance and Guarantee Fund (EAGGF) and amending and repealing certain regulations. No. L 160/80-102.

Official Journal of the European Union (2005). Council Regulation (EC) No. 1698/2005 of 20 September 2005 on support for rural development by the European Agricultural Fund for Rural Development (EAFRD). No. L 277/1-40.

Pickett, S. T. A., Cadenasso, M. L., Grove, J. M., Boone, C. G., Groffman, P. M., Irwin, E., Kaushal, S. S., Marshall, V., McGrath, B. P., Nilon, C. H., Pouyat, R. V., Szlavecz, K., Troy, A. and Warren, P. (2011). Urban ecological systems: scientific foundations and a decade of progress. *Journal of Environmental Management*, 92(3): 331-362.

Pouyat, R. V., Szlavecz, K., Yesilonis, I. D., Groffman, P. M. and Schwarz, K. (2010). Chemical, physical, and biological characteristics of urban soils. In: Urban ecosystem ecology. Aitkenhead-Peterson, J. and Volder, A. (Eds.). *Agronomy Monograph*, 55: 119-152.

Randrup, T. B., Konijnendijk, C., Dobbertin, M. K. and Prüller, R. (2005). The concept of urban forestry in Europe. In: *Urban Forests and Trees*. Konijnendijk, C. C., Nilsson, K., Randrup and T. B., Schipperijn, J. (Eds.), Springer, Verlag, Berlin, pp. 9-21.

Regulatory decree No. 11/2009 of 29 May (2009). Republic Diary - 1.ª Series, 2009, No. 104, pp. 3383-3389.

Salvati, L. (2014). The spatial pattern of soil sealing along the urban-rural gradient in a Mediterranean region. *Journal of Environmental Planning and Management*, 57(6): 848-861.

Sato, Y. and Zenou, Y. (2015). How urbanization affect employment and social interactions. *European Economic Review*, 75: 131-155.

Scalenghe, R. and Marsan, F. A. (2009). The anthropogenic sealing of soils in urban areas. *Landscape and Urban Planning*, 90(1-2): 1-10.

Setälä, H., Bardgett, R. D., Birkhofer, K., Brady, M., Byrne, L., de Ruiter, P. C., de Vries, F. T., Gardi, C., Hedlund, K., Hemerik, L., Hotes, S., Liiri, M., Mortimer, S. R., Pavao-Zuckerman, M., Pouyat, R., Tsiafouli, M. and van der Putten, W. H. (2014). Urban and agricultural soils: conflicts and trade-offs in the optimization of ecosystem services. *Urban Ecosystems*,17(1): 239-253.

Seto, K. C., Güneralp, B. and Hutyra, L. R. (2012). Global forecasts of urban expansion to 2030 and direct impacts on biodiversity and carbon pools. *Proceedings of the National Academy of Sciences of the United States of America*, 109(40): 16083-16088.

Skog, K. L. and Steinnes, M. (2016). How do centrality, population growth and urban sprawl impact farmland conversion in Norway? *Land Use Policy*, 59: 185-196.

Stone B., Hess J. J. and Frumkin H. (2010). Urban form and extreme heat events: are sprawling cities more vulnerable to climate change than compact cities? *Environmental Health Perspectives*, 118(10): 1425-1428.

Tavares, A. O. (2004). Geotechnical and natural hazard mapping on urban and outer urban planning. *Proceedings GéoQuébec 2004 Conference*, Eds, Demers, D., Leahy, D., Lefebvre, R., Leroueil, S. and Martel, R. CD – Session 4C, pp. 27-33.

Tavares, A. O., Mendes, J. M., Basto, E. and Cunha, L. (2010). Risk perception, extreme events and institutional trust: a local survey in Portugal. In: Briš, R., Soares, C. G. and Martorell, S. (Eds.). *Reliability,*

Risk and Safety: Theory and Applications Taylor & Francis Group, London, pp. 1245-1252.

Terakado, M. and Williams, H. K. (2014). *Investing in sustainable cities: challenges and opportunities.* International Development Finance Club, Special Interest Group on Sustainable Urban Development.

Tyrväinen, L., Pauleit, S., Seeland, K. and de Vries, S. (2005). Benefits and uses of urban forests and trees. In: *Urban Forests and Trees.* Konijnendijk, C.C., Nilsson, K., Randrup, T.B. and Schipperijn, J. (Eds.), Springer, Verlag, Berlin, pp. 81-114.

UN (2015). *World urbanization prospects: the 2014 Revision.* Department of Economic and Social Affairs, Population Division, United Nations. http://esa.un.org/unpd/wup/.

UN (2016). Draft outcome document of the United Nations Conference on Housing and Sustainable Urban Development (Habitat III), Quito, 17-20 October 2016. United Nations. http://habitat3.org/the-new-urban-agenda.

UN (2018). *World Urbanization Prospects: the 2018 Revision.* Department of Economic and Social Affairs, Population Division, United Nations. https://population.un.org/wup/.

Van Herzele, A., DeClercq, E. M. and Wiedemann, T. (2005). Strategic planning for new woodlands in the urban periphery: through the lens of social inclusiveness. *Urban Forestry and Urban Greening*, 3(3-4): 177-188.

While, A. and Whitehead, M. (2013). Cities, urbanisation and climate change. *Urban Studies*, 50(7): 1325-1331.

Zhang, X. (2016). Sustainable urbanization: a bi-dimensional matrix model. *Journal of Cleaner Production*, 134(Part A): 425-433.

In: Exploring Cities and Countries ...   ISBN: 978-1-53618-514-0
Editor: Kathie Summers   © 2020 Nova Science Publishers, Inc.

Chapter 3

STREET FOOD IN SOUTHERN ITALY: FROM THE PAST TO THE FUTURE

Maria Neve Ombra, Florinda Fratianni and Filomena Nazzaro*

Istituto di Scienze dell'Alimentazione, CNR, Avellino, Italy

ABSTRACT

Street food was born many centuries ago: already the ancient Romans sold it in their kiosks. Essential for travelers that at the time used to eat their meals standing up, quickly, stopping in places overlooking the street. Remains of these structures are in Rome and Pompeii (Southern Italy). In the city destroyed by the eruption of 79, more than 200 have been identified. Street food is an ancient invention still very current. Moreover, street food is one of the easiest ways to know the territory and a tasty, fast and cheap tradition. In a broad sense, street food has often been described as having some elements of the Mediterranean Diet. The famous chefs are well aware of the cultural value and the delicious flavors of these specialties and many of them have chosen to offer, in addition to haute cuisine, their own gourmet version of Southern Italy street food. As for

---

* Corresponding Author's Email: nombra@isa.cnr.it.

future street food, the advice is to choose healthier and sustainable food options.

Keywords: street food, pizza, lifestyle

1. INTRODUCTION

Street foods are ready-to-eat food for sale in streets, squares or markets, widespread around the world and throughout history. At present, around 2.5 billion people consume street food every day and its popularity has been increasing in recent decades (Fellows and Hilmi, 2019).

Street food is a typical cultural and socio-economic phenomenon of most urbanized areas. In urban areas, time spent cooking meals at home has declined dramatically and street foods are attractive due to their convenience, low cost and pleasant salty taste, making them a popular option/choice for food every day. Furthermore, the sale of street food represents an important source of livelihood for many vendors and their families, especially in the urban areas of developing countries.

Street foods are heterogeneous regarding their ingredients and degree of processing; they can vary greatly from fresh fruits, fresh vegetables and homemade cooked meals to highly industrialized packaged snacks and drinks. Because of their variety, street food provides options to meet diverse needs, lifestyles and food habits and contributes to a sizable proportion of the dietary intake in many populations worldwide (Steyn et al., 2014).

According to the FAO, street food has a determinant nutritional impact; therefore, consumers must be directed towards appropriate choices. The nutritional value of street food essentially depends on the ingredients used, which are country specific, as well as on their preparation and type of cooking. Street food presents some problems about its safety, as it is often prepared and sold in precarious hygiene conditions, so it would always be necessary to have sanitary and legal surveillance (Abrahale et al., 2018).

Street food has clearly acquired important economic, cultural and nutritional significance. In this chapter, we aimed to describe the street food consumption in the past, the actual street food and the next prepared foods in South-Italian area, where the Mediterranean Diet should continue to be the guide, the nutritional model forever in these territories, to be spread elsewhere.

2. PAST SOUTH-ITALIAN STREET FOOD

Street food was born centuries ago; already the ancient Romans sold it in their kiosks. Street food has always been essential for travelers and that at time they used to eat their meals standing up quickly, stopping in places overlooking the street. Remains of these structures are in Rome and Pompeii. In the city destroyed by the eruption of 79, more than 200 have been identified (Monteix, 2013). This is not surprising considering that, from the archaeological excavations, there were very few houses with kitchens, so almost all of them were forced to visit these places along the city streets. Bread was never missing from everyday foods. Charred remains of the latter have been found. In addition to bread, Pompeii's cuisine was also based on vegetables. From charred food finds, there is a large consumption of cauliflower grown in the gardens of ancient Pompeii, alongside different types of lettuce, broccoli, carrots, turnip and basil also used as a medicinal herb. Asparagus grew wild in the countryside of the city. The lava of Vesuvius has not only destroyed, it has also preserved, in fact, charred seeds of melon, beans, peas, chickpeas and lentils have been found. The fruit was of fundamental importance and figs were widespread, also used as a condiment for their sweet taste. The olives, on the other hand, were grown and preserved in salt or vinegar. Even the fruits that were preserved by drying for the long winter: pears, rowanberries, apples and peaches, were believed to have healing power. Walnuts, hazelnuts, almonds and pine nuts were also widespread. The fish was chosen and served fresh as well as mussels and oysters. From the blue fish typical of the Mediterranean coasts, a condiment was obtained which was highly appreciated by the inhabitants of Pompeii: Garum, a sauce obtained by fermenting the waste parts in salt. (Carannante, 2019). The milk obtained from sheep and cows was an indispensable ingredient for making seasoned and non-aged cheeses. From pigs, fresh meat was obtained which could be preserved by smoking. The *thermopolia* or *popinae* and the *cauponae* were the places where, at the time, soups, meat, fish, dried fruit were prepared, all food that was then sold to the patrons. The structures, some still visible in Pompeii, were composed of a counter that contained the dolia, large containers in which food was stored and on one side were, instead, arranged other vessels containing other dishes and a fire where to heat them, if necessary Figure 1. They were real stalls selling food, just like the ones we find on the streets of our cities for festivals. An invention, that of street food, ancient but still very current.

Figure 1. Thermopolium in Pompei.

However, over the centuries, it has undergone transformations and today the appeal lacks the so-called "spicaiola," the "tarallaro," the "zeppolaiuolo." There are no longer the voices, or rather the cries, of those who, with their carts, traveled along the various districts of Naples or other South-Italy cities. On the other hand, street food is something extremely theatrical, of being exhibited, as well as a real subversion of the times and ordered places provided by domestic consumption. Street food is linked to the people, to its desperation, to its need to fill swarming stomachs with a few coins.

2.1. "Mangiamaccheroni"

Between the end of the sixteenth century and the beginning of the eighteenth century, the Neapolitans were the protagonists of a real food revolution: from "leaf eaters" they became "mangiamaccheroni" completely transforming their way of eating (Sereni, 2015). By leaf, we meant at the time, that complex of foods used to indicate cauliflower and its subspecies: cabbage, sprouts, chicory, escarole, and broccoli. The name "leaf eater" lasted until 1600, when the consumption of macaroni began to spread. Initially the macaroni were served as a sweet dish, seasoned with sugar and cinnamon, then in the 18th century the pasta consumed in the ways we know today spread. On every street corner, the maccaronaro boiler appeared flanked by a bowl full of grated cheese and pepper, the only condiment for macaroni until the advent of tomatoes. Macaroni were served hard and were served on sheets of wax paper (a modern street food to eat with your hands). The strangers, the many travelers, were amazed at the ability of the people to bring the scorching macaroni to their mouths. It was mainly consumed on Sundays and public holidays. During the rest of the week the people ate pizza in the winter, and watermelon in the summer, nothing was thrown away from the latter, even the seeds, roasted, were used to fill the stomach and feed. Looking at archival photos and vintage postcards, often featured street scenes of mangiamaccheroni dangling fistfuls of pasta strands above their open mouths. Otherwise, contemporary travelers often commented on the city's popular dish. Perhaps the most notable is Goethe, who visited Naples in 1787 and commented on the local dried macaroni that could "*be bought everywhere and in all the shops for very little money. As a rule it is simply cooked in water and seasoned with grated cheese.*" Though Italy's most iconic dish is no longer a street food eaten by the fistful, it continues to be omnipresent, cheap, simply cooked in water, and best if seasoned with grated cheese (Figure 2). Some things never change.

Figure 2. Neapolitan "Mangiamaccheroni."

2.2. "Ricotta Fuscella"

There are flavors that remain etched in the memory and that recall the mind to childhood, to when everything was more genuine. One of these is the almost disappeared Ricotta 'e Fuscella, a type of cow ricotta produced exclusively in Campania. Its name derives from the term fiscella, which indicates the perforated truncated cone-shaped basket, made of woven wicker, in which it was transported and sold. Fuscella ricotta, to have this name, must have the characteristic trunk-pyramidal shape, not weigh more than 2 kg, from porcelain white to very light straw-colored, with no crust and doughy consistency, with a delicate and sweet taste (Cremona and Soletti, 2006). The production of this type of ricotta is consolidated in the area of the Municipality of Sant'Anastasia (NA), where in ancient times there was a flourishing sheep and goat breeding, with whose milk they were originally produced. Today it is instead produced with cow's milk from farms in the region. Once 'in Ricotta' and Fuscella was sold on the street-by-street vendors who came to Naples from the province with wicker baskets, full of ricotta, on their heads. They prepared and sold ricotta sandwiches, skewered in vertical wooden sticks and placed along the edge of the basket, while ricotta was served to passers-by on a vine leaf, thus accentuating the rustic flavor. The term "ricotta" comes from the Latin recoctus, which indicated the annealing of the whey after the production of the cheese. It is produced by heating the whey up to 80 degrees, until obtaining a clear and white mass, which is inserted in baskets called fuscelle. Ricotta is widely used throughout the region, eaten alone or as an ingredient in many traditional dishes: from filled pasta to desserts such as the pastiera. Contains about 146 kcal per 100 gr. of product and 10.9 gr. of fat. Fuscella ricotta is very lean and has a delicate taste, rich in calcium and vitamins, characteristics that make it perfect for feeding children, especially during the delicate phase of weaning.

2.3. Cooked Pears and Apples

In the past centuries, these fruits were consumed while walking on the street. They were in fact sold by street vendors who, once cooked, covered them with caramel. Then they skewered them with a stick so they could be consumed while walking. Nowadays they are no longer sold as street food.

2.4. "Bror 'e Purp"

"Bror 'e purp" was an ancient street food very common in cold periods. The broth was made from pieces of fresh boiled octopus flavored with pepper, served in the cup with the tentacles. Matilde Serao also mentions it in the literary work "*Il Ventre di Napoli*" (1884): "*with a little money you could buy a cup of boiling octopus broth "boiled in sea water" whose "women do business in the street, with a focolaretto and a small pignatta.*" Today it is still possible to find the octopus broth in the area of Porta Capuana, and slices of lemon accompany it. A simple dish that is prepared with just a few ingredients: the octopus is left to cook in a large saucepan filled with boiling water, salt, oil and pepper. The broth thus obtained can be sipped just as if it were a mulled wine or a punch, a seafood sauce that challenges the palate for a marine taste. The octopus broth has very ancient origins, apparently Greek. In Southern Italy, the news on its consumption date back to the mid-fourteenth century and Giovanni Boccaccio himself in 1339, in a letter addressed to his friend Francesco Bardi, tells that on the birth of a child the cronies had bought the most beautiful octopus and sent it to the "purpera." Women were in charge of the trade, that is, those who cooked octopus in the street and sold it to the hungry people.

2.5. Cooked Fava Beans

Even cooked beans were sold on cold days. People crowded to buy cooked broad beans; some carried directly a plate with bread, others, a "cozzetto" without breadcrumbs and let it be sprinkled with a ladle of boiling broth. Nowadays these vendors are no longer present on the streets.

2.6. Farinata

Farinata is the undisputed star of Genoa street food, golden, crunchy and soft at the same time. An ancient recipe made with few and simple ingredients - chickpea flour, water, salt and extra virgin olive oil mixed with abundance and left to rest enough before the last step in the oven. Still now, it is consumed in some regions of Southern Italy (https://www. taccuinigastrosofici.it/ita/news/contemporanea/panini-e-cibo-di-strada/ farinata-o-torta-di-ceci-nascita-del-mito.html).

3. MODERN STREET FOOD OF SOUTHERN ITALY

Actually, street food is one of the easiest ways to know a territory through its typical products. In Southern Italy arancini, crocchè, pizze are a tasty, fast and cheap tradition. The famous chefs are well aware of the cultural value and the delicious flavors of these specialties and many of them have chosen to offer, in addition to haute cuisine, their own gourmet version of street food. According to Coldiretti (Organization of agricultural entrepreneurs at Italian and European level), more than one in two Italians (52%) consume street food, driven by practicality and low cost, but also by the innovation of the formats and the expansion of the offer (as of December 20, 2017, the Coldiretti Organization listed on its website: https://www. coldiretti.it/economia/manovra-storico-via-libera-allo-street-food-contadino). In fact, the itinerant restaurant segment recorded significant performances and active companies grew by 13%. Moreover, about 70% of street food consumers buy traditional local specialties, another 30% opt for international food and ethnic specialties (e.g., hotdog, fish and chips, kebab). And the phenomenon had a real explosion with the appearance of technologically advanced mobile means, the so-called food trucks, for the preparation and offer of the different types of products, but also with the emergence of specialized chains." At the same time, dedicated events are also growing: for about twenty vehicles participating in every initiative of the street food festival. Street food is usually made fresh, or made of pre-mixed ingredients, then put together. Moreover, it can be unhealthy because of the high oil content and the fact that the same oil has been used all day and for various different dishes (Buscemi et al., 2011). In different parts of the world, street food is made and served differently, some cleaner than others, but the food always tastes delicious and retains the authentic local flavor. Street food in Southern Italy is very abundant, exhibiting high variability in the nutritional composition of foods (Figure 3). Generally, these foods contain high contents of fats, cholesterol, sodium, refined sugars and many calories. Public health policies should be targeted to improve the street food offer, promoting nutrient-dense foods and the reduction of added salt.

Figure 3. Modern street food: a) Pizza a portafoglio; b) cuoppo; c) panino ca meusa; d) arancino.

3.1. "Neapolitan Street Food"

Neapolitan street food has such strong roots in its people that it has been brought everywhere. Neapolitan emigrants have made pizza the most globalizing food in the world. (De Falco, 2018; Mattozzi, 2015) "The traditional art of Neapolitan pizza chefs," which has enjoyed the support of civil society and numerous institutions, with an extraordinary signature collection campaign open to all citizens of the world, represents the eighth Italian recognition in the list of UNESCO Intangible Heritage (2017). It is the third national inscription in the context of the food and wine tradition, after the "*Mediterranean Diet*" registered in 2013, and "*The Alberello di Pantelleria vine*" registered in 2014 (Deacon, 2018). Naples is known for its appetizing street food, from pizza al portafoglio (pizza folded twice into a practical triangle) to typical o' cuoppo (a paper cone filled with vegetable, potatoes and fish fried), thus prepared and served for eating it while walking. At the Neapolitan festivals around the world, such as the feast of San Gennaro and in the various Little Italy of the world, everything is accompanied by pastecresciute, armies of fried pizzas, crocché, "pizza a portafoglio." The latter also known as "pizza a libretto" is a pizza folded on itself, small in diameter, with less dressing, and the price is inexpensive. Usually it has little or no fiordilatte, little tomato and oil: a "light" version of a canonical margherita. "Fried cuoppo" is usually composed of some salty frittella, crocché made of potatoes and often enriched with cheese and ham, fried pumpkin flowers as well as a series of battered vegetables, fried polenta triangles. Often it has also been enriched with seafood, with fried fish, squid and rings. "Tarallo" is consumed at any time walking along the seafront, as an aperitif, a breaker and for some as a complete meal. In the shape of braided and rounded, corpulent braids, the taralli were born at the end of the eighteenth century when the bakers did not even throw away the pasta scraps obtained from their daily workings. Very caloric ingredients were added, ideal for facing long days of strenuous work: the suet, a lot of pepper and almonds. Roasted and greasy, they were sold by itinerant tarallari. Today, the taralli - which have become an iconic object of the Neapolitan street culture - are sold singly, by the package in bakeries.

3.2. Sicilian Street Food

One of the greatest traditions of the Sicilian island is street food. Walking among beaches, parks and monuments, there are many specialties to taste. "Arancini": there are hundreds of different recipes around the island. Being a popular dish, each city has its own secret recipe and uses different ingredients, mainly rice meat and vegetables. "Pane e panelle" is a simple dish to prepare, fast and cheap. As with the arancini, the Arabs introduced this delicacy. They began to grind the chickpea seeds to obtain a flour which, mixed with water and cooked on the fire, gave a dough. The dough spread in a thin and small sheet and cooked, gave a product with a unique flavor, which has now become a classic meal of Sicily. "Pane ca meusa" is one of the most loved dishes by Palermitans (Ribbene, 2017). The meusa (spleen) and the veal lung are fried in lard and then served with a soft sandwich (vastedda) and a splash of lemon. The "married" version provides for the addition of ricotta or flaky caciocavallo. The spleen sandwich is a poor dish that was born about 1000 years ago, when butchers of Jewish origin settled in Palermo. Not being able to receive money for their work, because of their religious faith, they kept the calf's entrails as a reward: guts, lung, spleen and heart. Jewish butchers had to find ways to utilize. They realized that Christians used to eat the entrails of animals, accompanying them with cheese or ricotta and they created a sandwich stuffed with lung, spleen and pieces of cartilage from the ox's trachea. The spleen sandwich, still today, is one of the most popular dishes in Palermo. It has been revisited, but maintains the characteristics of the past. This specialty is made up of soft bread, covered with sesame, called vastedda filled with thin slices of spleen. "U Pani cunzatu" (seasoned bread) is certainly one of the poorest dishes of the Sicilian gastronomic tradition (Lombardo et al., 2015). In the absence of more expensive condiments, the Sicilians began to season fresh bread with low-cost and easily available ingredients such as extra virgin olive oil, tomatoes, first salt cheese, oregano and anchovies in oil. The "iris" is a very soft fried donut without a hole with a soft heart of ricotta, sugar and pieces of chocolate, all sealed with a crispy external breading. In 1901 in occasion of Mascagni's "Iris" staged at the Massimo theater in Palermo, the pastry chef Antonino Lo Verso decided to create a new dessert. Since then, Iris becomes in demand throughout Palermo and still represents a symbol of the city and of all Sicily.

3.3. "Caciocavallo Impiccato" (Basilicata)

Caciocavallo is the symbol of southern dairy history. It comes from the "pasta filata" technique that Southern Italy has developed over the centuries to guarantee the shelf life of cow's milk cheeses. The curd, obtained by heating and coagulating the milk, is subjected to a second cooking, until it becomes elastic and can be handled without breaking (Uzun et al., 2020). Mozzarella, scamorze, provoloni and caciocavalli are all cheeses derived from this method. Caciocavallo Podolico is particularly valuable and is produced with milk from the Podolica breed. This breed bred in the wild or semi-wild is today not very numerous, but in the past, it was the most common breeds in Italy. This delicious seasoned pasta filata cheese is an excellent food to taste, and it is rich in vitamins and minerals. The classic form of ball-shaped cheese suspended in a noose on a bed of embers that, reached the melting point, is slid onto a slice of bread and tasted still hot (Figure 4). The cheese melted on the fire and accompanied with bread was the most popular meal among the shepherds in the transhumance period, when they moved through the pastures following the path marked by the sheep tracks. After a day of walking and waiting to continue the journey,

Figure 4. Caciocavallo Impiccato.

they ate simple dishes: among these pieces of cheese that were "sweated" on the flame and laid on slices of bread. Caciocavallo has a particular, aromatic flavor, and its intensity varies according to the seasoning. Heating the cheese by thermal radiation dissolves the pasta giving the cheese an incomparable creaminess. Caciocavallo Impiccato has a weight between 1.2 and 2 kg approximately. The stringy cheese gives way to the passage of the blade of a knife and is then spread on a slice of toasted bread.

4. THE FUTURE

Food has always exerted a fundamental role in human history and related social behavior. While in the next future the importance of food is surely not destined to decrease, the forms that people's relationship with food will take are different and somewhat difficult to predict. However, it is essential to comprehend which determinants/key factors will be of the future food scenario, since there are actions that can be implemented today to positively influence future developments. The phenomenon of climate change, (Yildiz, 2019), contribute to aggravate the agri-food scenario and the search for sustainable agricultural models is one of the important challenges of the next years (Bertoni et al., 2018). Next to the theme of scarcity of resources, there is also that of the loss and waste of resources. The good rules to be adopted to be sustainable in terms of food and nutrition, we could simplify them in three guiding tips: consume less; waste less; choose foods whose production has a reduced environmental impact. It is obvious that careful management of resources, processing and waste is synonymous with environmental sensitivity and the correct approach towards which to strive/commit. Scientists from several disciplines assess the global food system and set global scientific targets for shifting the world towards healthy diets and sustainable food production. In areas with informal markets, price incentives for street vendors to use healthy and sustainable ingredients and investment in sanitary locations have been recommended to increase the availability of safe, nutritious food. Second, healthy diets from sustainable food systems should be made more affordable. It will be necessary to popularize the concept/notion that it is possible to eat properly, maintaining an adequate food style to safeguard health, without sacrificing taste and pleasure in nutrition. Such a statement will have to coexist with coherent food proposals, the diffusion of correct information, for an improved education in taste and health. A 'universal' diet designed to protect our health and that of the Earth was proposed by a team of 37 scientists from 16 countries and published in the authoritative scientific journal The Lancet (Willett et al., 2019). The researchers focused on the future. The food model proposed by scholars is shaped around the skeleton of the Mediterranean diet that, thanks to the positive effects on longevity and the benefits for health, is recognized as an intangible cultural heritage of humanity by UNESCO, considered absolutely one of the healthiest and easier to follow. The Mediterranean diet is ranked first in fighting diabetes and promoting heart health: less meat, more fruit, and vegetables (Mazzocchi et al., 2019; Salas-Salvadó et al., 2019). In a flexible regime, the universal diet consists of increasing the consumption of vegetable and fruit based foods and substantially reducing the consumption of food of animal origin. The universal diet proposed by The Lancet recommends doubling the global consumption of fruit, vegetables, legumes and nuts and instead reducing by more than 50 percent that of red meats and sugars. As for the menu, the Mediterranean diet is used as an explicit example in the study. Several studies/accumulating evidence have associated bad eating habits and red meat consumption with metabolic disorders and cardiovascular diseases. Experts have shown that this shift in food style can improve the quality of life in terms of health and food sustainability. In addition to modifying the way people consume food, convincing them to prefer fruit and vegetables and to limit red meat as much as possible, it is important to restrict the use of land, water, and nutrients for production of sustainable agriculture. In fact, for the Planet, we must fight against climate change, the loss of biodiversity, pollution, the consumption of soil and water.

As street food is becoming more widespread, according to FAO data, it is consumed every day by around 2.5 billion people around the world and considering the importance of the Mediterranean diet, it is necessary to intervene at this level and adopt a model, closer to the med diet, especially in the past.

In fact, street food has many affinities/similarities with elements of the Mediterranean diet, especially of Southern Italy, given that the

Mediterranean Diet originated in these territories, as described by Ancel Keys, the first nutrition biologist in history (Keys and Keys, 1975). In 1962, he moved to Pioppi, in Cilento (Southern Italy) and, after decades of studies, he concluded that the type of diet in that area was responsible for the extraordinary beneficial effect on the local population (Dinu et al., 2018). An important opportunity for Italian food in the world to qualify the threatened offer from homologation but also to defend the national food identity that risks disappearing from the streets and squares invaded by other foreign specialties. Valuing the cultural identity of the historic centers is important for the inhabitants but also for the many Italian and foreign tourists who, when they arrive in these cities, expect to eat local traditional products that are the true strength of the Made in Italy holiday, conquered with the distinctiveness, biodiversity and the link with the territory.

As a general guideline, there is a return to the origins, especially on the raw material. *Enhance the past but in a modern key.*

The street food of the future must therefore be inspired by the proposals of the past, which included a greater consumption of fruit and vegetables, see for example cooked pears and apples, cooked legumes, described above. As shown in Table 1, four examples of the past with less calorie count and with a lower fat content than today. Moreover, the salt content of today's street food should not be overlooked. Nowadays salt consumption exceeds the level recommended by WHO (5 g/day), which is associated with negative effects on health (Cappuccio et al., 2019). Public health strategies to realize the WHO's objectives include salt content surveillance, improved nutritional labelling and product reformulation. Spices and aromatic herbs are a concentrate of active ingredients that flavor dishes naturally without covering the smells and flavors of the original ingredients, excellent alternatives to salt, for satisfied taste buds. Use of salt substitutes, is another potential strategy to prevent the adverse consequence of salt intake/consumption (Farrand et al., 2019). Thus there is need to raise awareness among food vendors and manufacturers about the importance for health of reducing sodium consumption.

Moreover, some preparations will be revised with the use of more sustainable basic elements available in the future (Dai et al., 2019). In Figure

5, how will the pizza of the future be more healthy and sustainable? For example, it could be prepared with a functional low glycemic index flour, tomatoes grown in urban gardens, functional oil and mozzarella or cheese obtained from vegetable milk (Galanakis, 2017).

Table 1. Comparison of nutritional values between typical South-Italy present and past street food

PRESENT					PAST			
Caciocavallo	Crocchè	Panino meusa	Pizza		Maccheroni	Ricotta	Bror purp	fava beans
439	150	690/>100g	235	Kcal/100g	167	146	60	146
2	80	32	44	%carbohydrates	61	9	9	58
64	7	52	36	% lipids/fats	20	11	16	8
35	14	15	18	% proteins	17	24	7	30

Nutritional facts including energy, protein, carbohydrate, and fat contents were based on the information given on: https://www.crea.gov.it/-/tabella-di-composizione-degli-alimenti.

Future Pizza: Health-Sustainable Pizza?

Flour: functional flower? (i.e. low glycemic index flower)

Tomatoes: from hurban garden?

Olive Oil : or a replacement oil?

Mozzarella/cheese: with vegetable milk?

Figure 5. Future pizza.

Following are the foods commonly associated with future nutrition and probably the recipes for street food will also be reviewed in light of these.

Algae rooted in oriental cuisine are slowly breaking through western tastes. Many nutritionists place them among the best candidates for "food of the future" based on their availability, ease of cultivation and beneficial properties of some species. Although rich in minerals and beneficial substances for our body, their limited caloric intake (less than 50 kcal per 100 grams) and protein, leads them to be considered, for most cases, a complementary food (Rai et al., 2018). *Mycoproteins* are proteins derived from mushroom cells (including yeasts and molds). The main source of mycoproteins is Fusarium venenatum. Available in various variations and flavors, it was introduced as a component of vegetarian burgers. Other food preparations are still in the experimental phase. In general, mycoproteins include 13 g of fats, 45 g of proteins, 10 g of carbohydrates, 25 g of fibers and several vitamins and minerals in 100 g of dry matter (Finnigan et al., 2017). Study on human volunteers has revealed that the biological value of proteins in mycoproteins is analogous to that of milk proteins. Furthermore, toxicology studies have verified that mycoproteins include no negative effects on normal growth of humans and animals. However, long or short-term consumption of the mycoproteins includes no general health concerns (Finnigan et al., 2017). *Great fruits:* excellent candidates for being "great fruits" capable of satisfying large masses. One of the most cited is certainly the jackfruit (Artocarpus heterophyllus). Originally, from India, it is also present in other countries of Southeast Asia, where it is known for its size and its nutritional characteristics (excellent source of potassium, calcium and iron). The jackfruit adapts very well even to very hot climates (which makes it, as some claim, proof of climate change) and trees need no special care (Lasekan and Abbas, 2012). *Jellyfish* extremely widespread in the main seas of the Earth, soon they could also be on our tables being easy to breed and rich in nutrients. Furthermore, with the decrease of predators such as tuna and turtles, the population of jellyfish is destined for exponential growth, being easily adaptable, so eating them could be a good strategy to counteract their indiscriminate increase. They are inexpensive, versatile and can acquire the charm of seafood in the tastes of the western consumer. The flavor is similar to that of a seafood such as the oyster, which also maintains its versatility in the kitchen. Jellyfish have a very wide range of nutrients. They are rich in collagen, as well as omega 3 and omega 6; an enviable percentage of protein (about 80%) and a balanced presence of fats (about 20%) for a product that, put in salt, guarantees about 40 calories per 100 grams (Leone et al.,2019). *Insects:* more immediately associate with the term "food of the future." Breeding is very easy, the minimum by-products (and reusable as compost) and the maximum nutritional yield. According to the FAO, more than 2 billion people already use insects for food, and there are over 1,900 edible species on the market. Insects feed on rotting food, mushrooms and plants, resulting highly eco-sustainable. For palatability, the crickets taste like shrimp and the moths of the flour have a nutty taste. They are highly nutritious, because they provide high quality proteins comparable to those of meat and fish (Jantzen et al., 2020). Among the "foods of the future," there are also the seeds, in particular those of chia, with their calcium content and the particularly balanced presence of essential fatty acids, omega 3 and omega 6. High consumption of meat is addressed as one of the most threatening problems (Ritchie et al., 2018; Rutten et al., 2018, Chalmers et al., 2019). In addition to health problems for the consumers, further consumption of meat can seriously affect climate change (Aschemann-Witzel et al., 2019; MacDiarmid and Whybrow, 2019). Many companies and start-ups are working on the production of synthetic meat in the laboratory, this food-engineering strand goes hand in hand with the sustainability of the livestock sector and the fishing industry, and it is known that this chain has a significant impact on the environment by producing greenhouse gases. The shrimp supply chain has a terrible environmental impact, which is why it focuses on plant-based products with a shrimp flavor, containing algae and sustainable ingredients. Categories of the artificial meats include cultured meats (produced using in vitro cultures of cells or tissues) and meat substitutes from plant and single-cell proteins (SCP) (Bhat et al., 2017; Maga and Murray, 2010; Van Der Spiegel et al., 2013).

In conclusion, one of the most pressing challenges of modern society concerns the search for well-being and sustainable living standards in light of the decrease in the quantity of available resources. Human health cannot be disconnected from the health of ecosystems. To meet the food and nutritional needs of a richer, more urbanized world with a growing population, people's eating habits will have to undergo transformations. Greater awareness of global environmental issues must be spread among people, with the awareness that the planet's natural resources are not unlimited and that the population will not be able, in the long term, to maintain the lifestyles currently most widespread, including in the food sector. The adoption of lifestyles and foodstuffs that favor the consumption of those foods that have a minor impact on the planet's ecosystem must be promoted, starting primarily from street food given its popular utilization. It is necessary to help people choose and implement a correct food style. The food of the future is the key to understanding how the man will survive.

REFERENCES

Abrahale, K., Sousa, S., Albuquerque, G., Padrão, P., Lunet, N. 2018. "Street food research worldwide: a scoping review." *Journal of Human Nutrition and Dietetics* 32(2):152-174.

Aschemann-Witzel, J., Ares, G., Thøgersen, J., Monteleone, E. 2019. "A sense of sustainability? – How sensory consumer science can contribute to sustainable development of the food sector." *Trends in Food Science and Technology* 90:180-186.

Bhat, Z. F., Kumar, S., Bhat, H. F. 2017. "In vitro meat: a future animal-free harvest." *Critical Reviews in Food Science and Nutrition* 57: 782-789.

Bertoni, D., Cavicchioli, D., Donzelli, F., Ferrazzi, G., Frisio, D. G., Pretolani, R., Ricci, E. C., Ventura, V. 2018. "Recent contributions of agricultural economics research in the field of sustainable development." *Agriculture* 8(12):200.

Buscemi, S., Barile, A., Maniaci, V., Batsis, J. A., Mattina, A., Verga, S. 2011. "Characterization of street food consumption in Palermo: Possible effects on health." *Nutrition Journal* 10(1):119.

Cappuccio, F.; Beer, M.; Strazzullo, P. 2019. "Population dietary salt reduction and the risk of cardiovascular disease. A scientific statement from the European Salt Action Network." *Nutrition Metabolism and Cardiovascular Disease.* 29:107-114.

Carannante, A. 2019. "The last garum of Pompeii: Archaeozoological analyses on fish remains from the "garum shop" and related ecological inferences." *International Journal of Osteoarchaeology* 29(3):377-386.

Chalmers, N., Stetkiewicz, S., Sudhakar, P., Osei-Kwasi, H., Reynolds, C.J. 2019. "Impacts of reducing UK beef consumption using a revised sustainable diets framework." *Sustainability* 11(23),6863.

Cremona, L., Soletti, F. 2006. *L'Italia dei formaggi*. Milano: Touring edition.

Dai, S., Jiang, F., Shah, N. P., Corke, H. 2019. "Functional and pizza bake properties of Mozzarella cheese made with konjac glucomannan as a fat replacer." *Food Hydrocolloids* 92:125-134.

Deacon, H. 2018. "Safeguarding the Art of Pizza Making: Parallel Use of the Traditional Specialities Guaranteed Scheme and the UNESCO Intangible Heritage Convention." *International Journal of Cultural Property* 25(4):515-542.

De Falco, S. 2018. "Vesuvius, pizza, coffee and...Innovation: Is a new paradigm possible for the creative "Vesuvius Valley," Naples, Italy?" *City, Culture and Society* 14:1-13.

Dinu, M., Pagliai, G., Casini, A., Sofi, F. 2018. "Mediterranean diet and multiple health outcomes: An umbrella review of meta-analyses of observational studies and randomised trials." *European Journal of Clinical Nutrition* 72(1):30-43.

Farrand, C., MacGregor, G., Campbell, N. R. C., Webster, J. 2019. "Potential use of salt substitutes to reduce blood pressure." *Journal of Clinical Hypertension* 21(3):350-354.

Fellows, P., Hilmi, M. 2019. *Selling street and snack food.* London: Food and Agriculture Organization of the United Nations.

Finnigan, T., Needham, L., Abbott, C. 2017. "Mycoprotein: A Healthy New Protein with a Low Environmental Impact." In *Sustainable Protein Sources*, edited by Sudarshan R. Nadathur, Janitha P.D. Wanasundara and Laurie Scanlin, 305-325. Amsterdam: Elsevier.

Galanakis, C. M. 2017. *Nutraceutical and Functional Food Components: Effects of Innovative Processing Techniques.* Amsterdam: Elsevier Inc.

Jantzen da Silva Lucas, A., Menegon de Oliveira, L., da Rocha, M., Prentice, C. 2020. "Edible insects: An alternative of nutritional, functional and bioactive compounds." *Food Chemistry* 311,126022.

Keys, A., Keys, M. 1975. *How to Eat Well and Stay Well the Mediterranean Way.* New York: Doubleday.

Lasekan, O., Abbas, K. A. 2012. "Distinctive Exotic Flavor and Aroma Compounds of some Exotic Tropical Fruits and Berries: A Review." *Critical Reviews in Food Science and Nutrition* 52(8):726-735.

Leone, A., Lecci, R. M., Milisenda, G., Piraino, S. 2019. "Mediterranean jellyfish as novel food: effects of thermal processing on antioxidant, phenolic, and protein contents." *European Food Research and Technology* 245(8):1611-1627.

Lombardo, G., Puglisi, V., Petrona Baviera, S. 2015. *Crocchè. Il cibo di strada di Palermo... nel mondo*. Rimini: NFC Edizioni.

MacDiarmid, J. I., Whybrow, S. 2019. "Nutrition from a climate change perspective." *Proceedings of the Nutrition Society* 78(3):380-387.

Maga, E. A., Murray, J. D. 2010. Welfare applications of genetically engineered animals for use in agriculture. *Journal of Animal Science* 88(4):1588-1591.

Mattozzi, A. 2015 *Inventing the Pizzeria: A History of Pizza Making in Naples*. Transl. Zachary Nowak. London: Bloomsbury Academic.

Mazzocchi, A., Leone, L., Agostoni, C., Pali-Schöll, I. 2019." The secrets of the mediterranean diet. Does [only] olive oil matter?" *Nutrients* 11(12), 2941 doi: 10.3390/nu11122941.

Monteix, N. 2013. "Cooking for others: The commercial spaces for food production in Pompeii." *Gallia* 70(1): 9-26.

Rai, S., Shrivastava, A. K., Ray, S. 2018. Secondary metabolites from algae: Benefits and future perspectives. Secondary Metabolite and Functional Food Components" In *Role in Health and Disease*, edited by Shashank Kumar, 123-152. New York: Nova Publisher, Inc.

Ribbene, R. 2017. *Pani câ meusa. La cucina di strada in Sicilia-The Sicilian street food*. Palermo: Marcello Clausi Editore.

Ritchie, H., Reay, D. S., Higgins, P. 2018. "Potential of Meat Substitutes for Climate Change Mitigation and Improved Human Health in High-Income Markets." *Frontiers in Sustainable Food Systems* 2, 16 doi.org/10.3389/fsufs.2018.00016.

Rutten, M., Achterbosch, T. J., de Boer, I. J. M., Cuaresma, J. C., Geleijnse, M., Havlík, P., Heckelei, T., Ingram, J., Marette, S., van Meijl, H., Soler, L., Swinnen, J., van 't Veer, P., Vervoort, J., Zimmermann, A., Zimmermann, K. L., Zurek, M. 2018. "Metrics, models and foresight for European sustainable food and nutrition security: The vision of the SUSFANS project." *Agricultural Systems* 163:45-57.

Salas-Salvadó, J., Becerra-Tomás, N., Papandreou, C., Bulló, M. 2019. "Dietary Patterns Emphasizing the Consumption of Plant Foods in the Management of Type 2 Diabetes: A Narrative Review." *Advances in Nutrition* 10:S320-S331.

Serao, M. 1884. *Il ventre di Napoli* [*The belly of Naples*]. Milano: Fratelli Treves, Editori.

Sereni, E. 2015. *I napoletani da mangiafoglia a mangiamaccheroni* [*The Neapolitans from leaf eaters to macaroni eaters*]. Napoli: Dante & Descartes.

Steyn, N. P., McHiza, Z., Hill, J., Davids, Y. D., Venter, I., Hinrichsen, E., Opperman, M., Rumbelow, J., Jacobs, P. 2014. "Nutritional contribution of street foods to the diet of people in developing countries: A systematic review." *Public Health Nutrition* 17(6):1363-74.

Uzun, P., Serrapica, F., Masucci, F., Barone, C., Yildiz, H., Grasso, F., Di Francia, A. 2020. "Diversity of traditional Caciocavallo cheeses produced in Italy." *International Journal of Dairy Technology* 73(1): 234-243.

Van der Spiegel, M., van der Spiegel, M, Noordam, M. Y., van der Fels-Klerx, H. J. 2013. "Safety of novel protein sources (insects, microalgae, seaweed, duckweed, and rapeseed) and legislative aspects for their application in food and feed production." *Comprehensive Reviews in Food Science and Food Safety* 12(6):662-678.

Willett, W., Rockström, J., Loken, B., Springmann, M., Lang, T., Vermeulen, S., Nishtar, S., Murray, C. J. L. 2019. "Food in the Anthropocene: the EAT–Lancet Commission on healthy diets from sustainable food systems." *The Lancet* 393(10170): 447-492.

Yildiz, I. 2019. Review of climate change issues: A forcing function perspective in agricultural and energy innovation. *International Journal of Energy Research* 43(6):2200-2215.

In: Exploring Cities and Countries …   ISBN: 978-1-53618-514-0
Editor: Kathie Summers   © 2020 Nova Science Publishers, Inc.

Chapter 4

THE CONFECTIONERY OF SOUTHERN ITALY: FROM THE TRADITION TO THE FUTURE

Maria Neve Ombra[*], *Florinda Fratianni* *and Filomena Nazzaro*

Istituto di Scienze dell'Alimentazione, CNR, Avellino, Italy

ABSTRACT

The confectionery tradition of Southern Italy is as wide as the abundant production of high-quality products: milk, cream, wheat, oil and butter, chocolate, must, fresh and dried fruit. Southern Italy is full of flavors and fragrances. From the sea to the mountains, from ancient Greece to the Middle Ages to contemporary society, many influences have led to the typical desserts we taste today. The cultural background is very rich with traditions that are different from each other, which eventually left their mark in the kitchen. Southern Italy really has a very huge tradition of typical sweets, ranging from poor cuisine to the finesse of Arab pastry. In this chapter, we describe some typical cakes, such as the cassata, the pastiera, etc. making some suggestive considerations on the products of the future. The bakery of the future will look more like an art gallery than a

[*] Corresponding Author's Email: nombra@isa.cnr.it.

sweet shop: crossing its threshold will involve a multi-sensorial experience. Finally, it should increasingly consider the health aspect and environmental sustainability.

Keywords: sweet products, cassata, pastiera

1. INTRODUCTION

In Southern Italy, each region has its particular and traditional sweet products with recipes that include typical ingredients to that agronomic territory (Pagani, et al., 2014). Moreover, in many cases and especially in small towns, desserts are typical fresh handmade products, an art handed down from generation to generation, representing an ancient tradition. Every family transmits it to their children, often linked to religious or pagan parties such as carnival, but undoubtedly, they cover an important aspect for every family. Cakes were offered in the past as a means of greeting, they were exhibited in patron saints and fairs, and they represented rural peasant life, respect for family and nature, all expressions of the pure feelings of the peasant people (Bordo and Surrasca, 2003).

In this chapter, some examples from the past will be reported, as the tradition regarding the use of acorns for preparing cakes, or the antiquities found in archaeological excavations as the cassata oplontina, and the sacrificial cakes from the Sanctuary of Demeter at Monte Papalucio (Oria). Furthermore, some actual typical sweets of the various regions will be described and finally the dessert of the future will be hypothesized.

2. PAST CAKES

Since ancient times the desserts constituted, not simply foods, but also an important ritual meaning, once linked to their use as a propitiatory gift offered to the gods during the great religious rituals. The first cakes derive from ancient Greeks, prepared with honey and mixing honey and white cheese. Among the Romans, the dessert ingredients were almost the same. Like the Greeks, even in the Latin world, the dessert had symbolic and auspicious significance: an example is the ritual in which the spouses offered to Jupiter Capitol a cake, somehow survived in the traditional wedding cake. From ancient Latin literature, art and archaeological data a diverse diet for both the upper and lower social classes was reported. Staple foods included bread, olives, cheese, vegetables and fruits, fish and poultry. For the Romans the honey (main sweetener as the sugar was not known) was used even to lengthen wine, as it was attributed healing qualities (VanderVeen, 2008). Honey, eggs, wheat flour or oats, milk and wine were the first ingredients of sweets, enriched with dry fruits, dates, figs, quinces or cheese. The first elementary sweet elaborations were for a long time reserved solely for the great solemnities. Still today, their use is a symbol associated with the most important celebrations and recurrences of man's life.

2.1. Example of Sacrificial Cakes: Offering Cakes at the Sanctuary of Monte Papalucio (Oria, Southern Italy)

Finds of cakes used in sacrifice are unearthed in a relatively good state of preservation from the Sanctuary of Demeter at Monte Papalucio in Oria, Southern Italy (Primavera et al., 2019). They represent the oldest cake remains, dating back to VI-III century B.C. from the Mediterranean region and a rare evidence of the food products offered during religious practices by the indigenous people. Moreover, these sacrificial cakes from Oria Sanctuary provides an exceptional occasion to correlate the finds and antique written sources, allowing for a deeper knowledge regarding cereal processing in the past as well as the role of these products among the ancient societies of the region.

2.2. "Acorn Cakes"

Several archaeo-botanical studies revealed that acorns were used as a food source in antiquity. In Italy, the culture of using oak acorns in human nutrition has practically disappeared nowadays. Sardinia is famous in Italy for its cork plantations (*Q. suber*) that produce also acorns, once locally eaten especially after roasting and as coffee surrogate (Mearelli and Tardelli, 1995). A manna-like substance used to be taken from branches of Italian oak (*Q. cerris*), which, after boiling, becomes a sweet syrup used in several recipes. In Sardinia, only elderly people have preserved the knowledge regarding the use of acorns as food; even the mid-age people are completely unaware of this use, and the younger generations ignore at all the possibility to eat these fruits. In Urzulei, an old woman still prepares a cake made from acorn flour. The preparation is quite complex. Acorns are collected, dry stored, and finally lightly toasted in an oven (Figure 1). For the preparation of the cake, the acorn shell is broken with a stone and the cotyledons placed in a sachet. The sachet is repeatedly beaten against a hard surface to free the cotyledons from their fibrous membrane. Subsequently, the cotyledons are boiled for 3–4 h, or longer, using water that has been previously "prepared". Water preparation consists in dissolving finely ground and sieved red clay in abundant water, and letting it sediment overnight. Using "prepared water" is necessary to ensure a proper cooking of the acorn cotyledons. During cooking, acorn cotyledons dissolve in a sort of dark brown porridge, which is poured into moulds to let it cool down. The acorn cake, dark brown to almost black in color, has a slightly granular consistency, a slightly bitter taste, and a typical flavor. The culture of using acorns in human nutrition has practically disappeared since it has been abandoned after World War II. Its memory is preserved in the area of Ogliastra, Sardinia. The knowledge remains in the minds of elder people who can still remember those times (Pignone and Laghetti, 2010). Most people try to remove the memories associated to the use of acorns from their minds, in view of its association to a period of extreme poverty. In fact, there was a kind of social order in the crops used for nutrition: richest people ate "white" bread (refined flour), less wealthy used "black" (whole-flour) bread, poor ones used chestnut cakes, often collecting from the wild, and the very poorest only used acorns.

Figure 1. Oak acorns and cake made from acorn flour.

2.3. "Cassata Oplontina": An Ancient Cheesecake from Roman Period

A remarkably well-preserved fresco of the II Pompeian style is located in the patrician residence called "Villa Poppea" in Oplontis (today Torre Annunziata-Naples), showing a table with over a round dessert (Ciardiello, 2009; 2012). Surprisingly similar to "Cassata" the iconic Sicilian cake, with colorful decorations made with fruit, the image became well-known with the name of "Cassata Oplontina". It may be considered an ancient cheesecake, preceding the Sicilian Cassata.

The Vesuvius area near Naples, in Southern Italy, is one of the richest places for archaeological ruins from Roman times, visited by millions of people. The 79 A.D. eruption preserved the daily life of Pompeii and Herculaneum and of the villas built around Vesuvius as in a snapshot, allowing us the possibility to investigate every aspect of their existence. In particular, Oplontis was a suburban area of nearby Pompeii, corresponding to the modern town Torre Annunziata and archaeological excavations have brought to light a magnificent villa (Thomas and Clarke, 2007). There are only very fragmented news on the ancient Oplontis. The name arises for the first time during the Middle Ages in the Tabula Peutingeriana (Figure 2). The site is indicated at three miles from Pompeii and Stabiae, and six miles from Herculaneum consisting of some holiday villas and thermal complexes, given the plenty of waters in the area. In fact, on the Tabula it was flagged by the symbol usually employed for the thermal places, still present in the area of Torre Annunziata. The absence of occupants and the finding of building material heaped in some rooms have suggested that, during the A.D. 79 eruption, the villa was probably abandoned and undergoing renovation following the A.D. 62 earthquake. The exceptional preservation of the remains of the former settlement has allowed us to know many aspects of their daily life. In the villa A, some frescoes depict bowls with fruits, or birds as peacocks and other animals and interestingly from the paintings to date twenty-one plants have been identified to the level of species (Moser et al., 2013). Among the various well-preserved frescoes, there is that shown in Figure 2 with a red-fringed dessert. In the Triclinium of Villa A-Oplontis, it is still perfectly visible the wall-painting that depicts a tripod, with over a dessert. Surprisingly it would seem like a Sicilian cassata of modern times, a part the edge that it is red rather than green. The recipe for this cake is not reported in any of the documents that came to us about the culinary customs of the ancient Romans, not even among the many recipes written by Apicio in "De re Coquinaria". It seems to be a sort of "cassata siciliana" with ricotta (or cheese), almond flour, honey and pieces of fruit and dried fruit, almost certainly a fine dessert served in the homes of the rich. As it would seem from the picture, it also contained dried fruits and pieces of fruit as decoration on surface. The dessert is disposed on a support with silver tray and folding handles. The color contrast is still alive that seems just painted, thanks to the Vesuvius lava that has protected it to this day. The amazement is great because the work performed 2000 years ago, still looks much like ours today. The table is richly worked, has feet in the form of hare legs and it adorns with other still life paintings, one of its triclinium, corresponding to our present dining room. We can imagine the servitude that in any occasional banquet placed the object here with extreme delicacy, locating it in the center of the room, available to diners disposing at horseshoe on the edges of the walls, very delighted at every lunch end. To emphasize how in the fresco is cared for in detail the exposure of the dessert, it almost seems to see the scene of the ancient diners gathered around it. Studying the dietary habits of the ancient romans and the range of ingredients, they could know and use, it was assumed a hypothetical recipe of the mysterious dessert, with plausible indications for local pastry chefs, which realized it. Latin literature recounts mainly the dining habits of the upper classes and the most famous description of a Roman meal is the Trimalchio's dinner party in *Satyricon* (Grimm, 2006). Knowledges on the dietary habits and on foodstuffs available to at least a part of people has been gathered from texts, wall-paintings or mosaics, and even from the remains of the food itself discovered in sites such as Pompeii (Pate et al., 2016). Walnuts, almonds, hazel nuts, pine nuts, chestnuts and sesame seeds were widespread. Nuts were used in pastries, for desserts sweetened with honey. Several fruits were dried to increase their shelf-life. Fig was a typical component of quotidian meals in the Mediterranean regions (Bakels and Jacomet, 2003), being abundant products, also easy to store and therefore available all year. Vineyards were also widely extended over the Vesuvius area. According to Pliny, a large number of cultivars were grown in that region. With the exception of the date palm, all the other products could be grown locally. Date was probably imported from North Africa since Phoenix dactylifera does not produce fruit in the region (Robinson, 2002). The quality and culinary uses of cheese are mentioned by a number of Roman authors, as Pliny the Elder in Historia Naturalis, Varro in De Re Rustica while a detailed description of Roman cheesemaking was reported by Columella in *De Re Rustica*. They used honey and wine-must syrup as sweetener in the sweet foods. They also added dried fruits (figs, dates and plums) and fresh berries. A likely recipe of Cassata Oplontis was extrapolated from all these informations. "Cassata Oplontina"- recipe: 1 kg ricotta cheese (better than sheep), 250 g of honey, 80 g dried apricots, 80 g dried plums, 70 g of grapes pass, 60 g pine nuts, 100 g shelled nuts, a dozen pounded dates. For the outer edge of the dessert, 150 g almond flour, 2 spoons of honey, red color with red fruits juice. The dessert had something more, something new to the time standard. It was an attempt to bring about something different adding an elaboration that, as far as we know, had never been seen before. Something that had its presence and its individuality. Above all, it was extremely innovative for those times, as the Sicilian Cassata will arise only later. Cassata Oplontina may be considered an ancient cheesecake, while the first "cheese cake" dates back to 2000 BC on the Greek island of Samos (Bovbjerg and Iggers, 1989). In Greece, cheesecake represented a good source of energy and there is evidence that it was served to athletes during the first Olympic Games in 776 B.C. In addition, greek spouses used cheesecake as a wedding cake. The simple ingredients of flour, wheat, honey and cheese were mixed and baked, very different from the more elaborated recipes available today. Later Romans modified the recipe and the ingredients were baked under a hot brick, they served it on special occasions. With the expansion of the empire, Romans brought cheesecake recipe to other populations. Great Britain and Eastern Europe began experimenting with ways to put their own tipical elements on cheesecake. In each country of Europe, the recipes started taking on different cultural shapes. Around the World, each region has its own take on the best way to make the dessert. Italians use ricotta cheese, while the Greeks use mizithra or feta. Germans prefer cottage cheese, while the Japanese use a combination of cornstarch and egg whites. There are special cheesecakes with blue cheese, seafood, spicy chilies and even tofu. Despite all the variety, the main ingredients: cheese, wheat and a sweetener, remain the same. From its beginnings on Samos to its actual distinguishing characteristics around the world this cake remains a favorite for sweet tooths of all ages.

Figure 2. (a) A fresco of Villa Poppea (Oplontis), with the "Cassata Oplontina" and (b) Tabula Peutingeriana.

Sweets contain high amounts of sugar, refined flour, and added fats. They can be extremely high in calories whereas considering the sweets of the past, described above, even though at high energetic content, they were healthier than the current cakes. At first, they contained various fresh and dried fruits, nuts, pine seeds, almonds, and dates with beneficial effects on human health. Secondly, given the absence of sugar in ancient Greece and Rome, only the honey was present as a sweetener. Moreover, we observed a low presence of animal fats in the past recipes, since ricotta of sheep was used, whereas the modern cakes often contain elaborated creams, rich in fats. Therefore, calculating the caloric content of an ancient dessert, we obtained a value of about 220 Kcal/100 g, at difference of a modern cheesecake, or chocolate cookies with a higher number of calories 321 Kcal/100 g and 492 Kcal/100g respectively. In Table 1, we reported the nutritional values for some common desserts and the comparison with an ancient cheesecake. An important concept must be adopted for the creation of healthy desserts without the addition of fats or sugars, for example by exploiting the natural sweetness of the fruits and vegetables and replacing whole milk with low-fat milk or vegetable milk, we could certainly reduce the calorie of a muffin.

3. TYPICAL DESSERTS OF SOUTHERN ITALY

In Southern Italy, there are hundreds of different sweets, (Costantino and Schacht, 2013) some of which associated with particular feast days. In this paragraph, we describe the most famous ones (Figure 3).

Table 1. Comparison of nutritional values between present and past sweet products

PAST	PRESENT		
	- Kcal +		
Ancient cheesecake	Value/100 g	Cheesecake	Muffin, chocolate	Chocolate cookies
220	Kcal/100g	321	389	492
13.5	Carbohydrates (g)	25.5	50.81	65.36
9.6	Total lipid (g)	22.5	18.16	24.72
8.6	Proteins (g)	5.5	6.4	5.1

(Nutritional values including energy, protein, carbohydrate, and fat contents were based on the information given on USDA National Nutrient Database for Standard Reference. Available online: https://fdc.nal.usda.gov/)

Figure 3. Typical sweets from Southern Italy.

3.1. "Cassata Siciliana"

Cassata Siciliana is a typical dessert with sponge cake, stuffed with ricotta cheese, completely covered with marzipan and decorated with candied fruits. It is one of the delicious dessert from Sicily that is traditionally eaten in winter or spring (around Easter time). The Cassata is rich in flavor and history, and as the cannoli, it is known all over the world. It has undergone changes, new and different influences, as the foreign dominions in Sicily. The origins date back to the Arab domination in Sicily between the 9th and the 11th centuries (Davidson, 2014). They introduced in Sicily sugar cane, lemon, cedar, and bitter orange, increased almond cultivation, previously initiated by the Phoenicians. Along with the sheep's ricotta, produced in Sicily from a long time, all the basic ingredients of the cassata were assembled. This traditional recipe would have roots attached to the religious cult of the sun, where the round shape of the dessert symbolized element of fertility, rebirth and resurrection. The name has uncertain origin. For some it would descend from the Latin "caseus" (cheese), for others by the arab "qas'at" (large and deep bowl). In any case, it was born from the encounter of the two cultures: the ricotta ingredient of the Roman pastoral world, the almond paste and the candied elements of Arab society (Dickie, 2008). In the Norman period, around the end of 1100, with the creation by the nuns of the Convent of the Martorana in Palermo, of the real pasta, called "martorana", a mixture of almond flour and sugar, colored green with herbal extracts, the previous casing was replaced, by a new wrap of real pasta said martoran. It was passed from the baked to the cold-baked cassata (Basile, 2004). The oldest text in which it appears the first time the word cassata is the" *Declarus"* (Sinesio, 1305-1386), the first dictionary Sicilian-Latin and in the entry "cassata" he wrote: *cibus ex pasta panis et caseus compositus"*.

3.2. "Cannoli"

Cannoli are famous sweets of Sicily, a land that produces an incredibly variegated and very fine pastry. Fried dough cylinders filled with a mixture of ricotta and candied fruit, flavored with cinnamon, but the variations are endless and all very tasty. Often the crunchy cylinder may be filled with creamy ricotta and chocolate flakes. A unique flavor, known worldwide that embodies aromas and pure essence of Sicily. Originally the dough was rolled around river canes (hence the name cannolo) and the first descriptions date back to 75 BC. Probably it was invented by the cloistered nuns, but for others it is an Arab or even Roman recipe (Di Leo, 2016).

3.3. "Pastiera"

Neapolitan pastiera is an Easter cake made with shortcrust pastry filled with a cream of wheat and ricotta, flavored with orange blossom water and spices, with the addition of candied fruit. Wheat is a symbol of richness and fruitfulness, and eggs symbolize nascent life, characterizing the pastiera as a dessert made of ingredients with meanings of prosperity and vitality. The origins take us far back in time to the rituals that celebrated the arrival of spring. There is no definite information but it was realized in a Neapolitan monastery, remained unknown: a nun of the monastery added to the cake the scent of the orange blossom of the convent, a little grain, eggs, symbol of new life, wildflower water, fragrant like spring, cedar and aromatic spices from Asia. Today the pastiera filling is composed of wheat kernels that, after a long soaking for 2–3 days and cooking in water, are added to milk, sugar, egg yolks, ricotta cheese, candied fruit, lemon rind, and cinnamon (Pignataro, 2016).

3.4. "Pasticciotto"

Pasticciotto is an ancient typical dessert of Salento (Puglia region) and the date of birth dates back to 1707. In fact, it was found in an inventory of the Curia of Nardò, on the death of the Bishop, a report that describes among other objects "copper barchiglie to make pasticciotti". According to another tradition, they date back to 1745, when in Galatina in the Ascalone family confectionery; they were prepared for the Saint Paul feast. Even today, this historic pastry shop produces delicious Pasticciotti, composed of shortcrust pastry filled with custard and sour cherries, baked in the oven. (Barletta, 2006).

3.5. Typical Sweets of Calabria

Mostaccioli are typical sweets of the area of Soriano Calabro, they are produced with natural ingredients, flour, honey and hot must, to which anthropomorphic forms are given, animals, flowers. Mostaccioli are consumed during fairs, Christmas and Easter parties.

Pignolata is a typical dessert of Calabria, made from fried dough balls covered with honey, traditionally made at Carnival. Chiacchere are prepared during the period of the Carnival celebrations. They are modeled in various forms, made with natural ingredients, such as flour, oil, fried or baked (Calabretta, 2015).

3.6. "Sardinian Products"

In Sardinia, products with semolina from durum wheat are still used, stuffed with honey and concentrated grape-must (named sapa) as alternatives to sugar (Fancello, 2018). This simple recipe can be enriched with grated lemon and orange rind and spices then formed as a small pocket for pistiddu; it can contain almonds, obtaining the so-called papassino, or candied fruits and nuts, making pani 'saba. Grape-must is also frequently utilized in Southern Italy where vine cultivation is very common. Other sweets are amaretti with an almond base. Sardinian sweets contain many ingredients with beneficial properties as nuts, almond, fruit, grape-must, honey.

4. FUTURE SWEETS

Sweets are a high-calorie food, with high sugar content. Sugar, like protein and fat, when consumed in excess leads to conditions such as obesity and related diseases and Dietary Guidelines recommend limiting dietary sugar less than 10% of total energy intake (World Health Organization, 2015). The quality of a cake is highly influenced by the quality and balance of ingredients. The primary ingredients are wheat flour, sugar, fat, milk, egg and leavening agents. Alternative sweeteners in a future pastry product formulation will replace sugar, and certain sweet proteins could be considered as sugar replacers. Furthermore, we hypothesize the future sweets like that in Figure 4. In the first place, a main objective will be the development of sweets based on a mixture of flours enriched of substances from vegetables, achieving alternative products with a low GI (Gbenga-Fabusiwa et al., 2019; Hussain, 2019). Foods that elicit a lower postprandial glycemic response may be beneficial to manage body weight (Schwingshackl and Hoffmann, 2013). The glycemic response that follows the consumption of a carbohydrate-containing food depends on the amount of carbohydrate consumed as well as its glycemic index (GI) (Jenkins et al. 1981). The carbohydrates in low GI foods are more slowly digested and absorbed and are thus beneficial in controlling postprandial blood glucose excursions (Jenkins et al. 2002). A partial replacement of wheat flour by functional ingredients rich in phenolics and fibers of fruits and vegetables, in biscuits, cakes or widely consumed bakery products, allowed decreasing the glycemic index. This reformulation intervention could represent an important dietary strategy. Chemopreventive actions of bioactive compounds of foods are currently objected to numerous studies. Bioactive compounds can interfere with biochemical processes at a molecular level. Because of their chemical structures, dietary phytochemicals exert multiple activities by interacting with several molecular pathways of glucose homeostasis. These mechanisms include slowing carbohydrate digestion and glucose absorption, stimulation of insulin secretion, modulation of glucose release, activation of insulin receptors and glucose uptake in the insulin-sensitive tissues. Numerous studies have shown that they can activate and/or silence transcription factors, and consequently influence gene expression, and regulate different signaling pathways in the muscle, the liver, pancreatic β-cells, the hypothalamus, and adipose tissue, thereby contributing to glucose homeostasis (Matsukawa et al., 2015). Furthermore, the modulation of microbial metabolism can synergically be beneficial to glucose homeostasis. The functional food science has gained great relevance, this field of nutrition combines food knowledge with health and human physiology to contrast or delay diseases (Galanakis, 2017). Several studies aim at the collection of more accurate data to improve the possible beneficial health effects of the consumption of functional foods, offering the possibility to improve human health thereby reducing healthcare costs. It would be desirable/attractive that the sweets of the future meet these requirements. Known since antiquity the close relationship between food and health, since the ancient Greeks already conscious of obesity as a health risk, observing that premature death was more common in people who were fat than lean (Haslam, 2016). Hippocrates argued: "Make food your medicine and medicine is your food". The Roman physician and philosopher Galen referred to the polysarkos, (obese) as people, which cannot walk without sweating, cannot breathe easily, etc. After all, by considering the sweets of the past, even though at high energetic content, they were healthier than the current cakes. In fact, they contained fresh and dried fruits, rich in bioactive compounds with positive effects on human health (Killgrove and Tykot, 2013). In addition, given the absence of sugar and the only presence of honey as a sweetener, they were certainly more acceptable from a health point of view. Honey contributed to the health and nutritional status of ancient people having a variety of components that are beneficial for human well-being (Crittenden, 2011). Egyptians, Greeks, Romans, and Chinese to heal wounds and diseases of the gut, including gastric ulcers, have traditionally used it. It has also been used as a remedy for cough, sore throat, and earaches (Ajibola et al., 2012). Accordingly, honey is well-known for its biological activities. These beneficial actions have been ascribed to its antimicrobial, anti-inflammatory and antioxidant potential. Natural honey contains on average 38.5% fructose, 31% glucose, 12% other sugars, 17% water, 0.5% protein, organic acids, minerals, amino acids, vitamins. Minor amounts of bioactive components with health benefits include phenolic acids, flavonoids, ascorbic acid, proteins, carotenoids (Pasupuleti et al., 2017). Finally, it should be emphasized the low presence of animal fats in the past desserts, not excessive as in modern cakes often containing elaborated creams, since ricotta of sheep was used. Very different from the modern cake, with the complicated architectures of different doughs and the ability to use an innumerable combination of creams and kinds of stuff (Figure 5). The modern desserts should go back to the ancient recipes. In fact, nutrients to limit in the diet as saturated fatty acids, added sugars and sodium were absent or effectively limited, while are included and sometimes excessive in modern sweets. On the contrary, healthy nutrients as fruits, nuts were abundant in the past, while are frequently absent in modern pastry products. Fruits and nuts possess great nutritional and functional importance due to the source of highly desirable macro-and micronutrients. Epidemiological studies have shown that dietary patterns, in which they are featured prominently, reduce the risk of cardiometabolic disease. Numerous evidence suggest that increased consumption of both could help to reduce the risk of chronic diseases, recommending an intake of at least five portions daily of fruits. (Ashfield-Watt et al., 2004). Nuts contain high amounts of vegetable proteins and fat-soluble bioactive. As well, they are rich in other nutrients and provide dietary fiber, vitamins, minerals and phytochemicals such as phenolic acids, flavonoids, lignin, proanthocyanidins, and carotenoids, among others. A synergistic interaction of all these bioactive constituents may all favorably influence human health (Salas-Salvadó et al., 2011; Donato, 2017). Finally, the future of pastry will be more creative, and we will resort to original formulas less sugar, water and cocoa will be used, due to water shortage and cocoa raised prices. Chocolates and various sweets will have little traditional colors, textures, and flavors. In addition, will the shapes be phantasmagorical because they are made with 3D printers? The bakery of the future will look more like an art gallery than a sweet shop: crossing its threshold will involve a multi-sensorial experience. In the future, climate change will have a further impact on agricultural yield, food quality and supply, with reduced resources and higher food prices. Climate change is straining agriculture and the entire production system. The expected decline in the production of three key cereals for global livelihood is very serious, namely maize, wheat, rice. Droughts and floods undermine production, against a 33% increase in demand in 2050. Two comfort foods, such as chocolate and coffee, are also in danger. (Gross, 2014). The first, in fact, grows only in territories with a rich and very humid soil. Many plantations, however, are found in regions where temperatures are becoming more volatile: this is why there is talk of a drastic drop in production by 2030. The second is put at risk by the crisis of bee moreover, coffee plants prefer the cool shade of trees and too hot does not help (Marshman et al., 2019). It also promotes "coffee rust" and other fungi. Latin America and Africa risk losing their plantations. Probably in the future, the cakes will be prepared with unconventional ingredients such as tomato, dandelion, and burdock or other vegetables with a sweet-soft taste. Among marine resources, algae will be more exploited, being valuable sources rich in minerals and beneficial bioactive compounds for our body, and for their limited caloric intake (less than 50 kcal per 100 grams) (Li et al., 2018; Rai et al., 2018). Likewise, jellyfish can be introduced in our diet and certainly, vegan confectionery will play a key role in innovation contest. Jellyfish are rich in collagen, with about 80% protein and a balanced presence of fats (about 20%), only giving 40 calories per 100 grams (Khong, 2016) Moreover, the edible flowers could have an interesting application as natural colorants, representing an alternative to the use of synthetic dyes in foods (Díaz-García et al., 2015). Replacement artificial dyes with natural coloring agents is one of the crucial interests of the food industry to satisfy the consumption trends. For example, some cream formulations require specific additives, as represented by dyes and the use of natural colorants, which are generally considered safer than the artificial ones, may be recommended (Pires et al., 2018; Ombra *et al.*, 2019). Anthocyanins water-soluble pigments extracted from plants, giving the blue, purple and red color of many plant tissues are authorized food colorants. These phenolic compounds are widely found in fruits (especially berries), as well as in flowers and leaves.

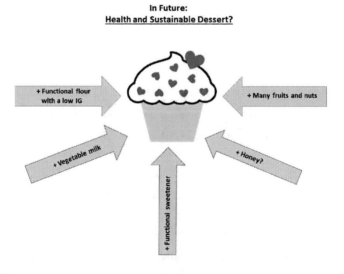

Figure 4. Future sweet.

Figure 5. Comparison between past and present cakes.

CONCLUSION

Even in the past, analogously today, food is brought to our tables in an endless array of shapes, colors, and recipes; it is designed. Men transform food for greater pleasure, for practical purposes such as longer shell life and additionally to convey values and tell myths. Food design helps to pass on cultural information collected by former generations and provides structures how to lay out life. We must endorse the idea that nice, delightful things may be done well knowingly, respecting our health and considering our well-being completely. Not only is a simple change taking place on sweet food, but a real metamorphosis. It is time to move from a logic of sacrifice to one of acceptance and gratification. From the logic of exclusion to awareness, which good does not exclude healthy. In this scenario, even on highly gratified indulgent foods, desserts, we will abandon an uncompromising attitude, because quality will make us feel good about ourselves: functional foods, special flours have a great future. As a general guideline, there is a return to the origins, especially on the raw material, improving the past in a modern key. Finally, a multisensoriality, which starts from the consistency of the papers chosen for the packaging of sweets to the perfumes that permeate the store.

ACKNOWLEDGMENTS

The authors would like to thank the "Archeoclub Torre Annunziata Oplontis" (No-profit association for the discovery, dissemination and enhancement of the artistic, cultural and archaeological heritage) and the friends A. Izzo, G. Izzo, R. Falanga, M. Matrone, A. Monaco.

REFERENCES

Ajibola, A., Chamunorwa, J. P. & Erlwanger, K. H. (2012). "Nutraceutical values of natural honey and its contribution to human health and wealth". *Nutrition & Metabolism, 9*, 61.

Ashfield-Watt, P. A., Welch, A. A., Day, N. E. & Bingham, S. A. (2004). "Is 'five-a-day' an effective way of increasing fruit and vegetable intakes?". *Public Health Nutrition, 7*(2), 257-61.

Bakels, C. & Jacomet, S. (2003). "Access to luxury foods in Central Europe during the Roman period: The archaeobotanical evidence". *World Archaeology, 34*(3), 542-557.

Barletta, R. (2006). *Dolci tipici salentini, Storia, folclore, curiosità, ricette.* [*Typical Salento sweets, history, folklore, curiosities, recipes*]. Lecce: Edizioni del Grifo.

Basile, G. & Musco Dominici, A. (2004). *Mangiare di festa.* [*Eat festive*]. Palermo: Kalos.

Bordo, V. & Surrasca, A. (2003). *L'Italia dei Dolci. Guida alla scoperta e alla conoscenza.* [*Italy of Sweets. Guide to discovery and knowledge*]. Bra (Cuneo): Slow Food.

Bovbjerg, D. & Iggers, J. (1989). *The Joy of Cheesecake*, New York: Barron's Educational Series.

Calabretta, A. (2015). *Calabria Eat sweet and savory*. Roma: GEDI Gruppo Editoriale.

Ciardiello, R. (2012). "Beryllos, the Jews and the Villa of Poppaea." In *Houses and Temples in Roman Antiquity and New Testament*, edited by David L. Balch and Annette Weissenrieder, 265-282. Tübingen: Mohr Siebeck.

Ciardiello, R. (2009). "La Villa di Poppea ad Oplontis: decorazioni dalla Repubblica all'Impero." [The Villa di Poppea in Oplontis: decorations from the Republic to the Empire]. In *Studies on Vesuvius' north slope and the bay of Naples*, edited by Girolamo F. De Simone, Roger T. Macfarlane, 64-76. Roma: Herder.

Costantino, R. & Schacht, J. (2013). *Southern Italian Desserts: Rediscovering the Sweet Traditions of Calabria*, Campania, Basilicata, Puglia, and Sicily. Emeryville: Ten Speed Press.

Crittenden, A. N. (2011). "The Importance of Honey Consumption in Human Evolution". *Food and Foodways*, *19*, 257-73.

Davidson, A. (2014). *The Oxford Companion to Food*. Oxford: Oxford University Press.

Díaz-García, M. C., Castellar, M. R., Obón, J. M., Obón, C., Alcaraz, F. & Rivera, D. (2015). "Production of an anthocyanin-rich food colourant from Thymus moroderi and its application in foods". *Journal of Science of Food and Agriculture.*, *95*(6), 1283-1293.

Dickie, J. (2008). Delizia! *The Epic History of Italians and Their Food*, New York: Free Press.

Di Leo, M. A. (2016). *I dolci siciliani in 450 ricette. [Sicilian sweets in 450 recipes]* Roma: Newton Compton Editori.

Donato, F., Romagnolo, D. F. & Selmin, O. I. (2017). "Mediterranean Diet and Prevention of Chronic Diseases". *Nutrition Today*, *52*, 208–222.

Fancello, G. (2018). Durches. Un viaggio nella storia dei dolci dall'antichità ai giorni nostri. [*Durches. A journey through the history of sweets from antiquity to the present day*]. Cagliari: Arkadia edizioni.

Galanakis, C. M. (2017). *Nutraceutical and Functional Food Components: Effects of Innovative Processing Techniques*. Amsterdam: Elsevier Inc.

Gbenga-Fabusiwa, F. J., Oladele, E. P., Oboh, G., Adefegha, S. A., Fabusiwa O. F., Osho, P. O., Enikuomehin, A. & Oshodi, A. A. (2019). "Glycemic Response in Diabetic Subjects to Biscuits Produced from Blends of Pigeon Pea and Wheat Flour". *Plant Foods for Human Nutrition, 74*(4), 553-559.

Grimm, V. E. (2006). "On Food and the Body." In *A Companion to the Roman Empire*, edited by David S. Potter, 354-368, Malden: Blackwell Publishing Ltd.

Gross, M. (2014). "Coffee and chocolate in danger". *Current Biology, 24*(11), R503-R506.

Haslam, D. (2016). "Weight management in obesity – past and present". *International Journal of Clinical Practice, 70*, 206–217.

Hussain, S. Z., Beigh, M. A., Qadri, T., Naseer, B. & Zargar, I. (2019). "Development of low glycemic index muffins using water chestnut and barley flour". *Journal of Food Processing and Preservation, 43*, e14049. doi.org/10.1111/jfpp.14049.

Jenkins, D. J. A., Wolever, T. M. S. & Taylor, R. H. (1981). "Glycemic index of foods: A physiological basis for carbohydrate exchange". *American Journal of Clinical Nutrition, 34*(3), 362-366.

Jenkins, D. J. A., Kendall, C. W. C., Augustin, L. S. A., Franceschi, S., Hamidi, M., Marchie, A., Jenkins, A. L. & Axelsen, M. (2002). "Glycemic index: overview of implications in .health and disease". *American Journal of Clinical Nutrition, 76*(1), 266S-273S.

Killgrove, K. & Tykot, R. H. (2013). "Food for Rome: A stable isotope investigation of diet in the Imperial period (1st-3rd centuries AD)". *Journal of Anthropological Archaeology, 32*(1), 28-38.

Khong, N. M. H., Yusoff, F. M., Jamilah, B., BasriaI, M., Maznah, I., Chan, K. W. & Nishikawa, J. (2016). "Nutritional composition and total collagen content of three commercially important edible jellyfish". *Food Chemistry*, 196: 953-960

Li, Z. S., Zheng, J. W., Manabe, Y., Hirata, T. & Sugawara, T. (2018). "Anti-obesity properties of the dietary green Alga, Codium cylindricum, in high-fat diet-induced obese mice". *Journal of Nutritional Science and Vitaminology, 64*(5), 347-356.

Marshman, J., Blay-Palmer, A. & Landman, K. (2019). "Anthropocene crisis: Climate change, pollinators, and food security". *Environments – MDPI, 6*(2), 22

Matsukawa, T., Inaguma, T., Han, J., Villareal, M. O. & Isoda, H. (2015). "Cyanidin-3-glucoside derived from black soybeans ameliorate type 2 diabetes through the induction of differentiation of preadipocytes into smaller and insulin-sensitive adipocytes". *Journal of Nutritional Biochemistry, 26*(8), 860-867.

Mearelli, F. & Tardelli, C. (1995). "Maremma mediterranea". [Mediterranean Maremma]. *Erboristeria domain*, 45-47.

Moser, D., Allevato, E., Clarke, J. R., Gaetano Di Pasquale, G. & Nelle, O. (2013). "Archaeobotany at Oplontis: woody remains from the Roman Villa of Poppaea (Naples, Italy). *Vegetation History and Archaeobotany, 22*, 397–408.

Ombra, M. N., d'Acierno, A., Nazzaro, F. & Fratianni, F. (2019). "Health attributes of ten edible flowers used in Mediterranean diet: anti-proliferative and enzyme-inhibitory properties". *Trends in Phytochemical Research, 3*(4), 251-260.

Pagani, M. A., Lucisano, M. & Mariotti, M. (2014). Italian Bakery Products. *Bakery Products Science and Technology*: Second Edition 9781119967156, edited by Weibiao Zhou, Yuan H. Hui, 685-721. Hoboken: Wiley-Blackwell.

Pasupuleti, V. R., Sammugam, L., Ramesh, N. & Gan, S. H. (2017). Honey, Propolis, and Royal Jelly: "A Comprehensive Review of Their Biological Actions and Health Benefits". *Oxidative Medicine & Cellular Longevity, 1259510*. doi.org/10.1155/2017/1259510.

Pate, F. D., Henneberg, R. J. & Henneberg, M. (2016). "Stable carbon and nitrogen isotope evidence for dietary variability at Ancient Pompeii, Italy". *Mediterranean Archaeology Archaeometry, 16*(1), 127-133.

Pignataro, L. (2016). *I dolci napoletani. [The Neapolitan sweets]*. Roma: Newton Compton ed.

Pignone, D. & Laghetti, G. (2010). "On sweet acorn (Quercus spp.) cake tradition in Italian cultural and ethnic islands". *Genetic Resources and Crop Evolution*, *57*, 1261–1266.

Pires, T. C. S. P., Dias, M. I., Barros, L., Barreira, J. C. M., Santos-Buelga, C. & Ferreira, I. C. F. R. (2018). "Incorporation of natural colorants obtained from edible flowers in yogurts". *LWT*, *97*, 668-675.

Primavera, M., Heiss, A. G., Valamoti, M. S., Quarta, G., Masieri, M. & Fiorentino, G. (2019). "Inside sacrificial cakes: plant components and production processes of food offerings at the Demeter and Persephone sanctuary of Monte Papalucio (Oria, southern Italy)". *Archaeological and Anthropological Sciences*, *11*(4), 1273-1287.

Rai, S., Shrivastava, A. K. & Ray, S. (2018). Secondary metabolites from algae: Benefits and future perspectives. Secondary Metabolite and Functional Food Components" In *Role in Health and Disease*, edited by Shashank Kumar, 123-152. New York: Nova Publisher, Inc.

Robinson, M. (2002). "Domestic burnt offerings and sacrifices at Roman and pre-Roman Pompeii, Italy". *Vegetation History and Archaeobotany*, *11*, 93-100.

Salas-Salvadó, J., Casas-Agustench, P. & Salas-Huetos, A. (2011). "Cultural and historical aspects of Mediterranean nuts with emphasis on their attributed healthy and nutritional properties". *Nutrition Metabolism & Cardiovascular Diseases*, *21*, S1-S6.

Schwingshackl, L. & Hoffmann, G. (2013). "Long-term effects of low glycemic index/load vs. high glycemic index/load diets on parameters of obesity and obesity-associated risks: A systematic review and meta-analysis". *Nutrition, Metabolism and Cardiovascular Diseases*, *23*(8), 699-706.

Thomas, M. L. & Clarke, J. R. (2007). "The Oplontis Project 2005-6: Observations on the construction history of Villa A at Torre Annunziata". *Journal of Roman Archaeology*, *20* (1), 223-232.

VanderVeen, M. (2008). "Food as embodied material culture: diversity and change in plant food consumption in Roman Britain". *Journal of Roman Archaeology*, *21*, 83-110.

World Health Organization. (2015). *Guideline: Sugars Intake for Adults and Children*. Geneva: Department of Nutrition for Health and Development World Health Organization, (http://apps.who.int/iris/bitstream/10665/149782/1/9789241549028_eng.pdf).

In: Exploring Cities and Countries …   ISBN: 978-1-53618-514-0
Editor: Kathie Summers   © 2020 Nova Science Publishers, Inc.

Chapter 5

GASTRONOMIC PUBLIC POLICY: MINAS GERAIS ON THE SCENE

Lelis Maia Brito[1,] and Lidiane Nunes da Silveira[2, †]*

[1]Department of Public Management, Ouro Preto Federal University
Ouro Preto, Minas Gerais, Brasil
[2]Social Sciences Coordination, Minas Gerais Federal Institute
Ouro Preto, Minas Gerais, Brasil

ABSTRACT

Considering the material and immaterial heritage as a reflection of the identity of a community, local gastronomy can be analyzed as an immaterial heritage that involves unique know-how, places and actions that represent local, historical and cultural aspects of a given population. Regarding the relevance of recognizing gastronomy as an intangible heritage, there is a trend towards the rescue of the traditional cook and the revaluation of cultural roots. In this sense, public policies aimed at cultural tourism aim to strengthen the cultural values of a society, since cultural heritage is the expression of people's identity, their territory, their history,

---
* Corresponding Author's Email: lelis@ufop.edu.br.
† Corresponding Author's Email: lidianenunes@ymail.com.

tradition and civilization. In this sense, this article proposes to analyze and discuss public policies and actions of gastronomy actors focused on local cuisine. This article highlights that policies of this nature consider that sustainable tourism can represent a considerable instrument of social strength and economic development through employment and income generation, combined with cultural preservation and the increase in tourist and economic activities in general. Thus, for this theoretical essay, the case of Minas Gerais gastronomy, in Brazil, is used as an example, due to the Gastronomy Development Policy created by that State and other mechanisms proposed by public institutions, private institutions and civil society. This theoretical essay concludes that the strengthening of Minas Gerais gastronomy as a public policy enhances the expertise of the region and provides the State, in terms of participation and promotion of public actions, and all sectors involved, conditions to institutionalize gastronomy, not only family farming, but also chefs and, mainly, consumers, as a tourist destination in a specific and competitive market.

Keywords: gastronomy, public policy, intangible heritage and Minas Gerais

INTRODUCTION

The recognition of gastronomy as an intangible heritage is directly related to the geographical, historical and cultural aspects of a population. The process of patrimonialization and the appropriation of these items can contribute significantly to an effective local economic development.

The actions promoted by the Brazilian government are carried out by the National Institute of National Historical and Artistic Heritage (IPHAN), through the listing, registration and listing of cultural assets. The patrimonializing process of material and immaterial properties reaffirms the idea of belonging and appreciation, being characterized as an instrument capable of strengthening local development and considerably increasing the quality of life of the citizen.

Considering material and immaterial heritage as a reflection of the identity of a community, local gastronomy can be analyzed as an intangible heritage that involves unique know-how, places and doings that represents local, historical and cultural aspects of a certain population. However, nowadays these procedures and doings that constitute part of the identity of communities have been set aside by citizens, as a direct consequence of new modern life habits, lack of time and the increase of industrialized, frozen and multiprocessed products 'offer and consumption.

In this context, behaviors, trends and attitudes towards food become less local and more globalized. Due to the fast food culture, regional culinary practices are losing space for "ready meals", which do not require manipulation and preparation, so that people no longer enjoy the consumption of local products (which involves identity, history and tradition) and, instead, consume items with a global identity, low nutritional value and no level of community representation.

Due to this loss, governmental interventions are needed, which are developed through public policies that intend to revitalize cultural heritage, bringing as a consequence of a well succeeded implementation the local cultural reaffirmation.

In Brazil, the promotion of popular participation and decentralized government offer the public administration the opportunity to listen to the demands of the community and decide on social proposals, through the proximity between the governor and the governed. Thus, this research proposes to analyze and discuss the importance of public policies aimed at local gastronomy and how they can contribute to the economic development of the communities involved, through the creation of jobs and income and the increase of economic and tourist activities in general.

PUBLIC POLICIES AND GASTRONOMY

Concerning the relevance of the recognition of gastronomy as an immaterial heritage, a tendency to rescue of traditional culinary can be observed along with cultural roots. This fact becomes necessary on account of the observance that the prepares and unique know how of typical cuisine have been losing its space and historical and cultural characteristics, due to market globalization, homogenization of menu and the current population interest on fast and cheap food, and on the facilitation of the access to items that once were not accessible by local culture (Beluzzo 2004).

It is worth mentioning that this whole discussion can be considered a movement in favor of strengthening cultural values related to the typical cuisine of a country or region. It is believed that this type of movement, in a way, rescues the cultural importance of food and, in another, considers that this sector is important for social and economic development, since it covers many contexts / areas. This movement can be seen from the implementation of several public policies aimed at food, such as the European Union and Latin America.

European Union case is related to European Parliament's Committee on Culture and Education, which, in 2014, has mobilized itself about the European Parliament Resolution concerning European gastronomic heritage, portraying its cultural and educational aspects and recognizing the importance of food and gastronomy as an artistic and cultural expression and one of the fundamental pillars of families and social relations. (Cavicchi & Stancova 2016).

In Latin America, intangible heritage has been recognized as a potential area for sustainable tourism development, which can be particularly important for the income generation of local communities. This is because culinary heritage has been valued in different parts of the continent, such as the recognition of Mexican cuisine as an immaterial world heritage and the development of Novoandina cuisine in Peru (OECD 2012). For UNESCO's list of intangible cultural heritage, Mexican cuisine, the Mediterranean diet and French gastronomy, due to the knowledge and techniques used by them, which express the identity of the community, strengthening social ties, local, regional and national identities. (Gordin and Trabskaya 2013).

What is observed is that this movement for the development of gastronomy as a cultural identity has an important pillar: the role of food in the social and economic development of a community. This means that food is a way to discover the local history and culture of a given region, providing tourists with a fun way to familiarize themselves with the chosen destination. This means that, for these authors, gastronomy is part of the local character and product of the mentality of a particular region, reflecting myths, religious peculiarities, family relationships and local characteristics. (Gordin and Trabskaya 2013; Leigh 2000).

The use of local foods can directly or indirectly contribute to the sustainability of a region, by stimulating and supporting agriculture and food production. In addition, for these authors, all this stimulus results in the empowerment of the community through the creation of jobs and the encouragement of entrepreneurship, creating local pride in their production and reinforcing the identity of a local brand (OECD 2012; Telfer & Wall 1996).

Thus, cultural identity and gastronomy are totally linked, since food is configured as a language related to people's culture, practices and regional behaviors (Garcia, 1999). One of the relevant aspects of preserving local gastronomy is the fact that it allows the economic development of local communities, which defines it as an instrument for generating income, healthy eating and strengthening cultural identity.

In this context, it is important to mention that most of the time the local economic development caused by the stimulation of local practices is sustainable, which means that it allows, simultaneously, to obtain profit and to protect the environmental balance. This is caused by the use of better ecological methods than those used by industries in the production process, by the consumption of typical foods exactly where they are produced, which is healthier than the consumption of multi-processed, frozen and industrialized items, and also because it approximates citizens of their cultural identity, consequently strengthening the preservation of intangible heritage.

The public policies aimed to cultural tourism tends to strengthen cultural values of a society, once intangible heritage is the expression of people's identity, its territory, history, tradition and civilization. Furthermore, this kind of public policy considers that sustainable tourism may represent a considerable instrument for social power and economical development through jobs and income generation. (Klein 2001)

Gastronomic tourism goes beyond the exclusive benefits for this sector, which means that tourism cannot be developed before the existence of an adequate infrastructure, linked to access, lodging and meals, leisure, entertainment, cultural activities, health and well being. -being, buying, preserving and developing historic and archaeological sites, etc., (Dulau et.

Al. 2010). This means that all agents involved in the implementation and formulation of public policies have an important role in local development. These agents are public and private institutions and, mainly, citizens, one of the most important agents in the process of elaborating gastronomic policy.

From this tourist context, gastronomy can be associated with cultural tourism. According to these authors, these associations allow economic and social development through many different opportunities, such as the exploration of traditional dishes, specific cultural activities related to agriculture and other fields related to food production, experimentation of the local tradition in production processes, tales and stories, organic products, etc., (Dulau et. Al. 2010). Considering these arguments, public policies aimed at gastronomy can also be considered actions developed in tourism and consumer behavior in relation to food.

Based on this context, it is possible to expand the discussion on citizen behavior and engagement, given the changes in the food market. This citizen engagement is defined by the author as food citizenship, which means the practice of involving behaviors related to food, which, instead of posing a threat, support the development of socially and economically fair democracy and a sustainable food system. (Wilkins 2005).

This citizen-citizen movement makes it possible to establish a relationship between society's awareness of food and, at the same time, society's engagement in the public policy agenda involving this topic. This means that society is concerned with food and, for this reason, is participating, gaining space, promoting actions and increasingly influencing the initiatives of the States on this subject.

Despite the integration between State and society in relation to public gastronomy policies, engaging in local development at the federal level can be uncomfortable and difficult. However, to promote food citizenship, incentives and tools from the population are needed to promote effective change. (Wilkins 2005).

In the same direction, gastronomy, traditional folklore and the natural landscape were considered to be key factors for strengthening intangible heritage in that region, especially through "consumer empowerment" in relation to receiving marketing (Klein 2001). The idea is possible to understand that consumer empowerment, or even the engagement proposed by Wilkins (2005), in a context of cultural tourism, may be related to citizen empowerment as an important agent, inserted in the gastronomic chain, capable of measuring the performance of products and services offered by the gastronomic sector. This also means that "citizen behavior" (or consumer, when it comes to a market view of gastronomy) can influence the formulation and implementation of public policies in the gastronomic sector (Klein 2001).

While public policies on gastronomy are proposed, the local culture develops from new products and services for tourists and agents that make up this sector. According to these authors, gastronomy has an important role to play, not only because food is a central element of the tourist experience, but also because gastronomy has become a significant source for the formation of the identity of postmodern societies (Dulau et al., 2010).

In view of this process of society's engagement in the elaboration and implementation of public policies on food, a great concern involving the quality of the food offered and its historical cultural identification started to demand from public managers the elaboration of public policies aimed at creating opportunities for development local economy and the protection of typical foods as intangible heritage, which must be protected from globalized food culture, as will be demonstrated.

GASTRONOMIC PUBLIC POLICY: MINAS GERAIS ON THE SCENE

The heritage phenomenon of national and regional gastronomy often presupposes their reconstruction, reinvention and appreciation as a result of a certain economic and social history (Hernandes & Garcia-Arnaiz 2005).

The gastronomic sector is very important for the cultural development of Minas Gerais and is also extremely positive in the tourist activity of that state, since its cuisine is the result of a historical fusion started in the gold cycle that occurred in the 18th century. For this reason, it contains elements that show the mixture of Portuguese, indigenous and African habits, which, over time, have been transformed into a unique food culture in the region. Since then, the way of using local ingredients, the mixing of elements, the use of specific items (such as soapstone pans) and methods of preparation have been passed down from generation to generation and have become a relevant aspect of the inhabitants of this State and a concrete representation of their traditions.

In order to value the intangible heritage, satisfy the public interest and observe the goals established by UNESCO and the Constitution of the Republic, the State of Minas Gerais, in 2014, included gastronomy in the structure of the State Tourism Secretariat and, subsequently, many actions became economic, social, tourist and cultural began to be developed.

Since then, the first step in the gastronomic segment was taken as a public policy by the public administration, obtaining greater relevance as a vector of economic development in all regions of the State.

The first initiative was the institutionalization of the Minas Gerais Gastronomy Day, instituted by Law no. 20,577, on December 21, 2012. This day is celebrated on July 5, in honor of the writer Eduardo Frieiro, who had written the first book on Minas Gerais gastronomy, entitled "Feijão, Angu e Couve", which approaches Minas General. cuisine related to historical, anthropological and sociological aspects.

The Minas Gerais Gastronomy Day not only contributes to tourist exploration and income growth, but also intends to strengthen its identity, since Minas Gerais cuisine expresses the cultural diversity of the State and brings together, in a syncretic way, food and ingredients typical of the region. indigenous, African and Portuguese dishes (Instituto Eduardo Frieiro).

Alongside this day, there is also the Week of Gastronomy from Minas Gerais, an event designed by chef Edson Puiati. In this special week, aimed at rescuing the cultural values of Minas Gerais cuisine, according to the Minas Gerais State Department of Culture, various activities take place, such as training, culinary demonstrations and cultural interventions in many places in Belo Horizonte, the capital of the state. State. Edson Puiati states that "this project's objective is to involve Minas and show its cultural diversity through gastronomy". This is a way of recovering the cultural values of your cuisine and emphasizing that this appreciation is the result of the involvement and participation of society; it is a space where the empowerment of society and its values can be seen.

In 2015, project No. 1,618 / 2015 was presented to the Legislative Assembly. The central idea of this initiative was focused on stimulating the entire productive chain of the sectors and gastronomic actions that fuses the State's cuisine with the economic and tourism expansion through the development of State's gastronomic policies.

Concomitantly with the procedural protocol, public hearings were organized, where professionals, institutional representatives and the general public met to publicize the proposal and share ideas, suggestions, challenges and perspectives of the sector to improve the project, since this is central. objective, to guide government actions aimed at strengthening gastronomy. In addition, the process was attended by the Minas Gerais Gastronomy Association and the Minas Gerais Gastronomic Front, an intersectoral movement formed by voluntary actions, composed of united institutions and groups of people who are interested in promoting and preserving the environment. United States gastronomy.

The project was approved and converted into Law No. 21,936 / 2015 and had as an important factor for its approval the presentation of a petition, in which many people, from public and private institutions, were strongly in favor of its content. This is due to the notorious recognition of the importance of strengthening gastronomy for the State and for all sectors of its production chain, its power to create jobs, the development and distribution of income in the regions.

Since then, the State of Minas Gerais has specific legislation that governs the development of public policies aimed at gastronomy. Therefore, it is a pioneering initiative that aims to guide and systematize permanent government actions, reconciling economic development and the preservation of the State's socio-cultural identity.

The State's Gastronomic Development Policy will guide the elaboration and implementation of the State's Gastronomic Development and will guide the government's actions aimed specifically at strengthening the gastronomy of Minas Gerais. From the analysis of the second article of this new law, it is possible to observe, through the principles, the institution of values that intend to guarantee the promotion of sustainable economic development, the preservation of intangible heritage and the involvement of society in the implementation of policies, according to the development plan.

Art. 2nd The States' Gastronomic Development Policy is based on the following principles:

    i. socioeconomic and environmental sustainability to guarantee food security, the establishment of fair prices, balanced socioenvironmental standards, throughout the gastronomic production chain;

    ii. articulation between public power and private initiative, in order to provide gastronomic production with competitiveness in the domestic and foreign market;

    iii. enhancement of the territory as a guarantee of authenticity and uniqueness of the local cuisine;

    iv. preservation of gastronomic traditions and reinforcement of local identity and community sense;

    v. connection between local and global culture;

    vi. recognition of the multidimensional character of the gastronomic production chain and the importance of related segments;

    vii. social participation in the formulation, execution and monitoring of public policies aimed at the development of gastronomy, as a necessary condition to guarantee the legitimacy of these policies;

    viii. decentralization of public policies, in order to reach segments that are part of the gastronomic production chain;

    ix. recognition, by the public authorities, in its actions to define characteristics, diversity, structures, conditions and skills of enterprises related to gastronomic activity.

In addition to recognizing these principles, social participation in the development of gastronomic policies was reinforced by the third paragraph of the first article and also by the fourth article, which established the possibility of a call from civil society and from all sectors involved in the gastronomic production chain (commodities, supply and storage, industry, commerce and services - which respond in different ways to public policies and the market) for the implementation of this new policy:

Article 1. (...)

§ 3. The Gastronomy Development Policy will be developed, in conjunction with the guidelines of public tourism policies, civil society, agencies and councils of the gastronomy segments of the production chain.

(...)

Article 4. The State, through its competent body, will formulate and implement the Program of States for the Development of Gastronomy, and the participation of civil society will be guaranteed whenever possible.

In addition, to promote the preservation of the values defined in article three, article four of this law establishes the objectives of the development plan, consisting of an exemplary number of many actions that must be promoted by the public administration in close collaboration with society. At this point, it is possible to highlight three fundamental objectives: protecting the authenticity and identity of local gastronomy as an intangible heritage to be preserved, recognizing the importance of this sector for economic development and encouraging the participation of society in the creation and implementation of these actions.

Article 3. The objectives of the development policy mentioned in this Law are:

i.   transform the State of Minas Gerais as a gastronomic destination known nationally and internationally;
ii. revitalize and diversify tourism and promote economic development;
iii. create productive opportunities for the primary sector;
iv. protect the quality and authenticity of local cuisine;
v.   define gastronomy as a creative industry;
vi. to safeguard the gastronomic heritage of the State of Minas Gerais in all its diversity and origin;

vii.   guarantee the sustainability of the activities of the sectors of the gastronomic production chain;

viii. develop an intersectorial network to position it nationally and internationally;

ix.   connect gastronomic production to tourist demand;

x.   create and improve tax and credit instruments that stimulate gastronomic production;

xi.   build and reinforce public-private partnership models;

xii.   creating gastronomic-tourist products and adding value to those already existing;

xiii. develop innovative marketing promotion strategies;

xiv.   identify and attract new markets for gastronomic tourism;

xv.   promoting good practices in artisanal production.

The innovative legislation of Minas Gerais recognizes the activities related to gastronomy as one of the most important segments of the economy and presents itself as a substantial reinforcement to the formulation of a sustainable gastronomic model allied to all sectors of the production chain, stimulating actions that integrate the cuisine mining tourism expansion and protection of this important intangible heritage that makes up the state's cultural identity.

Thus, the proposal is that not only an intersectorial network be developed for the recognition of the national and international cuisine of Minas Gerais, but also the protection and enhancement of its authenticity and uniqueness through the executive and legislative power with organized civil society.

It is important to note that there are other government policies and programs in Brazil that aim to recognize gastronomy as a cultural activity, such as Law No. 8,313, of December 23 (Law Rouanet); Federal Law 9.279 / 1996 and Federal Decree 3.551 / 2000. In addition to these laws and decrees, there are also public policies in the area of tourism, which highlight gastronomy in a certain way (Minasse 2015).

The Rouanet Law (Law No. 8,313, of December 23) instituted the National Program to Support Culture, known as PRONAC, and aims to enhance it through measures to preserve, safeguard, promote and finance cultural production in the country. In 2015, approved bill No. 6,562 / 13 established the inclusion of gastronomy and food culture among the beneficiaries of the State's tax incentive policy. In addition, according to the National Congress, the concept of traditional and popular food culture was also included.

Another law that involves this discussion is Federal Law 9.279 / 1996, which regulates rights and obligations related to industrial property. Articles 176 and 182 of this law present the constitution of an indication of geographical origin and denomination of origin, considering the National Institute of Intellectual Property (INPI) to be the agency responsible for establishing conditions for the registration of geographical indications in Brazil. "This appreciation directly contributes to the perspective of gastronomic tourism, since it distinguishes these products and permanently associates them with a locality, creating and strengthening gastronomic territorialities (Minasse 2015, p. 5).

Finally, there is also Federal Decree 3,551, of August 2000, which institutes the registration of intangible cultural assets and constitutes Brazilian cultural heritage, based on the National Intangible Heritage Program, supervised by IPHAN. This immaterial process of patrimonialization addresses the classification related to cultural goods and local knowledge, celebrations, rituals, legends, habits and many cultural practices.

Once the legal context of public instruments for indirect strengthening of gastronomy in Brazil has been presented, although these instruments are not specifically targeted at gastronomy, they can be used as a way to formally recognize this sector. Based on this recognition, it is possible, in a more effective and specific way, to create public policies that intercede in favor of these manifestations and become fundamental for the awareness of a larger group of people about the importance of these manifestations (Minasse 2015)

Thus, the author concludes that "a wide recognition and appreciation of Brazilian gastronomy as a cultural practice is a construction movement that necessarily passes through official channels (federal institutions and entities) and their respective public policies, as had already occurred in countries like France and Spain "(Minasse 2015, p. 7), in the European Union and in some Latin American countries.

Although there is such a diversified legal apparatus, it is important to highlight that this policy of valuing gastronomy (Law 21.936 / 2015) is presented in an incipient context of public actions directed specifically to this sector. Therefore, it is important to emphasize that, even in such an incipient context of public policies aimed at food, it can be observed that these legal instruments proposed by the State, which had the support, empowerment and co-creation of civil society, are going in the same way as the movement that can be observed in other countries towards recognizing food as a cultural aspect.

For this exclusivity and in view of the importance of gastronomy for the State of Minas Gerais, it is important to highlight, once again, the role of this policy as a way of guaranteeing the empowerment of a society that culturally and historically experiences tradition, knowledge and "mineiridade" (term used to describe the peculiar characteristics of the inhabitants of Minas Gerais).

CONCLUSION

The promotion of public policies aimed at gastronomy as an instrument of local economic development is part of a movement to value immaterial culture in the food context, countering, in a way, the development of food industrialization and the risks of diluting local and national identities by globalization phenomenon.

Following a worldwide trend, which can be observed through the proposal of some countries, such as France, Mexico and Peru, the institution of the State Policy for Gastronomic Development (PDG) and the institution of the State Plan for Gastronomic Development (PEDG) bring as a consequence, at the same time, the recognition of the importance of intangible heritage for local identity, the reconnection of citizens with their own history and culture through eating habits, the encouragement of sustainable economic development and the empowerment of citizens, the encouragement of practices inherent to its socio-cultural identity, the expansion of entrepreneurial opportunities and the calling and hearing of people in the implementation and formulation of public policies.

This democratic movement allowed the realization of values related to the empowerment and co-creation of citizens, through a governmental opening that guarantees, through skilled instruments, such as public hearings, the listening of associations and representatives of the area, active participation of the citizen and society in general, instead of a mere role of spectator before the public administration by the governors (Farazmand, 2012).

The strengthening of gastronomy by the State of Minas Gerais as a public policy reinforces the expertise of the region and gives it conditions, in terms of participation and promotion of public actions, and to all the agents involved, to institutionalize gastronomy as a brand - by family farmers, chefs, consumers - and as a tourist destination and competitive advantage in the market.

Despite the pre-existence of government policies that intend to recognize gastronomy as a cultural activity, the proposal of the State of Minas Gerais represents an innovation in public management, which can become more democratic, participatory, objective and institutionalized, and can be used as a paradigm for other countries Latin America and the world, since it is about meeting the need to preserve intangible cultural heritage, the exact direction recommended by the United Nations through UNESCO, against the phenomenon of globalization and the weakening of local cultural identities in society Modern.

According to what is shown, it is necessary that the typical gastronomy is thought not only by the local communities involved, but also by the Public Administration, so that sustainability, socio-cultural identity and economic development become the result of a social construction. Therefore, it is necessary for many sectors of society to come together to face challenges effectively in order to achieve the good of all.

REFERENCES

Bonomo, J. R. (2013). The cuisine of Minas Gerais as a sign and intangible cultural heritage. In: *International Interdisciplinary Congress on Social and Humanities*. Belo Horizonte-MG.

Cavicchi, A., & Stancova, K. C. (2016). *Food and gastronomy as elements of regional innovation strategies* (No. JRC99987). Institute for Prospective and Technological Studies, Joint Research Centre.

Dulău, A. V., Coroş, M. M., & Coroş, M. E. (2010). The place of the public administration and gastronomic heritage in the destination branding and tourism promotion. *WSEAS Transactionson Business and Economics*, 4(7), 402-413.

Fagliari, G. S. (2005). *Turismo e Alimentação: Análises Introdutórias*. Ed. Roca, São Paulo.

Farazmand, A. (2012). *Sound governance: Engaging citizens through collaborative organizations*. Public Organization Review, 12(3), 223-241.

Gordin, V., & Trabskaya, J. (2013). *The role of gastronomic brands in tourist destination promotion: The case of St. Petersburg*. Place Branding and Public Diplomacy, 9(3), 189-201.

Horng, J. S., & Tsai, C. T. S. (2012). Culinary tourism strategic development: An Asia-Pacific perspective. *International Journal of Tourism Research*, 14(1), 40-55.

Khoo, S. L., & Badarulzaman, N. (2014). *Factors determining George Town as a city of gastronomy*. Tourism Planning & Development, 11(4), 371-386.

Klein, R. (2001, March). Public Policies and Cultural Tourism-EU activities. In *First Conference on Cultural Tourism, Economy & Values in the XXI Century*, Enterprise directorate general Tourism (pp. 29-31).

Lee, I., & Arcodia, C. (2011). The role of regional food festivals for destination branding. *International Journalof Tourism Research*, 13(4), 355-367.

Minasse, M. H. (2015). Eu como cultura? Notas sobre políticas de valorização da gastronomia no Brasil. In. *Seminário Nacional de*

Pesquisa e Pós-Graduação em Turismo [Do I eat culture? Notes on gastronomy valuation policies in Brazil. In. *National Seminar on Research and Graduate Studies in Tourism*].

OECD (2012). *Food and the Tourism Experience: The OECD-Korea Workshop, OECD Studies on Tourism*, OECD Publishing.

Pearson, D., & Pearson, T. (2015). Branding Food Culture: UNESCO Creative Cities of Gastronomy. *Journal of Food Products Marketing*, 1-14.

Telfer, D. J., & Wall, G. (1996). Linkages between tourism and food production. *Annals of Tourism Research*, 23(3), 635-653.

In: Exploring Cities and Countries …   ISBN: 978-1-53618-514-0
Editor: Kathie Summers   © 2020 Nova Science Publishers, Inc.

Chapter 6

GASTRONOMY AS A MARK OF A TOURIST DESTINATION

Lelis Maia Brito[1,] and Odemir Vieira Baeta[2,†]*
[1]Department of Public Management,
Ouro Preto Federal University Ouro Preto, Minas Gerais, Brazil
[2]Department of Languages and Fine Arts,
Viçosa Federal University, Viçosa, Minas Gerais, Brazil

ABSTRACT

Destination Marks is a multi and interdisciplinary field of study for addressing various variations and interpretations in terms of place identity. One of these understandings is gastronomic tourism, also known as 'gastrotourism,' or culinary tourism, which has been strengthened based on the appreciation of local cultural and culinary aspects. If gastronomy was considered as a support element for tourism, at that moment, the movement is to consider it as the main attraction, an alternative to present the place, create its identity and attract visitors. With this, this area has become an important brand element capable of promoting tourism and

[*] Corresponding Author's Email: lelis@ufop.edu.br.
[†] Corresponding Author's Email: odemirvieirabaeta@gmail.com.

local cultural values. This theoretical article relates destination mark approaches and gastronomy and discusses the role of gastronomy as a destination mark. This aims to discuss, theoretically, the relationship between gastronomy and destination brands. This discussion relates the destination mark elements to gastronomy, aiming to explore the main theoretical approaches in the literature on the subject. The article establishes a connection between the theoretical discussions about destination marks and gastronomy, points out the main researches in the area and expands these reflections by contextualizing Minas Gerais gastronomy in face of the propositions presented.

Keywords: gastronomy, destination brand, tourism and Minas Gerais

INTRODUCTION

Destination brands or place marks can be understood as a multi and interdisciplinary field of study by addressing several variations - "destination branding, place branding, destination image, location branding and place marketing" (Gertner, 2011; Khoo & Badarulzaman, 2014; Mak 2011; McCabe & Stokoe, 2004) - and interpretations in terms of place identity (Kavaratzis & Hatch, 2013). For some authors, it is a concept that is associated with aspects related to the tradition of a particular place, an identity which relates to the intrinsic characteristics, histories, cultural values, symbols and other specific elements of a place (Kalandides), 2011; Kavaratzis & Hatch, 2013; Khoo & Badarulzaman, 2014; Mayes, 2008). While for others, it is a concept linked to the image of a destination which influences tourists in the decision making process about which place to visit and possibly what kind of perception they may have before visiting the city or referred region (Nelson, 2016). In general, a destination mark can be understood as an identification attributed to a product or service, whether tangible or intangible, that allows it to be recognized and strengthened by local consumers or visitors through values and characteristics (Pearson & Pearson, 2015).

The idea of strengthening and promoting local cultural identity comes from the global competitiveness of tourist destinations, both for leisure and work or study. Institutionalizing an identity that allows highlighting the expertise of the place and, at the same time, creating sustainable competitive advantages has been the main attention of cities (Khoo & Badarulzaman, 2014). For Dulău, Coroş and Coroş (2010), highlighting the competitive advantages are fundamental due to the 'competition' that exists between tourist destinations to attract foreign investors, financial resources, maintain existing investments, attract and retain tourists and other actions.

Destination brands or the institutionalization of a particular tourist destination as a brand are made in the face of the global economic and social vision of the market. This means that, given this globalization, it has been strategic for specific countries, cities or regions to create unique identification tools on these environments. This identification is a way of creating a distinctive image and promoting competitive advantage of the site over others (Dulău et al., 2010). In this context, one can cite examples from South Africa, Australia, Canada, Croatia, South Korea, Hong Kong, Macao, Singapore, Thailand, and Taiwan (Horng & Tsai, 2012); Romanian (Dulău et al., 2010); Russia (Gordin & Trabskaya, 2013); India (Khoo & Badarulzaman, 2014); Germany, Spain, USA, France, Czech Republic and Turkey (Caldwell & Freire, 2004).

Analyzing the tourism market and aiming to strengthen regional competitive advantages, Dulău et al. (2010) comment that tourism considered classic - by promoting various attractions linked to leisure time, sports activities, visits to historical monuments, landscapes, geographical and historical contexts - has been presenting changes. For these authors, a new type of tourism has been designed, emphasizing both the classic attractions and promoting other cultural values, such as gastronomy. In this case, gastronomic tourism, also known as 'gastrotourism' or 'culinary tourism,' has been strengthened based on the appreciation of local cultural and culinary aspects. The identity or brand of gastronomy as a destination tourism has been built on these values, thus creating a competitive differential in the tourism market. If gastronomy was considered as a support element for tourism, now the movement is to consider it as the main element, an attribute that influences the decision of the tourist to visit a certain place. In some studies, the focus is on discussing and promoting gastronomy as a cultural experience (Hall & Mitchell, 2000; Mykletun & Gyimóthy, 2010; Nelson, 2016).

Importantly, the competitiveness of a local gastronomy also involves discussions on the adoption of strategies aimed at the tourism sector that value the regional attributes of local cuisine, emphasizing aspects of creativity and the allocation of scarce resources. For Gordin and Trabskaya (2013), given the importance of gastronomy as a destination tourism, local cuisine can not be considered just as a prop or a tourist point, it is a differential, a key or decisive factor regarding tourist's choice of this destination.

In this sense, gastronomy can be seen as a means of valuing an identity, a regional brand, due to the cultural values that surround it. In addition, this area has been presenting itself as an important aspect of destination tourism and as a 'sense of place' (Hall & Mitchell, 2005). In this context, the UNESCO classification is cited as regards the identification of a city focused on gastronomy, such as the "Creative Cities of Gastronomy" program, by defining cities that value cultural and identity-based aspects. in gastronomy. This is the case of the cities Belém and Florianópolis (Brazil), Bergen (Norway), Chengdu and Shunde (China), Dénia and Burgos (Spain), Ensenada and Tucson (Mexico), Gaziantep (Turkey), Jeonju (South Korea), Ostersund (Sweden), Parma (Italy), Phuket (Thailand), Popayán (Colombia), Rasht (Iran), Tsuruoka (Japan) and Zahlé (Lebanon).

Although the discussion about destination brands and gastronomy is incipient in the academic environment (Caldwell & Freire, 2004; Pearson & Pearson, 2015), this relationship has been studied by several areas, such as marketing, management, tourism and urban development. For Kavaratzis and Hatch (2013), despite this evolution, academic contributions are still scattered in both theoretical and practical sense.

In a practical sense, according to Nelson (2016), tourist destinations or 'gastrotourism' can be considered as successful by establishing connections between food and place. This means that they have a defined identity, a local culture that involves gastronomy with regional traditions and values.

In the theoretical sense, the thematic mark of destiny has been presenting importance in terms of publications and as construction of a theoretical field.

Such a proposal may be interesting, on the one hand, in understanding the emerging field of action and, on the other, in considering that there is a discrepancy between theoretical discussions and practical actions. Studies presented in this area aim to explore and discuss the role of gastronomy as a means of enhancing local image, enabling business opportunities and differentiating the place as a 'authentic' gastronomic destination (Khoo & Badarulzaman, 2014; Parkerson & Saunders; 2005).

For Berg and Sevón (2014), there are in the literature a diversity of examples of how gastronomy has been used as an attraction for visitors, local people and as business opportunities for companies and investors. Based on these studies, Berg and Sevón (2014) comment that published research presents results that discuss indirect activities or side effects of the role of gastronomy in city brands. For these authors, research mainly involves regional foods and wine as tourism-related activities, citing the studies by Kivela and Crotts (2006) and Croce and Perri (2010). In addition, the authors argue that research using food or gastronomy as a strategic marker and positioning of cities is still incipient. This may be related to the absence of conceptual models that take into consideration the role of food/gastronomy in the process of building a city brand.

Thus, it can be said that gastronomy plays an important role in the process of institutionalization and strengthening of an image for a territory, an aggregation of value in the identity of a place as destination tourism. To this end, Anholt (2010), Berg and Sevón (2014) and Kavaratzis (2005) generally assume that a 'gastronomic brand' is a strategic way of producing a placemark effect capable of generating positive effects on a destination place or image.

Given the importance that gastronomy has been presenting in the market as a means of economic and social development and as an instrument of valorization of the destination brand, the following question arises: 'How can gastronomy be used as a destination brand element?'

Tourism promotion institutions and tourists themselves regard food and all values involved in gastronomy as a niche market, as a factor in promoting a place, a region, a dissemination and appreciation of a tourist destination (Horng & Tsai, 2012). One of the explanations for this cultural appreciation involving gastronomy, according to the authors, is the understanding that cuisine and food are a representation of the (intangible) heritage of a destination, from which it is possible to demonstrate local and regional cultural characteristics. and be developed as a brand.

Importantly, the competitiveness of a local gastronomy also involves discussions on the adoption of strategies aimed at the tourism sector that value the regional attributes of local cuisine, emphasizing aspects of creativity and the allocation of scarce resources. One can also, according to Horng and Tsai (2012), associate competitiveness with the integration between the agents of the gastronomy chain, with emphasis on society.

Given the above, this chapter aims to discuss the relationship between gastronomy and destination brands. For this essay, the discussion is summarized in relating the destination mark elements to gastronomy, aiming to explore the main theoretical approaches in the literature on the subject.

GASTRONOMY AS A BRAND AND VALORIZATION STRATEGIES

The discussion between gastronomy as a brand and strategies for valuing this sector in the context of destination tourism has been fragmented in the literature (Horng & Tsai, 2012; Kavaratzis & Hatch, 2013). Despite the diversity of concepts and theoretical approaches that involve this area of study, 'discussing the use of gastronomy as a means of enhancing and promoting a city brand has been common in academic research on this theme' (Berg & Sevón, 2014, p. 3).

Regarding classifications or dimensions of gastronomy as an element of a destination mark, it can be said that all expressions involving the construction and promotion of a proposed destination mark can be better explored according to the context in which they are being studied (Caldwell & Freire, 2004). This means that gastronomy plays an important role in the process of institutionalizing and strengthening an image for a territory, adding value to the identity of a place as a destination tourism (Gordin & Trabskaya, 2013).

It is understood that to develop a 'gastrotouristic' identity it is necessary to present basic infrastructure to make such attractiveness possible. It is in this context that Gordin and Trabskaya (2013) question whether the lack of resources or infrastructure would be an obstacle, a limitation, for the development of a gastronomic brand. In this sense, the authors comment that the development of regional gastronomy brand (RGB) is based on the tourist experience with this type of service, a consumer involvement with products and services related to local traditions and values and the brand participation and promotion by public, private and third sector institutions. It is this identity and involvement that assist in the promotion and institutionalization of gastronomy as a brand.

GASTRONOMY CLASSIFICATIONS AS BRAND

This chapter considers Gordin and Trabskaya' (2013) theoretical approach to classifications of gastronomy as a brand. For these authors, gastronomy, under the branded brand approach, can be initially analyzed through two central criteria. The first criterion defines brand as internal or external from the analysis of residents and nonresidents. From this analysis, brands can be classified into export, tourist and domestic. The second criterion is defined based on the type of region in which cuisine is involved. In this second criterion, brands can be classified into rural gastronomy, single product region and cultural cities. For the authors, defining classifications and types of gastronomy as brands enables the development of specific promotion strategies in the domestic/domestic and foreign markets.

First criterion. Types of gastronomy brands: export, tourist and domestic. Trademark related to the type of export gastronomy involves agriculture products, seafood as well as industrialized products. It is understood that this type of gastronomy brand makes it possible to associate food products with specific production regions, emphasizing the identification "country of origin," which is a synonym of quality assurance by consumers. Gordin and Trabskaya (2013) comment that this discussion about origin and intellectual property about gastronomic brands is complex, both about the role of the producer and the regulatory institutions as well as the consumer. In any case, this kind of gastronomic brand appreciation is a way of strengthening a region's identity regarding the production of a particular product or service and the community's involvement in this production and tradition.

Another type of gastronomic brand is tourism, which comprises the identification of a particular tourist region from which only one visit is possible to associate with and recognizes its competitive gastronomic differential. This means that the product produced in these regions can be purchased anywhere. However, better tasting and understanding of the production process and product appreciation can be done authentically only in the specific region (Gordin & Trabskaya, 2013).

In these two types of gastronomic brands it is possible to analyze that the technical aspects of production and the edaphoclimatic conditions are valued in the foreign market environment, while the cultural values, tradition, know-how and personal involvement of the consumer in the environment. production are aspects valued in tourist brands of the tourist type.

Regarding the third type of gastronomic brand, Gordin and Trabskaya (2013) comment that these brands are considered significant from the point of view of regional identity by internal consumers, who regularly consume the product. For the authors, this type of brand is valued only in the domestic market, presenting no projections for foreign markets or even as a tourism product.

Second criterion. As for the creation of the gastronomic brand in relation to the type of population, Gordin and Trabskaya (2013) present three types: rural territory, single product territory and multicultural (cosmopolitan) territory.

In the rural territory type, the focus is on agricultural production of diversified products in a given region. In this region are also emphasized the technical aspects of production, the community involvement around this product and the knowledge and tradition about the production process and preparation of the product. For the authors, this type of gastronomic brand definition has been addressed given the appreciation in the market of issues associated with health and well-being, which may be related to this rural environment.

In the other gastronomic brand group, single product territory, regions are defined by highlighting particular product and types of restaurants. The definition of this product is understood in the identity or brand of that region. You now recognize the location based on your product.

In the third group, multicultural or cosmopolitan territory, there is a combination of diverse cultures, customs, traditions and values. This process of cultural diversification reflects the historical aspects of the gastronomy of this territory, which enables the integration of various culinary products and techniques. For Gordin and Trabskaya (2013), this multicultural process has been contributing to global trends related to gastronomy because it absorbs various types of cuisine in a single environment. This cultural context, according to these authors and based on research by Scarpato and Daniele (2003), can be called "new global cuisine." However, such studies point out that there is a difference between "new global cuisine" and multicultural cuisine. For the authors, "new global cuisine" involves an artificial proposal of various types of cuisine in a single environment, unique cuisine. While multicultural cuisine proposes the creation of a diverse and organic culinary environment over a significant period, ie multicultural cuisine is part of the purpose and ambience of the kitchen in question.

For Gordin and Trabskaya (2013), the idea of multicultural territory may, on the one hand, have positive aspects regarding the promotion of culinary cultural diversity to consumers, on the other, it has a negative aspect that is precisely not present a unique cultural identity gastronomically. That is, in territories of this type it is not possible to create a unique gastronomic brand identity, which, in fact, represents and symbolizes the place in an authentic way.

The positive aspect of this type of gastronomic brand is that it presents consumers with a diversity of culinary cultures, emphasizing both local and other types of cuisine, in which case the idea of minimizing tourist culture shock is associated. Anyway, the gastronomic brand in territories of this nature is not valued and promoted. The highlight is the fact that the city has a cultural diversity, disregarding gastronomy as an element of identity.

In addition to the classification proposed by Gordin and Trabskaya (2013), there are other definitions and analyzes of gastronomy as a mark of destination element. Among them is the research by De Chernatony and Mc William (1990) also discussed by Caldwell and Freire (2004). De Chernatony and Mc William (1990) propose a brand box model by which brands are defined in two dimensions: representativeness and functionality. From this model, it is possible to evaluate the brands of products or services from the understanding of consumers and marketing managers (Caldwell & Freire, 2004). Brands defined as representative are built from the idea that consumers use brands as a means or element of expression about themselves, about their personalities. Brands of this nature explore meanings that go beyond the technical or physical aspects of products or services, involving subjective attributes valued by consumers. The second dimension, functionality, explains that consumers would opt for brands that further exploit the physical, technical attributes, and performance of the product or service, such as quality, reliability, and other utilitarian factors.

CONCLUSION

From these brief theoretical discussions, this essay aims to understand how gastronomy can be considered a destination brand element. The classifications presented reinforce that the value added from the institutionalization of gastronomy as a brand must take place from the context of local food and culture. That is, the cultural aspects that involve cooking are as important as the services that involve cooking. This means that the place must have its own identity linked to cooking, a cultural identity that further strengthens gastronomy as a brand (Horng & Tsai, 2012). At this point, it is important to emphasize that the cuisine has history, values, cultures, symbols and identity. Strengthening gastronomy as a brand is a way of strengthening the historical aspects of a society's cooking, so that such identification can preserve cooking as an intangible heritage.

The development of future research, such as this essay involves, will allow a detailed analysis of the construction and promotion of gastronomy as a brand from the perspective of its stakeholders - representatives of public, private and third sector institutions and directly acting professionals. in the area; local consumers and visitors. To this end, mining gastronomy will be considered as an object of study given its social, economic, political and cultural importance to the state.

REFERENCES

Anholt, S. (2006). The Anholt-GMI city brands index: How the world sees the world's cities. *Place Branding and Public Diplomacy*, 2(1), 18-31.

Berg, P. O., & Sevón, G. (2014). Food-branding places - A sensory perspective. *Place Branding and Public Diplomacy*, 10(4), 289-304.

Caldwell, N., & Freire, J. R. (2004). The differences between branding a country, a region and a city: Applying the Brand Box Model. *Journal of Brand Management*, 12(1), 50-61.

Croce, E. and Perri, G. (2010) *Food and Wine Tourism: Integrating Food, Travel, and Territory*. Cambridge, MA: CAB International.

De Chernatony, L., & McWilliam, G. (1990). Appreciating brands as assets through using a two-dimensional model. *International Journal of Advertising*, 9(2), 111-119.

Dulău, A. V., Coroş, M. M., & Coroş, M. E. (2010). The place of the public administration and gastronomic heritage in the destination branding and tourism promotion. *WSEAS Transactions on Business and Economics*, 4(7), 402-413.

Gertner, D. (2011). Unfolding and configuring two decades of research and publications on place marketing and place branding. *Place Branding and Public Diplomacy*, 7(2), 91-106.

Gordin, V., & Trabskaya, J. (2013). The role of gastronomic brands in tourist destination promotion: The case of St. Petersburg. *Place Branding and Public Diplomacy*, 9(3), 189-201.

Hall, C. M., & Mitchell, R. (2005). Gastronomic tourism: Comparing food and wine tourism experiences. *Niche tourism: Contemporary issues, trends and cases*, 73-88.

Hall, C. M., & Mitchell, R. (2000). We are what we eat: Food, tourism and globalization. *Tourism, Culture and Communication*, 2(1), 29-37.

Horng, J. S., & Tsai, C. T. S. (2012). Culinary tourism strategic development: An Asia-Pacific perspective. *International Journal of Tourism Research*, 14(1), 40-55.

Kalandides, A. (2011). The problem with spatial identity: revisiting the "sense of place." *Journal of Place Management and Development*, 4(1), 28-39.

Kavaratzis, M. (2005). Place branding: A review of trends and conceptual models. *The marketing review*, 5(4), 329-342.

Kavaratzis, M., & Hatch, M. J. (2013). The dynamics of place brands an identity-based approach to place branding theory. *Marketing Theory*, 13(1), 69-86.

Khoo, S. L., & Badarulzaman, N. (2014). Factors determining George Town as a city of gastronomy. *Tourism Planning & Development*, 11(4), 371-386.

Kivela, J., & Crotts, J. C. (2006). Tourism and gastronomy: Gastronomy's influence on how tourists experience a destination. *Journal of Hospitality & Tourism Research*, 30(3), 354-377.

Mak, A. K. (2011). An identity-centered approach to place branding: Case of industry partners' evaluation of Iowa's destination image. *Journal of Brand Management*, 18(6), 438-450.

Mayes, R. (2008). A place in the sun: The politics of place, identity and branding. *Place Branding and Public Diplomacy*, 4(2), 124-135.

McCabe, S., & Stokoe, E. H. (2004). Place and identity in tourists'accounts. *Annals of Tourism Research*, 31(3), 601-622.

Mykletun, R. J., & Gyimóthy, S. (2010). Beyond the renaissance of the traditional Voss sheep's-head meal: Tradition, culinary art, scariness and entrepreneurship. *Tourism Management*, 31(3), 434-446.

Nelson, V. (2016). Food and image on the official visitor site of Houston, Texas. *Journal of Destination Marketing & Management*, 5(2), 133-140.

Parkerson, B., & Saunders, J. (2005). City branding: Can goods and services branding models be used to brand cities? *Place Branding and Public Diplomacy*, 1(3), 242-264.

Pearson, D., & Pearson, T. (2015). Branding Food Culture: UNESCO Creative Cities of Gastronomy. *Journal of Food Products Marketing*, 1-14.

Scarpato, R., & Daniele, R. (2003). New global cuisine: Tourism, authenticity and sense of place in postmodern gastronomy. *Food tourism around the world: Development, management and markets*, 296-313.

In: Exploring Cities and Countries
Editor: Kathie Summers

ISBN: 978-1-53618-514-0
© 2020 Nova Science Publishers, Inc.

Chapter 7

SCIENCE RESEARCH IN SINGAPORE

*Sameen Ahmed Khan**
Department of Mathematics and Sciences,
College of Arts and Applied Sciences (CAAS),
Dhofar University, Salalah, Sultanate of Oman

Abstract

Singapore has made rapid progress in industrial and sustainable development. This would not have been possible without government patronage for science and research. The government agencies responsible
for science funding and research policy have played a crucial role in the
scientific growth of the nation. Singapore has several premier institutions
dedicated to the emerging fields of science and technology. Along with
these, Singapore has learned societies and science museums. Singapore
has received international recognition in its scientific and environmental
endeavours. This Chapter describes the status of science research in Singapore and the crucial role it has played in making Singapore a model for
sustainable development.

Keywords and Phrases: Science; Research; Science Policy; Singapore; Synchrotron; National Parks Board of Singapore, Climate Change; UNESCO; UN-
ESCO Sultan Qaboos Prize for Environmental Preservation

*Corresponding Author's Email: rohelakhan@yahoo.com; Website: http://orcid.org/0000-
0003-1264-2302.

1. INTRODUCTION

Science is undoubtedly the greatest collective endeavour of the human race. It has contributed to our understanding of life and has provided cures for many diseases. It has contributed to basic needs including water, food, energy, and housing. In recent decades, science has revolutionized the communication technologies impacting our indulgences in sports, music and entertainment, among other spheres of life. Apart from the very basic necessities, science has enabled us to explore the understanding of nature from the subatomic world to the universe itself (to the extent, we know it now). Science has a specific role, as well as a variety of functions for the benefit of our society: creating new knowledge, improving education, and increasing the quality of our lives. Science needs to respond to societal needs and numerous global challenges. Public understanding and engagement with science, and participation on a larger scale are essential to prepare citizens to make informed personal and professional choices. Likewise, the ministries/governments make use of science in various sectors such as health and agriculture. We quote from Pandit Jawaharlal Nehru, the first Prime Minister of Independent India:

> *It is science alone that can solve the problem of hunger and poverty, of insanitation and illiteracy, of superstition and deadening customs and traditions, of vast resources running to waste, of a rich country inhabited by starving people. Who indeed can afford to ignore science today? At every turn we have to seek its aid. The future belongs to science and to those who make friends with science.* [1]

With the rapid progress in science and industrialization, there are also accompanying issues such as arms races, climate change and ocean health, to name a few. Such issues affect the whole world in one way or the other. In this Chapter, we shall have a closer look at Singapore's journey with science. Singapore has made rapid progress in industrial and sustainable development. This would not have been possible without government patronage to science and research. The government agencies responsible for science funding and research policy have played a crucial role in the scientific growth of the nation. Singapore has several premier institutions dedicated to the emerging fields of science and technology. Along with these, Singapore has learned societies and science museums. Singapore has received international recognition in its scientific and environmental endeavours. This Chapter describes the status of science research in Singapore and the crucial role it has played in making Singapore a model for sustainable development [2]-[4].

2. SINGAPORE: FACTS & FIGURES

First and foremost, let us look at a few facts and figures related to Singapore [2]. It is to be noted that Singapore is a city-state and an island-country with an area of 725.1 $kilometers^2$ or 280 $miles^2$ and a population of less than six million (2018). The population density is $7,804/km^2$ or $20,212.3/mile^2$. The *Ethnic groups* as of the 2015 data comprised Chinese (74.3%), Malay (13.3%), Indian (9.1%) and others (3.3%). The prevalent *List of religions* is Buddhism (33.2%), Christianity (18.8%) Irreligious (18.5%), Islam (14.0%), Taoism and folk religion (10.0%), Hinduism (5.0%) and others (0.6%). Singapore has the *Official languages*: English (main language), Malay, Chinese, Tamil accompanied with the *Official scripts*: Latin script (English and Malay), Simplified Chinese and Tamil respectively.

Singapore has an ancient history with written records as old as the third century CE (Christian Era). Singapore was a *Sultanate* for over four centuries, Malacca Sultanate (1400-1511) and Johor Sultanate (1528-1819), respectively. With the arrival of the British colonialism, there were relatively short-lived occupations including: Singapore under British control (1819-1826), Japanese occupation of Singapore (1942-1945), Straits Settlements (1826-1942), British Military Administration (1945-1946) and Colony of Singapore (1946-1963). Singapore was one of the 14 states of Malaysia (also known as Malaya) from 1963 to 1965. Since 1965, Singapore is an independent republic.

At the time of independence, Singapore's per capita income was US$800. The Gross National Income per capita (PPP international) for the year 2017 was $90,570. The life expectancy at birth male/female (year 2016) is 81/85, respectively. The infant mortality rate for Singapore is remarkably low at 2.2, one of the lowest in the world. Its literacy rate is 95.45%, again one of the highest in the world.

3. SCIENCE POLICY AND FUNDING

Singapore became an independent republic from Malaysia on 9 August 1965. Lee Kuan Yew and Yusof bin Ishak served as the first prime minister and president, respectively. The foremost concern and focus of the leaders then was the survival of the new nation constrained with limited natural resources. It was realized that science could serve as a vehicle for the efficient utilization of available natural resources. Science was seen as a panacea for the economic survival of the new nation, as it would lead to industrial and technological progress in a timely manner [3]-[4].

The efforts towards research & development predate Singapore's independence in 1965. We note some of the landmark events in Singapore's journey with science. In 1961, the Economic Development Board (EDB) was created with the aim to attract investors/industrialists to Singapore. An Industrial Research Unit was formed within the EDB under the guidelines of the Colombo Plan with aid from New Zealand. In 1966, the Industrial Research Unit of Singapore became a full member of International Organisation for Standardisation. In 1967, a Science Council was created to enhance the national advancement of science & technology and build up human resources in scientific Research & Development. In 1967, Singapore became a member of the Commonwealth Scientific Committee, whose main goal was to bring about cooperation among the Commonwealth countries in science and technology. The Science Council of Singapore in 1968 organized a landmark event under the name *National Conference on Scientific and Technical Cooperation between Industries and Government Bodies*. The event brought together over 200 local scientists, technologists, industrialists and economic planners. The event lead to the identification of areas of mutual interests and found ways to foster cooperation. This conference set the agenda for the upgrading of industry through science and technology, technical manpower development, and the direction of Research & Development in Singapore. Singapore Institute of Standards and Industrial Research (SISIR) was formed in 1969. In 1968, the National Industrial Training Council was established to make policy for technical education and industrial training to meet manpower requirements of new industries. In 1969, a Placement Agency was established by the Science Council of Singapore. The agency was assigned the task of matching the number of graduates in science and engineering with the requirements of the industries. It was also asked to create a database of overseas undergraduates, then expected to return to Singapore. The Agency also began work on evaluating the supply and demand for technical manpower at the middle and higher levels respectively. In 1971, Applied Research Fellowship Scheme was introduced to foster links between scientists and engineers in industry with their counterparts in educational institutions. Fellowships were awarded for specific research projects which could be part-time in nature. From 1975, these research projects had to be full-time research projects. The scheme was phased out in 1977.

At the time of independence, Singapore's per capita income was US$800. In 2017, the figure had increased to $90, 570 for the Gross National Income per capita (PPP international). Since the National Science and Technology Board was formed in 1991, gross expenditure on research and development increased from 1.00% of GDP in 1991 to 1.76% in 1998. In 2018, the Research & Development expenditure as a percentage of GDP for Singapore was 2.16%, which brings it closer to countries famed for their focus on research, such as Denmark and Switzerland. It is to be noted that the world average was 2.10% for the year 2018. This is consistent with the recommended norm of 2%. Singapore has a target to raise the Research & Development funding to 3.5% of GDP, which will place the small city-island-state among the top five research-intensive countries, including Israel, Sweden and Japan [3]-[4].

Singapore is determined to integrate science and technology into its overall economic strategy plan and this move has been greatly influenced by numerous changes. The desire to bridge the technological gap also reflects the prevalent ideology to survive and to catch up in view of the dynamic changes in economic relations between countries, in which technology has become a dominant competitive force. Singapore's economic growth now centres on an innovation-driven industrial strategy [3]-[4].

3.1. Singapore's Agency for Science, Technology and Research – A⋆STAR

The Singapore's Agency for Science, Technology and Research (A⋆STAR, https://www.a-star.edu.sg/) is a statutory board under the Ministry of Trade and Industry of Singapore. A⋆STAR drives mission-oriented research that advances scientific discovery and technological innovation. It plays a pivotal role in nurturing and developing talent and leaders for the Research Institutes, the wider research community, and industry. The agency supports Research & Development that is aligned to areas of competitive advantage and national needs for Singapore. These span the four technology domains of Advanced Manufacturing and Engineering (AME), Health and Biomedical Sciences (HBMS), Urban Solutions and Sustainability (USS), and Services and Digital Economy (SDE) set out under the nation's five-year Research & Development plans. The agency's research institutes are located mostly in Biopolis and Fusionopolis. The total strength of the A⋆STAR community, including scientists and researchers, technical and non-technical staff, and industry development and commercialization staff is over five thousand.

A⋆STAR was established in 1991 with the primary mission to advance the economy and improve lives by growing knowledge-intensive biomedical research, along with scientific and engineering fields. It was formerly known as the National Science and Technology Board (NSTB) until January 2002. The Agency serves as a catalyst, enabler and convener of significant research initiatives among the research community in Singapore and beyond. Through open innovation, A⋆STAR collaborates with its partners in both the public and private sectors, and bring science and technology to benefit the economy and society [3]-[4].

3.2.   National Research Foundation

The National Research Foundation (NRF, https://www.nrf.gov.sg/) was established in 2006. It is a department within the Prime Minister's Office. The NRF sets the national direction for research and development (R&D) by developing policies, plans and strategies for research, innovation and enterprise. It also funds strategic initiatives and builds up Research & Development capabilities by nurturing research talent. The NRF aims to transform Singapore into a vibrant Research & Development hub that contributes towards a knowledge-intensive, innovative and entrepreneurial economy; and make Singapore a magnet for excellence in science and innovation. The *Vision: Singapore as a vibrant science & technology hub, with Research & Development contributing significantly to a knowledge-intensive, innovative and entrepreneurial economy.* The *Mission*: The National Research Foundation (NRF) sets the national direction for Research & Development by: (a) Developing policies, plans and strategies for research, innovation and enterprise; (b) Funding initiatives that strengthen research and scientific capabilities, and achieve economic and national impact; (c) Building up Research & Development capabilities and capacities through nurturing its people and attracting foreign researchers and scientists; and (d)

Coordinating the research agenda of different agencies to transform Singapore into a knowledge-intensive, innovative and entrepreneurial economy.

The National Research Foundation is the secretariat to the Research, Innovation and Enterprise Council (RIEC), chaired by the Prime Minister, the Deputy Prime Minister and the Minister for Finance. The *Strategic Thrusts*: The plan to grow Singapore's economy through research, innovation & enterprise is underpinned by its strategic thrusts of: Strengthening foundational capabilities; Developing talent; Driving research excellence through competition; and Ensuring impact through public-private collaborations, industry-oriented Research & Development, and commercialisation [3]-[4].

3.3. Mathematics Education in Singapore

Over the decades (particularly, after its independence in 1965), Singapore's Education System has evolved. Likewise, Mathematics education in Singapore has also evolved. Today, all children receive at least ten years of general education in over 350 primary, secondary and post-secondary schools across Singapore. Mathematics is a compulsory subject from primary to the end of secondary education. In the early grades (lower classes), about 20% of the school curriculum time is allotted to mathematics. This is with the aim to lay a strong foundation in order to support further learning in higher classes and beyond. The present-day School Mathematics Curricula strives to cater to the needs of every child in the school. This is undoubtedly a big challenge not only in Singapore but across the globe. It is based on a framework that has mathematical problem solving as its primary focus. Singapore has an outstanding performance in international benchmark studies, for school education, particularly in mathematics [5].

The Ministry of Education (MOE, https://www.moe.gov.sg/) and the National Institute of Education (NIE, https://www.nie.edu.sg/) collectively share the responsibility for mathematics education in Singapore. The MOE focuses on the design and implementation of the curriculum. NIE takes care of the teacher preparation and development along with the research in mathematics education. The curriculum is centrally planned by the MOE. At the same time schools are given some flexibility in the process of implementation, taking into account the abilities and interests of students. Every six years, the mathematics curriculum is reviewed in consultation with various key stakeholders and partners to ensure that it meets the diverse needs of the nation.

The National Institute of Education (NIE, https://www.nie.edu.sg/) is an autonomous institute within the Nanyang Technological University (NTU, https://www.ntu.edu.sg/) and the only teacher education institution in Singapore! It provides education programmes (both pre-service and in-service) ranging from diploma to doctorate levels. In order to be abreast of the knowledge and required skills, teachers in Singapore are provided over hundred hours of training. This programme of training the trainer started in 1998. This personal development programme is generously funded by the MOE. Teachers have an opportunity to avail these programmes and upgrade themselves. The MOE works in tandem with NIE to design these special courses for practicing teachers. Moreover, some of these courses offered by NIE lead to postgraduate degrees. This is an extra incentive for the teachers to acquire higher degrees. Research is undertaken by graduate students and university scholars. Since 2002, the National Institute of Education has actively funded research in order to improve education in Singapore, particularly in the sciences [3]-[4].

4. UNIVERSITIES IN SINGAPORE

Industrialization required highly competent engineers produced locally in Singapore. Consequently, engineering diploma courses at Singapore Polytechnic were upgraded to full degree courses in 1965. In 1968, the National Industrial Training Council was established to make policy for technical education and industrial training to meet manpower requirements of new industries. The School of Postgraduate Medical Studies was established in 1970, offering master-level degrees in medicine, surgery, paediatrics, and internal medicine. In 1971, the Science Council instituted the Science Teachers' Awards to recognise inspiring science teachers.

There are 34 universities in Singapore, out of which six are autonomous. These receive funding from the government and are given the flexibility to strategise, innovate, and differentiate themselves. Besides, there are institutions offering external degree programmes along with polytechnics. We shall elaborate on the six autonomous universities of Singapore [3]-[4].

4.1. National University of Singapore

The National University of Singapore (NUS) is the first autonomous research university in Singapore. NUS is a comprehensive research university, offering a wide range of disciplines, including the sciences, medicine and dentistry, design and environment, law, arts and social sciences, engineering, business, computing and music at both the undergraduate and postgraduate levels. It was founded in 1905 as the Straits Settlements and Federated Malay States Government Medical School. The National University of Singapore is the oldest higher education institution in Singapore. As of 2018, it had 2,555 academic staff and 35,908 students (for further details, visit http://www.nus.edu.sg/).

4.2. Nanyang Technological University

The Nanyang Technological University (NTU) is the second oldest public autonomous research university in Singapore. NTU is the second largest university in Singapore. The University is organised into eight colleges and schools, including the College of Engineering, College of Science, Nanyang Business School, Lee Kong Chian School of Medicine, and College of Humanities, Arts and Social Sciences. NTU is also home to several autonomous institutions such as Singapore's National Institute of Education, S. Rajaratnam School of International Studies, Earth Observatory of Singapore, Singapore Centre on Environmental Life Sciences Engineering, Institute on Asian Consumer Insight, and the recently launched NTU Institute of Science and Technology for Humanity. NTU's main campus covers 200 hectares (490 acres) of land, making it the largest university campus in Singapore. The primary campus grounds are located in the western part of Singapore, along 50 Nanyang Avenue. It also has two other campuses in Singapore's healthcare and start-up districts, Novena and One-North respectively. It has 33,500 students and 10,000 faculty and staff (for further details, visit https://www.ntu.edu.sg/).

4.3. Singapore Management University

Singapore Management University (SMU) is the third autonomous university in Singapore. The university provides broad-based business programmes modelled after the Wharton School of the University of Pennsylvania. SMU was established on 29 July 2000 and is located in the Downtown area of Singapore. It has a city campus with a total enrollment of about 10,000 undergraduate and postgraduate students and comprises six schools offering undergraduate, graduate and PhD programmes in business administration, business analytics, financial services, accountancy, economics, information systems management, law and social sciences. The university has over 30 research institutes and centres of excellence, and customised corporate training and lifelong learning for individuals are available through the university's professional and executive development programmes. SMU is accredited by the AACSB International, EQUIS, and AMBA (for further details, visit, https://www.smu.edu.sg/).

4.4. Singapore University of Technology and Design

The Singapore University of Technology and Design (SUTD) is the fourth autonomous university in Singapore. It was founded in 2009. It is one of the first universities in the world to incorporate the art and science of design and technology into a multi-disciplinary curriculum. Established in collaboration with the Massachusetts Institute of Technology (MIT), SUTD seeks to nurture technically-grounded leaders and innovators in engineering product development, engineering systems and design, information systems technology and design, and architecture and sustainable design, to serve societal needs. The University, also in collaboration with Zhejiang University (ZJU) and Singapore Management University (SMU), is distinguished by its unique East and West academic programme which incorporates elements of technology, entrepreneurship, management and design thinking. It also offers an MIT-SUTD Dual Masters' Degree Programme, a full-time programme leading to a degree from MIT and another from SUTD. Graduate opportunities also include the SUTD PhD Programme (for further details, visit https://www.sutd.edu.sg/).

4.5. Singapore Institute of Technology

The Singapore Institute of Technology (also known as Singaporetech) is the fifth autonomous university in Singapore. It was established in 2009. SIT is Singapore's first university of applied learning. The university offers industry-focused, applied degree programmes. It confers its own degree programmes as well as specialised degree programmes with overseas universities. The university's degree programmes are grouped into five clusters: Engineering (ENG), Chemical Engineering and Food Technology (CEFT), Infocomm Technology (ICT), Health and Social Sciences (HSS), and Design and Specialised Businesses (DSB). It has 146 academic staff and 6,000 Students (for further details, visit https://www.singaporetech.edu.sg/).

4.6. Singapore University of Social Sciences

The Singapore University of Social Sciences (SUSS) is the sixth autonomous university in Singapore. It was established in 2017. SUSS focuses on applied degree programmes primarily in social sciences. In 2017, SUSS received its inaugural class of 2,137 graduates. SUSS academia is organised into five schools, Institute for Adult Learning (IAL), College for Lifelong & Experiential Learning (CLEL), UC and five centres. It has 280 academic staff and 15,000 Students (for further details, visit http://www.suss.edu.sg/).

5. RESEARCH INSTITUTIONS IN SINGAPORE

Science and innovation have enjoyed a special high priority by both government as well as the industry in Singapore. Science and Technology (S&T) has been serving as a key pillar of Singapore's national strategy for growth. The sustained patronage to science has enabled the transfer of knowledge into the market place. This in turn is contributing to the economy, which in turn is supporting science. Research Centres of Excellence (RCEs) were established within the universities to build and leverage their existing strengths to create world-class research centres. We have seen the description of the universities in Singapore in the previous section. There are many academic faculties and departments across Universities active in research. A detailed description of these is beyond the scope of this Chapter. In this section, we shall describe some of the prominent research centres [3]-[4].

5.1. Institute for Mathematical Sciences

The Institute for Mathematical Sciences (IMS, https://ims.nus.edu.sg/) was established at the National University of Singapore (NUS, http://www.nus.edu.sg/) in 2000. The mission of the Institute is to foster mathematical research, both fundamental and multidisciplinary, in particular, research that links mathematics to other disciplines, to nurture the growth of mathematical expertise among research scientists, to train talent for research in the mathematical sciences, and to serve as a platform for research interaction between the scientific community in Singapore and the wider international community. Since its inception, the IMS assumed an international profile, hosting visitors from many parts of the world. Today it organizes programmes and workshops attended by more than 700 mathematical scientists each year and is a major node in the mathematical research community in the Asia-Pacific region. There are typically six programmes and twenty workshops organized in a year, with up to 60 participants for each of them. A programme lasts between one and three months, while workshops are of one week duration. The purpose of each programme is: (a) to bring together mathematical scientists and researchers from different disciplines in activities around common themes; (b) to bring to Singapore leading researchers in selected fields to interact and do joint research with local scientists; and (c) to provide training for graduate students and young scientists through tutorial sessions.

For training of graduate students, the Institute for Mathematical Sciences also conducts summer schools every year. Each summer school lasts from three weeks to a month. Some of the summer schools are associated with thematic programmes and held during the respective programme periods. The Institute also organizes conferences, stand-alone workshops, colloquium lectures and ad-hoc seminars. These workshops and seminars are normally focused on specific topics with the objective of attracting smaller groups of participants and encouraging intensive interaction among them.

The Institute for Mathematical Sciences produces a *Lecture Notes Series* published by the World Scientific Publishing Company (https://www.worldscientific.com/). The main objective of the Lecture Notes Series is to make available to a wider audience the original or revised notes of the tutorial lectures given during the Institute's programmes. The Institute also publishes, two to three times a year, a newsletter called *Imprints* (https://ims.nus.edu.sg/resourceimp.php), which reports on IMS' programmes and activities and features interviews with distinguished visitors to the Institute. In addition, IMS maintains a preprint series of research papers by visitors that were either initiated or written fully or in part during their participation in the Institute's programmes. As a part of its outreach programme, the Institute organizes public lectures, school lectures and math camps. Through these means and interview articles in the newsletter, the Institute seeks to raise public awareness and understanding of the role of mathematics in science, engineering, technology and industry, and to encourage talented students in the study of mathematics leading to the pursuit of careers in research in mathematical sciences [4, 5].

The Institute for Mathematical Science in Singapore seems to have been inspired by the *Institute of Mathematical Sciences* (MATSCIENCE, IMSc) in

Chennai (Madras), India, both in its name and spirit! The Institute of Mathematical Sciences (MATSCIENCE/IMSc) was founded by Alladi Ramakrishnan in 1962. It is an autonomous national institution for fundamental research in the areas of Theoretical Physics, Mathematics, Theoretical Computer Science and Computational Biology [6]-[8]. It is funded mainly by the Department of Atomic Energy (http://dae.nic.in/). (for further details, visit https://www.imsc.res.in/).

5.2. RISP–The Centre for Remote Imaging, Sensing and Processing

The Centre for Remote Imaging, Sensing and Processing, better known as CRISP (https://crisp.nus.edu.sg/), is a university-level research centre of the National University of Singapore (NUS, http://www.nus.edu.sg/). It was established in the early 1990s as a centre for the reception and processing of images received from earth observation satellites. It is well-known in the region as the source of many of the satellite images, which have revealed details of both natural and man-made disasters, such as the Indian Ocean tsunami of 2004 and the fires in Indonesia, which had caused widespread hazy conditions in much of South-East Asia. CRISP's remote sensing satellite ground station is one of the first multi-mission ground stations built around the open system concept, with a high level of flexibility to accommodate future satellite missions. It is able to acquire images of the earth's surface within a radius of about $3000km$ (for satellites orbiting at heights of about $800km$) or about $2300km$ (for satellites orbiting at heights of about $700km$). These vast areas enable satellites to cover a number of countries: Brunei, Indonesia, Cambodia, Laos, Malaysia, Myanmar, Philippines, Singapore, Thailand, Vietnam, Sri Lanka, and the southern regions of China.

The CRISP facility is currently receiving and processing data from the satellites: FENGYUN; TERRA, AQUA and SUOMI-NPP; WORLDVIEW-1 and WORLDVIEW-2; and CBERS. Users of remote sensing data can search the complete data catalogue of CRISP through the Internet. *Quick look images* and location maps are provided together with textual information through the catalog-browse system. CRISP is prepared to provide training or consultation services in the fields of remote sensing technology or applications. CRISP is open to proposals from interested organisations to jointly develop applications of remote sensing data [4].

5.3. The NUS Nanoscience and Nanotechnology Initiative

The Nanoscience and Nanotechnology Initiative (NUSNNI, https://www.nusnni.nus.edu.sg/) began functioning in January 2002 and was officially opened in July 2004. It is located in the National University of Singapore (NUS, http://www.nus.edu.sg/). The aim of NUSNNI is to initiate and coordinate long-term nanoscience and engineering research. The NUSNNI has the following objectives: (a) to develop research human capital and long-term research capabilities in the strategic field of nanoscience and nanotechnology; (b) to galvanize and coordinate multidisciplinary research effort (across departments, faculties and with the Research Institutes) in nanoscience and nanotechnology; and (c) to help set research priorities and directions for high impact nanoscience and nanotechnology research. In order to fulfill these objectives, NUSNNI has done interdisciplinary collaborations among the various disciplines within the university faculties and interested research partners. NUSNNI provides the necessary support to facilitate efforts by faculties, researchers and students interested in pursuing research in nanoscience and nanotechnology.

In the light of the University's strong commitment to nanoscience and nanotechnology research, NUSNNI's role in its development and promotion is to optimise resources and focus on multidisciplinary strategic programmes [4].

5.4. The Centre for Quantum Technologies

The Centre for Quantum Technologies (CQT, https://www.quantumlah.org/) in Singapore is a Research Centre of Excellence, hosted by the National University of Singapore (NUS, http://www.nus.edu.sg/). It has significant autonomy both in pursuing its research goals and in its governance. The Centre has its own Governing Board and a Scientific Advisory Board. The Centre brings together physicists, computer scientists and engineers to do basic research in quantum physics and to build devices based on quantum phenomena. Experts in quantum technologies are applying their discoveries in computing, communications and sensing. Research in quantum information science in Singapore took a turning point in 1998, in the form of a series of informal seminars at the National University of Singapore. The seminars attracted local researchers and as a result, the Quantum Information Technology Group (informally referred to in Singlish as *quantum lah*) was formed. A formal setup took shape in 2002, with support from Singapore's Agency for Science, Technology and Research

(A★STAR, https://www.a-star.edu.sg/). This led to a number of faculty appointments. In 2007, the Quantum Information Technology Group was selected as the core of Singapore's first Research Centre of Excellence. The Centre for Quantum Technologies was founded in December 2007 with $158 million to be spent over ten years. The Centre for Quantum Technologies is funded by the Singapore National Research Foundation (https://www.nrf.gov.sg/) and the Ministry of Education (https://www.moe.gov.sg/).

The Centre for Quantum Technologies pursues insights into the physics that describes light, matter, and information. It has developed novel tools to study and control their interactions. CQT's research goals range from understanding the properties of materials to working out new encryption schemes. CQT has built technologies for secure communication, quantum computing, and precision measurement. It creates its own software and control systems that push the boundaries of what is possible. Moreover, CQT collaborates and consults with industry. CQT has training programmes ranging from undergraduate to postdoctoral level. This enables training of the next generation of practitioners in these emerging fields and provides support to those in the frontiers. The members of the institute are skilled in planning and problem-solving, with diverse skills such as coding, circuit design, and systems engineering. The alumni have successfully moved on to jobs in academia as well as in industry [4].

5.5. Tropical Marine Science Institute

The Tropical Marine Science Institute (TMSI, https://www.tmsi.nus.edu.sg/) is an institution formed within the National University of Singapore (NUS, http://www.nus.edu.sg/). TMSI is a centre of excellence for research, development and consultancy in tropical marine science as well as environmental science. With its multi-disciplinary research laboratories and active international links, it handles projects relevant to Physical Oceanography, Acoustics, Marine Biology, Marine Mammals, Biofuels, Water Resources and Climate Change. TMSI also provides postgraduate research opportunities. The Institute's funding comes from a variety of sources which enables the TMSI to undertake a wide spectrum of research in tropical marine science. The major research areas are in marine environmental management, underwater remote sensing and oceanography. Through active collaboration with academic, government and industrial sectors, TMSI aims to play a strong role in promoting integrated marine science, in Research & Development, as well as to establish itself as a regional and international education and training centre.

The Tropical Marine Science Institute arose from the need to have a multi-disciplinary research team to scientifically address the diverse yet interconnected problems and opportunities faced by Singapore's coastal waters. Singapore is an island nation on the equator, with one of the world's busiest shipping industries and has one of the most advanced coastal development strategies, and yet it is located in one of the richest regions in the world for marine biodiversity. Under these circumstances, there is a need to reconcile these factors to benefit the maximum number of people and accommodate their diverse interests. Currently located on the NUS campus, the TMSI also has coastal facilities on St. John's Island, which greatly extend its research and teaching capabilities [4].

5.6.   The Mechanobiology Institute

The Mechanobiology Institute (https://mbi.nus.edu.sg/) is hosted by the National University of Singapore (NUS, http://www.nus.edu.sg/). Its goal is to develop new models of biomedical research by focusing on the quantitative and systematic understanding of dynamic functional processes. With a systems-level perspective, it is working to identify, measure and describe how the forces for motility and morphogenesis are expressed at the molecular, cellular and tissue levels.

The Mechanobiology Institute has leading-edge core and support facilities to enable novel and innovative research in mechanobiology. Equipment, staff and services are provided to support and overcome the experimental and computational challenges that the principal investigators (PI), researchers and students may face. MBI is committed to developing better ways to bring together the multi-disciplinary expertise that is needed to understand the systems biology of mechanical functions. In approaching integrated functions such as biomechanics, a single laboratory often does not have the resources to study all of the relevant parameters; however, innovation and insights will continue to be driven most rapidly by single investigators in a collaborative environment. MBI's Microscopy Core is the largest of MBI's core facilities, serving as the backbone for most of the experimental work at the Institute. The Core supports image related research, offering a wide range of microscopes and image analysis resources. The Nano and Microfabrication Core helps with the design and fabrication of innovative devices to further our biological understanding of the cell. MBI's Microfabrication Core was formed to support the microfabrication needs of the principal investigators, collaborators, research fellows and graduate students through direct fabrication or recommendation of suitable solutions. Their process starts with a discussion with PIs or students about their design. They help them draw the lay-out of the photo-mask (when applicable) using AutoCAD/L-edit software, and according to the fabrication process requested, they write or outsource the mask, and use it for photo-lithography. The MBI laboratories' design is based on the bold concept of an *open laboratory*. There are no walls or partitions separating one principal investigator's group from another and benches are communal, as are the core facilities and common shared equipment such as autoclaves, deep freezers, centrifuges and other common bench-top equipment. The MBI's laboratories cover protein expression, microscopy, computation, nanofabrication, cell culture and other essential services to better serve the Institute members. They provide equipment, staff and service to support and overcome the experimental and computational challenges that MBI's principal investigators, researchers and students may face [4].

5.7. Singapore Synchrotron Light Source

The Singapore Synchrotron Light Source (SSLS, http://ssls.nus.edu.sg/) is a University-level Research Centre at the National University of Singapore (NUS, http://www.nus.edu.sg/). This is a coveted facility and is covered in a separate section [4].

6. LEARNED SOCIETIES AND SCIENCE MUSEUMS

A learned society (also known as a learned academy, scholarly society, or academic association) is an organisation that exists to promote an academic discipline, profession, or a group of related disciplines such as arts and science. Membership may be open to all, may require possession of some qualification, or may be an honour conferred by election. Learned societies in the sciences have a long history of activism, particularly in the western world. Some of the oldest learned societies are the Académie des Jeux floraux (founded 1323), the Sodalitas Litterarum Vistulana (founded 1488), the Accademia della Crusca (founded 1585), the Accademia dei Lincei (founded 1603), the Académie Française (founded 1635), the Academy of Sciences Leopoldina (founded 1652), the Royal Society of London (founded 1660) and the French Academy of Sciences (founded 1666). But in Asia and Africa, such learned societies were formed much later. In this section, we briefly describe some of the learned societies in Singapore [3]-[4].

6.1. Singapore National Academy of Science

Way back in 1967, the Singapore National Academy of Science (SNAS) co-existed with the Institute of Physics Singapore (IPS), the Singapore National Institute of Chemistry (SNIC), the Singapore Mathematical Society (SMS) and the Singapore Institute of Biology (SIBiol) as a single entity (a learned society) to promote and popularise science and technology in Singapore. At that time, SNAS was in charge of publishing the SNAS Journal and conducting the SNAS Congress. During the mid-seventies, the four societies were integrated into SNAS [4].

In 1976, SNAS was re-purposed, when some functions were invested into the Singapore Association for the Advancement of Science (SAAS, a constituent member of SNAS). The year 1976 is considered the official date for the founding of the Singapore National Academy of Science (SNAS, https://snas.org.sg/). It is a government funded body in Singapore. Thus, SNAS became an umbrella organisation with the dual objectives of: (a) promoting the advancement of science and technology in Singapore; and (b) representing the scientific opinions of its members. SNAS endeavours to promote the advancement of science and technology in Singapore. SNAS also represents the scientific opinions of its members. From the outset, SNAS was conceived to be an umbrella organization, which would not only have its own series of programmes but would also oversee the activities of its constituent societies. Since 2011, SNAS has begun to elect its own fellows.

The constituent organisations of SNAS are: (i) the Chapter of Clinician Scientists, Academy of Medicine (CCS); (ii) the Institute of Physics Singapore (IPS); (iii) the Materials Research Society Singapore (MRSS); (iv) the Science Teachers Association of Singapore (STAS); (v) the Singapore Association for the Advancement of Science (SAAS); (vi) the Singapore Institute of Biology (SIBiol); (vii) the Singapore Institute of Statistics (SIS); (viii) the Singapore Mathematical Society (SMS); (ix) the Singapore National Institute of Chemistry (SNIC); (x) the Singapore Society for Biochemistry and Molecular Biology (SSBMB); and (xi) the Singapore Society for Microbiology and Biotechnology (SSMB).

The Singapore National Academy of Science is a member of

several international organizations including: *International Council of Science* (http://www.icsu.org/); *Pacific Science Association* (http://www.pacificscience.org/); *Association of Academies and Societies of Sciences in Asia* (http://aassa.asia/). For further details, see the comprehensive accounts in [4].

6.2. Singapore Women in Science Network

Women make up about half of the world's population. About 24% of the scientists and engineers in the United States and the European Union are women. In the case of Singapore, this figure is significantly better at 30% (see [2] for details). Very few women make it to the top awards particularly in the field of mathematics [9, 10]. The Singapore Women in Science is a network of women working in science, technology and academia. This include women who are working or studying in academia, patent law, business development, technology transfer, pharmaceutical and personal care industries. The network has universities, industries and other organizations as its members. The network is strong and serves as an effective support group, facilitating collaboration, mentorship and friendships. Its members have exposure to networking opportunities with leaders in the field. It hosts regular events such as monthly talks by professional women, who hold diverse leadership positions in the field of science and technology. These talks are followed by informal networking happy hours. The Network holds regular events such as gender summits and also partners in such events with other organizers. These summits are designed to bring together stakeholders who shape Singapore's scientific ecosystem, including funders, research institutions, scientists, and policymakers. They aim to bring together professionals in the Singaporean science landscape onto a global platform to showcase the positive impacts of gender diversity in science and raise awareness of the real challenges faced by women in science, connecting grassroots with policy (for further details, visit, https://www.singaporewomeninscience.org/).

6.3. The Lee Kong Chian Natural History Museum

The Lee Kong Chian Natural History Museum (LKCNHM, https://lkcnhm.nus.edu.sg/) is a museum of natural history at the Kent Ridge Campus of the National University of Singapore (NUS, http://www.nus.edu.sg/). It was officially opened in April 2015. It houses the Raffles Natural History Collection. The idea for a natural history collection was first proposed by Sir Stamford Raffles, and the collection of Southeast Asian biodiversity was begun in 1849 at the Raffles Museum (now the National Museum of Singapore). In 1972, the Government of Singapore removed the natural history collections from the National Museum and gave them to the Zoology Department of what was then the University of Singapore. They were housed in various temporary premises, including the Nanyang Technological University for seven years. Subsequently, they were returned to the NUS and housed in the Raffles Museum of Biodiversity Research. LKCNHM inherited the natural history collections from the Raffles Museum of Biodiversity Research. The Museum currently has more than 560,000 catalogued lots in its collection and over a million specimens from throughout the region. About 2,000 of these are exhibited in the museum's galleries.

Importantly, the Lee Kong Chian Natural History Museum offers a range of curriculum-based educational workshops and other programmes for teachers and students in the area of natural history and ecology. These activities seek to arouse curiosity and educate students about the rich natural history and heritage in Singapore, facilitate a better appreciation and understanding of conservation in Singapore, foster experiential learning and creative thinking in students, and provide students with opportunities to carry out research projects and interact with scientists. The museum also has a research and publication programme including books magazines and journals [4].

6.4.   Science Centre Singapore

The Science Centre Singapore (SCS, https://www.science.edu.sg/) was previously known as Singapore Science Centre. It is a scientific institution in Jurong East, Singapore, specialising in the promotion of scientific and technological education for the general public [4]. Science Centre Singapore was opened in 1977. With over 850 exhibits spread over eight exhibition galleries, it sees over a million visitors a year. Every year, Science Centre initiates new activities. The Science Centre was carved out of the National Museum of Singapore as a separate institution, so that the latter could focus on its artistic and historical collections. We note two of the many activities organized by the Science Centre Singapore.

6.4.1. Singapore Science & Engineering Fair

The Singapore Science & Engineering Fair (SSEF) is a national competition organised by the Ministry of Education (MOE, https://www.moe.gov.sg/), the Agency for Science, Technology and Research (A★STAR, https://www.a-star.edu.sg/) and the Science Centre Singapore (SCS, https://www.science.edu.sg/). The SSEF is affiliated with the prestigious International Science and Engineering Fair (ISEF), which is regarded as the Olympics of science competitions. This competition is an excellent platform for budding scientists and engineers to showcase their passion in their respective fields by communicating their findings to industry experts. Winners get an excellent opportunity to represent Singapore and compete at the ISEF. The SSEF award winners are eligible to move on to the A★STAR Talent Search (ATS) competition. The SSEF is open to all secondary and pre-university students between 15 and 20 years of age. Participants submit research projects, which are student-initiated or from programmes such as the Youth Research Programme (YRP), the Nanyang Research Programme (NRP), the Science Mentorship Programme (SMP), the Science Research Programme (SRP), the Technology & Engineering Research Programme (TERP) and the Young Defence Scientists Programme (YDSP) or projects done at A★STAR research institutes and schools [4]. The project topics range across all areas of science and engineering. The Intel ISEF is held annually in May and attracts over 1,300 students from 40 nations to compete for scholarships of over two million US$, tuition grants, scientific equipment and scientific fieldtrips.

6.4.2. Singapore Science Festival

The Singapore Science Festival is an annual national event to celebrate the dynamism of science, engineering, technology and bio-medicine. It is jointly organised by the Agency for Science, Technology & Research (A★STAR) and Science Centre Singapore (SCS, https://www.science.edu.sg/). The Singapore Science Festival celebrates the role science, technology, engineering and mathematics (STEM) play in shaping the lives and in sculpting the future of societies. The festival attracts persons, who love to inquire, imagine and invent to make the future brighter for one and all [4].

7. SINGAPORE AND THE INTERNATIONAL YEAR OF LIGHT AND LIGHT-BASED TECHNOLOGIES

The international years are year-long observances to observe certain issues of international interest or concern. Such years are generally established by international bodies such as the United Nations (UN, https://www.un.org/). The specific agencies are the United Nations Educational, Scientific and Cultural Organization (UNESCO, https://en.unesco.org/), the World Health Organization (https://www.who.int/), among others.   The first year was the World Refugee Year (1959) in the context of refugees and migration after the Second World War.   The science related years include: the International Health and Medical Research Year (1960), the World Year of Physics (2005, http://www.wyp2005.org/), the International Year of Astronomy (2009, https://astronomy2009.org/), the International Year of Chemistry (2011, http://www.chemistry2011.org/), and the International Year of Sustainable Energy for All (2012, https://www.seforall.org/ and https://www.un.org/en/events/sustainableenergyforall/). It is interesting to note that there is yet be an International Year of Mathematics!   The year 2014 was the International Year of Crystallography (https://www.iycr2014.org/). The year 2015 was the International Year of Light and Light-based Technologies (IYL2015, http://www.light2015.org/). The year 2016 was the International Year of Pulses.   The year 2019 is the International Year of the Periodic Table (https://iypt2019.org/). The same year was also the International Year of Indigenous Languages and the International Year of Moderation. The upcoming years include the International Year of Plant Health (2020), the International Year of Peace and Trust (2021), the International Year of Artisanal Fisheries and Aquaculture (2022) and the International Year of Camelids (2024). The year-long celebrations stimulated worldwide interest in light and related sciences & technologies [11]-[18].

Singapore took an active part in the International Year of Light and Light-based Technologies. It was one of the 93 *National Nodes*, which organised local campaigns, activities and events. Nanyang Technological University served as the *Primary National Organizer*. Singapore organized about sixty events. Nanyang Technological University was a Gold Sponsor of the International Year of Light. It organized more than 40 technical and 20 social events in Singapore with support from regional organizations/societies. John Michael Dudley (President of the Steering Committee of the IYL2015) was the keynote speaker for one of these events. For the first time, an IEEE Photonics Society Chapter Forum was hosted in Singapore. Various training workshops and industry networking sessions were organized to provide a platform for students, researchers, and academics to meet and exchange ideas on photonics. The LUX Photonics Consortium was established in 2015 to create a platform to promote translational research and industry collaborations in Singapore. Among the many events, the *Photonics Global Conference* and the *Photonics Global Student Conference* were a grand success. All these activities enabled to spread awareness about light and light-based sciences across Singapore. It also led to collaborations among students, researchers and other professionals [18].

The *International Day of Light* is a direct and enduring legacy of the International Year of Light and Light-based Technologies (IYL2015). On 14 November 2017, the UNESCO proclaimed 16 May as the International Day of Light (IDL, https://www.lightday.org/), during the 39th Session of the UNESCO General Conference [19]. The first laser was demonstrated on 16 May 1960 by engineer and physicist Theodore Harold Maiman using a synthetic-ruby crystal. The *inaugural* International Day of Light was marked in a grand ceremony at the UNESCO Headquarters in Paris, France on 16 May 2018. IDL will be an excellent opportunity to recognize and present contributions to light and light-related sciences nationally and internationally (for further details, visit https://www.lightday.org/).

8. SINGAPORE SYNCHROTRON LIGHT SOURCE

Charged-particles, when accelerated, radiate electromagnetic energy. This interesting physical phenomenon, now known by the name *synchrotron radiation* had its theoretical beginnings a long time ago at the time of classical electrodynamics. At that time, only the very basic features of this physical phenomenon were studied and expressions were derived for several quantities such as the *total radiation intensity*, *spectral distribution* and *angular distribution* [20]-[23]. These theoretical studies had to wait for about half a century till the development of charged-particle accelerator technology for a direct observation and experimental verification. Synchrotron radiation has very special properties, which are not to be found in the traditional X-Rays and the lasers. Hence, synchrotron radiation with its unique properties has found numerous uses beyond the reach of the X-Rays and laser sources.

Let us recall that the X-Ray images are a major medical diagnostic tool.

They date back to more than a century. It is to be noted that X-Rays are one part of the electromagnetic spectrum just as visible light is. But X-Rays are far more energetic than the visible light. Hence, they form good probes. Synchrotron radiation is much more powerful than the traditional X-Rays [24]-[33]. A synchrotron radiation facility is based on the technology of charged-particle accelerators. Bunches of charged particles (usually, electrons) are made to circulate for several hours inside a ring-shaped, long tube under high vacuum. These rings have several beam lines with experimental stations and serve several sets of users simultaneously. Contrary to expectation, there are not very many synchrotron facilities to meet the huge demands of numerous users. Synchrotron radiation facilities are expensive (about a hundred million US $) and technologically challenging to construct and maintain. Now, we have about eighty synchrotron radiation facilities in twenty-eight countries: Armenia, Australia, Brazil, Canada, China, Denmark, England, France, Germany, India, Iran, Italy, Japan, Jordan, Korea, Netherlands, Poland, Russia, Singapore, South Korea, Spain, Sweden, Switzerland, Taiwan, Thailand, Ukraine, United Kingdom, and USA [33]. The geographic distribution is as follows. Europe: 10 countries with synchrotrons; USA: 12 synchrotrons; Asia: 30 synchrotrons in 9 countries; Japan: 17 synchrotrons; South America: one synchrotron; Australia: one synchrotron; Middle East: two synchrotrons (Jordan and Iran). It is to be noted that the African continent does not have any synchrotrons. Synchrotron facility are expensive and also require substantial technological expertise. Consequently, many countries pool their technical and financial resources to have *international synchrotron radiation facilities* [24]-[29]. It is relevant to note the wavelength-dependent effects arising from the *Quantum Mechanics of Charged Particle Beam Optics* [34]-[?] and the *Quantum Methodologies in Light Beam Optics* [55]-[70], respectively. The Quantum-*like* Methods serve as useful for modelling some of the accelerator systems [71]-[74]

The Singapore Synchrotron Light Source (SSLS, http://ssls.nus.edu.sg/) is a University-level Research Centre (see Figure 1). It is located in the National University of Singapore (NUS, http://www.nus.edu.sg/). It is under the office of the Deputy President (Research & Technology), with activities involving local and international groups from many universities, research institutes, and industry. Since SSLS was commissioned in the year 1999, its scope of activities has evolved and broadened as the number of beam lines and users has increased. It currently has Research & Development programmes featuring micro/nanofabrication, a variety of analytical applications, and the development of

Figure 1. Singapore Synchrotron Light Source.

advanced synchrotron radiation instrumentation [75].

Singapore Synchrotron Light Source comprises of a compact superconducting storage ring with $700MeV$ electron energy and $4.5Tesla$ magnetic field to produce synchrotron radiation with a characteristic photon energy of $1.47keV$ and characteristic wavelength of $0.845nm$ (8.45Å). The useful X-Ray spectrum extends from about $10keV$ down to the far infrared at wave numbers of less than $10cm^{-1}$. While the flux is maximum in the soft X-Ray and adjacent harder X-Ray range, the roll off to harder photons is such that $10keV$ is considered a practical limit, depending on the requirements of a specific experiment. At the other end of the spectrum, in the far infrared, the edge effect is used, that is, the source point is chosen at about half of the maximum bending field in the entrance region of one of the two superconducting dipoles and this provides high flux and brilliance throughout the whole infrared spectral range [75].

The research at SSLS involves Micro/nanofabrication using deep X-Ray lithography and the LIGA process, which is of relevance in biotechnology, X-Ray optics, micro-optics, micro-fluidics, and gigascale micro-electronic packaging. The analytical applications are based on X-Ray absorption and fluorescence spectroscopy, X-Ray diffraction, infrared spectroscopy and microscopy, phase contrast imaging, photoemission spectroscopy, and include surface, interface, and nanostructure studies, catalyst development, speciation of elements for environmental and materials science, characterization of molecules on surfaces and in the gas phase, and imaging biological and technological systems. SSLS's development of advanced synchrotron radiation instrumentation are focused on the superconducting mini-undulator. The aim of this is to produce tunable brilliant light in the $2eV$ to $50eV$ spectral range for surface science and nanoscale microscopy [75].

9. National Parks Board of Singapore Awarded the 2017 UNESCO Sultan Qaboos Prize for Environmental Preservation

The very prestigious *2017 UNESCO Sultan Qaboos Prize for Environmental Preservation* [76]-[82] was awarded to the *National Parks Board of Singapore*, Singapore [83]-[86]. The award ceremony took place on the first day of the 8th World Science Forum, which took place at the Dead Sea, Jordan, from 7-11 November 2017, under the auspices of UNESCO [87]-[88]. Her Excellency Dr. Madiha Al Shaibani, Minister of Education, Sultanate of Oman, presented the award to the National Parks Board of Singapore (see Figure 2).

Figure 2. Award Ceremony of the 2017 UNESCO Sultan Qaboos Prize for Environmental Preservation.

The *National Parks Board of Singapore* (NParks) promotes biodiversity in a highly urbanized and land-scarce landscape, the recovery of habitats and species and supports the incorporation of biodiversity into all levels of the education system. Let us recall that Singapore is a city-state and an island-country with an area of about 725 square-kilometers and population of less than six million (2018). The NParks is one of the numerous statutory boards of the Government of Singapore. In this system, the statutory boards are organizations, which have substantial autonomy. The origins of the NParks can be traced to the exercise of tree-planting in the 1960s, which enjoyed the patronage of Lee Kuan Yew, then Prime Minister of Singapore. The massive tree planting continued into the 1970s resulting in the *National Tree Planting Day* (observed in the first week of each November) in 1971. The *Singapore Botanic Gardens* (created in 1859) was a natural choice in providing expertise and plant materials. There were several organizational changes, notably, the merger of the tree-planting initiative with the *Parks & Trees Unit* in 1973. This merger led to the creation of the *Parks and Recreation Department* under the auspices of the Ministry of National Development in 1975. The *1975 Parks and Trees Act* provided another boost to the greening exercise. The *Parks and Recreation Department* was renamed as the *National Parks Board* in 1996. With significant achievements in greenery, the vision and mission of the NParks has evolved from a "Garden City" to a "City in a Garden". Notably, the NParks manages Singapore's first UNESCO World Heritage Site [89], namely the *Singapore Botanic Gardens*, along with four nature reserves and together with more than 350 parks [84].

In 2008, the *National Parks Board of Singapore* along with the Secretariat of the *Convention on Biological Diversity* (this convention was conceived by United Nations Environment Programme) has developed the *Singapore Index on Cities' Biodiversity* (also known as the *City Biodiversity Index* or simply *Singapore Index*). Other environmental indices are centered around indicators including clean water, sanitation, energy efficiency, air quality, and waste management. The Singapore Index consolidates the various biodiversity indicators and provides a single index (see Ref. [85] and the User's Manual therein). Singapore Index is an effective self-assessment tool to help cities evaluate and benchmark their biodiversity conservation efforts. Further details about the NParks is to be found at https://www.nparks.gov.sg/.

The *National Parks Board of Singapore* are much more than the greening of the city-state of Singapore. They have conducted significant conservation biology research that has resulted in the discovery of new endemic plant and terrestrial invertebrate species [86]. These results have been used by the NParks to design better management plans and facilitate science-based decision making. National Parks Board of Singapore has an active publication programme and has a wide range of books/manuals/guides on various aspects of environmental concerns [84]. The annual reports of the NParks are freely available from its website [84]. NParks conducts training programmes, provides scholarships and career guidance in environment and related fields. NParks is also involved in legislation and administration of certain laws related to the environment. The diverse activities and the rich experience of the *National Parks Board of Singapore* is an excellent example to emulate [79]-[80]. Its experience can benefit many cities across the globe in growing a variety of plants such as dates in the deserts [90] and olives in the Mediterranean climate [91], respectively.

9.1. About the UNESCO Sultan Qaboos Prize for Environmental Preservation

We note the origins and the significance of the UNESCO Sultan Qaboos Prize for Environmental Preservation (see Figure 3).

Figure 3. Logo, UNESCO Sultan Qaboos Prize for Environmental Preservation.

His Majesty Sultan Qaboos Bin Said, Sultan of Oman — May Allah Almighty Bless Him — made a historic impact on the United Nations Educational, Scientific and Cultural Organization (UNESCO) during his visit to the Organization's Headquarters, in Paris, France on the first of June 1989. During that momentous visit, he expressed his support to UNESCO's objectives to preserve humanity from natural disasters through a donation to establish a *Prize for Environmental Preservation* [77]. UNESCO established the Statutes of the Prize, adopted by the Executive Board at its 132nd session in November 1989. According to the Statutes, the UNESCO's *Man and the Biosphere Programme* (MAB) was given the responsibility of selecting the laureates through a jury of members from the MAB office [76]. The *inaugural* Prize was awarded in 1991 to the *Instituto de Ecología*, Veracruz, Mexico [92]. Since then, it has been awarded very regularly every biennium (once in two years). During the period 1991-2017, the prize was awarded fourteen times. The laureates are from 18 countries across the continents. Mexico is the only country to get the prize twice (the inaugural prize in 1991, unshared; and the 2005 prize shared with Australia). The complete list of the laureates is in [76]-[82]. The Prize consists of a diploma, a medal and a cash endowment of US$100,000, thanks to the very generous endowment by His Majesty Sultan Qaboos Bin Said Al Said of Oman. In 2007, His Majesty increased the value of the Prize from US$20,000 to US$30,000. This was further increased to US$70,000 in 2013 and US$100,000 in 2019.

Between 1991 and 2001, the Prize awarding ceremony took place at the UNESCO Headquarters, Paris, France. During 2003-2011, it was awarded under the auspices of UNESCO, during the biennial *World Science Forum* (WSF, https://worldscienceforum.org/) held at Budapest, Hungary [87]. The 2013 WSF was held in Rio de Janeiro, Brazil, starting a rotation of venues between Budapest and elsewhere. The 2015 WSF was held at Budapest and the 2017 WSF at Dead Sea, Jordan [88]. The 2019 WSF is scheduled to take place in Budapest, during 17-22 November 2019. The grand success of the WSF in Jordan has prompted the creation of the *Arab Science Forum* to bring together science and research communities to address critical regional challenges [88]. The Arab Science Forum (ASF) is scheduled to be held every two years, starting with the first one in Jordan in 2020. This would be another venue to address environmental issues (see http://www.rss.jo/ for details). The purpose of the UNESCO Sultan Qaboos Prize for Environmental Preservation is to afford recognition to outstanding contributions by individuals, groups of individuals, institutes or organizations in the management or preservation of the environment. Nominations for the Prize can only be made by UNESCO Members States and by International Organizations or by Non-Governmental Organizations, which have consultative status with UNESCO, each of which may make only one nomination. Others can propose their candidate to their country's *National Commission* for UNESCO. It is the first Arab environmental protection prize to be awarded at the international level [78]-[80]. The other major science prizes instituted by the Middle Eastern region are the *King Faisal International Prize* by Saudi Arabia established in 1979 [93]-[104]; and the Mustafa Prize for Science by Iran launched in 2015 [105].

10. WORLD SCIENTIFIC PUBLISHING COMPANY, SINGAPORE

World Scientific Publishing Company Private Limited was established in 1981 with only five employees in a tiny office. Now, the company employs about 200 staff at its headquarters in Singapore and another 450 world-wide. The offices of the World Scientific can be found in New Jersey (USA); London (UK); Munich (Germany); Geneva (Switzerland); Tokyo (Japan); Beijing, Hong Kong, Shanghai and Tianjin (China); Taipei (Taiwan); and Chennai (India). Within three decades, it has established itself as one of the leading academic and professional publishers in the world, and the largest international scientific publisher in the Asia-Pacific region. For further details, visit https://www.worldscientific.com/.

World Scientific Publishing is an academic publisher of scientific, technical, and medical books and journals. World Scientific publishes about 600 new titles a year and 140 journals in various fields. World Scientific has published more than 12,000 titles. Many of its books are recommended texts adopted by renowned institutions such as Harvard University, California Institute of Technology, Stanford University and Princeton University.

World Scientific broke new ground in 1991, when it signed a memorandum of agreement with the Nobel Foundation (https://www.nobelprize.org/) to publish the entire series of Nobel Lectures in all subjects of the Nobel Prize. The five subjects are: physics and astronomy, chemistry, physiology or medicine, economic sciences and literature. The company had published and distributed the Nobel Lectures series (1901-2005) worldwide, making accessible the scientific, literary and humanitarian achievements of numerous Nobel laureates to a wide audience. Recently, World Scientific signed a new memorandum of agreement with Nobel Media (Nobel Foundation) to publish the latest series from 2006 to 2010.

In 1995, World Scientific co-founded the London-based Imperial College Press together with the Imperial College of Science, Technology and Medicine. In 2016, World Scientific Publishing Group restructured the brand and consolidated the various imprints under the World Scientific branding. This also applied to the Imperial College imprint. This smart move enables World Scientific Publishing Group to better serve its authors and customers by streamlining marketing, distribution and production of the Group's titles and products. World Scientific is also the exclusive distributor for The National Academies Press (based in Washington, DC) in Asia-Pacific (except Japan, New Zealand and Australia).

One cannot think of a University library, which can do without the books from World Scientific. Many of the books and journal articles cited in this Chapter are from the World Scientific! These include: [4], [10], [42], [43], [45], [46] and [47].

11. SINGAPORE CHANGI AIRPORT AND SINGAPORE AIRLINE

One may wonder about the presence of this section on the Singapore Changi Airport and Singapore Airline in this Chapter! Transport systems have played an important role in development of commerce and economies since ancient times. The scientific endeavour has directly and indirectly benefitted from transport systems. It is in terms of the transport of personnel, who carry ideas & expertise with them, the transport of literature and tools/equipment.

Singapore Changi Airport (http://www.changiairport.com/) is a major civilian airport in the Asia-Pacific region. It serves not only Singapore, but is also one of the largest transportation hubs in Asia. It is one of the world's busiest airports for international passenger and cargo traffic. The airport is operated by Changi Airport Group and it is the home base of Singapore Airlines, Singapore Airlines Cargo and several other airlines. Singapore Changi Airport had a passenger movement of sixty-six million for the year 2018.

Singapore Airlines Limited (SIA, https://www.singaporeair.com) is the flag carrier airline of Singapore with its hub at Singapore Changi Airport. The airline uses the Singapore Girl as its central figure in corporate branding. It has been ranked as the world's best airline year after year.

Many across the globe have benefitted from the Singapore Airport not only for business & tourism travels, but for the numerous conferences in the Asia-Pacific region. If not for Singapore Changi Airport and Singapore Airlines, many of the conferences in the Asia-Pacific region would be short of participants. This would be truer for the international participants from the distant lands! The author is one of the many beneficiaries of such travels through Singapore Changi Airport and Singapore Airline for a conference in Japan [36].

CONCLUSION

It is beyond the scope of this Chapter to cover the diverse science activities in Singapore. We have covered the major universities, science centres and learned societies. There would definitely be some which we have missed listing in this Chapter. Along with the facilities within its boundaries, Singapore has also played a pivotal role in international organizations. The concept for the Association of Asia Pacific Physical Societies (AAPPS, http://www.aapps.org/) began in 1983 with the first Asia Pacific Physics Conference (APPC) in Singapore. With an effort over several years, the AAPPS was formally established in 1989. The *Institute of Physics, Singapore* (http://ipssingapore.org/) is one of the seventeen *Member Societies* of AAPPS. The aims of AAPPS set at the start have been realized. AAPPS, together with the European Physical Society (EPS, https://www.eps.org/) and the American Physical Society (APS, https://www.aps.org/) are the three major important continental physical associations in the world. Singapore is one of the *Core Members* of the *Division of Plasma Physics* under the AAPPS (AAPPS-DPP, http://aappsdpp.org/AAPPSDPPF/). Singapore is represented by the Institute of Physics, Singapore. Since 2014, the AAPPS-DPP has been awarding the *Subrahmanyan Chandrasekhar Prize of Plasma Physics*. The prize is to recognize outstanding contributions to experimental and/or theoretical research in fundamental plasma physics and plasma applications in all fields of physics [106]-[108]. We have briefly cited the AAPPS as an example. There are many more such examples, where Singapore is playing an active role.

The journey of each country with science is a unique experience. In this Chapter, we have recorded the essential features of Singapore's journey with science. We have seen the development of science education, and scientific research activities in Singapore over recent decades accompanied by the rapid growth of the country. Scientific enterprise in Singapore has come a long way and it is in an active state now, with the promise to go much further. Among various achievements, Singapore can boast of numerous universities/polytechnics, science parks [3]-[4], and the coveted synchrotron radiation facility [75]. There is a thriving community of scientists, scientific industries, science education and many other science activities. Singapore serves as a prime example for its achievements in scientific enterprise. Singapore's scientific success is accompanied by its handling of environmental concerns. Singapore has achieved the status of a *City in a Garden* starting from a *Garden in a City*! This environmental success earned Singapore the very prestigious *2017 UNESCO Sultan Qaboos Prize for Environmental Preservation* [76]-[82]. Singapore has won many other prestigious awards such as the *2015 Mustafa Prize* launched by Iran in 2015. It was awarded to Jackie Yi-Ru Ying in the field of Nano-biotechnology sciences and she is from the Institute of Bioengineering and Nanotechnology in Singapore (https://www.a-star.edu.sg/ibn). Her corecipient was Omar Mwannes Yaghi [105].

Looking ahead, Singapore will need to collaborate with other countries in order to achieve a much greater impact than it has today. The collective wisdom of science and other fields of expertise definitely have the potential to deliver comprehensive and impactful solutions benefitting one and all. Science needs to be communicated to the bulk of the population. In many places, the majority of the population may not be conversant in the English language. In order to make the population more scientifically advanced and to embed scientific temper in people, science communication must reach the audience in the languages they know. The diverse experience of India in this endeavour can serve as a model elsewhere [109]-[111].

In just less than six decades (since the independence in 1965), Singapore has transformed itself from a developing economy with few natural resources to a thriving global metropolis. Singapore's Research & Development efforts have led it to be consistently ranked in the top ten in the *Global Innovation Index* (see https://www.globalinnovationindex.org/ for further details).

It would require an encyclopedia to do justice to the exemplary journey of Singapore with science. This Chapter is only a *summary of summaries*! I as a humble author wish Singapore continued success in its scientific endeavours.

ACKNOWLEDGMENTS

I am grateful to Professor Ramaswamy Jagannathan (Institute of Mathematical Sciences, Chennai, India) for my training in the field of accelerator physics, particularly in the emerging field of *quantum theory of charged-particle beam optics* [51, 52], which was the topic of my doctoral thesis. This work is now part of the book, *Quantum Mechanics of Charged Particle Beam Optics: Understanding Devices from Electron Microscopes to Particle Accelerators* [52] (Figure 4). He gave the brilliant suggestion to employ the Foldy-Wouthuysen transformation technique to investigate the scalar optics (Helmholtz optics) and vector optics (Maxwell optics). The new formalism of light optics using quantum methodologies was selected for the *Year in Optics 2016* by the *Optical Society* [of America]. The summary of the two selected papers [61, 62] is available in the special issue of *Optics & Photonics News* [63]. The author is grateful to *Nova Science Publishers* for their continued encouragement, which has resulted in this Chapter. SAK has eight chapters with *Nova Science Publishers*, which are listed in [14], [32], [58], [82], and [112]-[114].

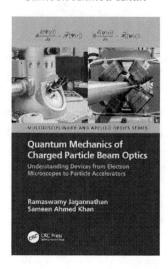

Figure 4. Book Cover, Quantum Mechanics of Charged Particle Beam Optics: Understanding Devices from Electron Microscopes to Particle Accelerators.

REFERENCES

[1] Sorell Tom, *Scientism: Philosophy and the Infatuation with Science*, Routledge, London, UK, (1991); https://isbn.nu//978-1138160934.

[2] *Department of Statistics*, Government of Singapore, https://www. singstat.gov.sg/.

[3] Boon Goh Chor, *From Traders to Innovators: Science and Technology in Singapore since 1965*, ISEAS–Yusof Ishak Institute, Singapore, (2016); https://bookshop.iseas.edu.sg/publication/2191.

[4] *50 Years of Science in Singapore*, Editors: B.T.G. Tan, Hock Lim and K.K. Phua, World Scientific, (2017); https://doi.org/10.1142/10057.

[5] *The Proceedings of the 12th International Congress on Mathematical Education: Intellectual and Attitudinal Challenges*, (8-15 July, 2012, COEX, Seoul, Korea), Editor: Sung Je Cho, Springer (2015); http://isbn.nu/978-3-319-10685-4 and http://dx.doi.org/10.1007/978-3-319-12688-3.

[6] Jagannathan R., The Institute of Mathematical Sciences, Chennai, India, *Resonance*, **4** (1), 89-92 (January 1999); https://doi.org/10.1007/BF02837161.

[7] *The Legacy of Alladi Ramakrishnan in the Mathematical Sciences*, Editors: Krishnaswami Alladi, John R. Klauder, and Calyampudi R. Rao, Springer (2010); http://isbn.nu/978-1-4419-6263-8 and http://dx.doi.org/10.1007/978-1-4419-6263-8.

[8] Khan Sameen Ahmed, Institute of Mathematical Sciences Celebrates Jubilee, *Muscat Daily*, page 22 (20 January 2013), (The Apex Press and Publishing, Muscat, Sultanate of Oman). http://www.muscatdaily.com/.

[9] Khan Sameen Ahmed, Maryam Mirzakhani (1977-2017), *Current Science*, **113** (5), 982-983 (10 September 2017); https://www. currentscience.ac.in/Volumes/113/05/0982.pdf.

[10] Khan Sameen Ahmed, Fields Medallist Maryam Mirzakhani (1977-2017), *Asia Pacific Mathematics Newsletter*, **7** (1), 36-39, (December 2017); http://www.asiapacific-mathnews.com/07/preserved-docs/0701/0036_0039.pdf.

[11] Khan Sameen Ahmed, 2015 declared the International Year of Light and Light-based Technologies, *Current Science*, **106**(4), 501 (25 February 2014); http://www.currentscience.ac.in/Volumes/106/04/0501.pdf.

[12] Khan Sameen Ahmed, *International Year of Light and Light-based Technologies*, LAP LAMBERT Academic Publishing, Germany (2015); http://isbn.nu/9783659764820/.

[13] Khan Sameen Ahmed, Medieval Arab Contributions to Optics, *Digest of Middle East Studies* (DOMES), **25**(1), 19-35 (Spring 2016); http://dx.doi.org/10.1111/dome.12065.

[14] Khan Sameen Ahmed, International Year of Light and History of Optics, Chapter-1 in: *Advances in Photonics Engineering, Nanophotonics and Biophotonics*, Editor: Tanya Scott, (Nova Science Publishers, New York, 2016, http://www.novapublishers.com/), pp. 1-56 (April 2016), http://isbn.nu/978-1-63484-498-7.

[15] Khan Sameen Ahmed, Reflecting on the International Year of Light and Light-based Technologies. *Current Science*, **111**(4), 627-631 (2016); http://dx.doi.org/10.18520/cs/v111/i4/627-631 and http://www.currentscience.ac.in/Volumes/111/04/0627.pdf.

[16] Khan Sameen Ahmed, Medieval Arab Achievements in Optics, Chapter-14 in: *Light-Based Science: Technology and Sustainable Development*, Proceedings of The Islamic Golden Age of Science for today's Knowledge-based Society: The Ibn Al-Haytham Example, UNESCO Headquarters, Paris, France, 14-15 September 2015, Editors: Azzedine Boudrioua, Roshdi Rashed and Vasudevan Lakshminarayanan, pp. 195-204 (2017), CRC Press, Taylor & Francis; http://isbn.nu/9781498779388.

[17] Siddiqui Azher Majid and Khan Sameen Ahmed, Need to Create International Science Centres in Arab Countries, Chapter-15 in: *Light-Based Science: Technology and Sustainable Development*, Proceedings of The Islamic Golden Age of Science for today's Knowledge-based Society: The Ibn Al-Haytham Example, UNESCO Headquarters, Paris, France, 14-15 September 2015, Editors: Azzedine Boudrioua, Roshdi Rashed and Vasudevan Lakshminarayanan, pp. 207-219 (2017), CRC Press, Taylor & Francis; http://isbn.nu/9781498779388.

[18] Dudley John, González Jorge Rivero, Niemela Joseph, and Plenkovich Krisinda, *The International Year of Light and Light-based Technologies 2015*, A Successful Community Partnership for Global Outreach Final Report (October 2016). Document code: SC/2016/IYL; Catalog Number: 246088; http://unesdoc.unesco.org/images/0024/002460/246088e.pdf and http://www.light2015.org/dam/About/IYL2015-FInal-Report.pdf.

[19] Khan Sameen Ahmed, The International Day of Light, *ICFA Beam Dynamics Newsletter*, **76**, 210-212, (April 2019), (ICFA: International Committee for Future Accelerators); http://www.icfa-bd.org/Newsletter76.pdf.

[20] Griffiths David J., *Introduction to Electrodynamics*, Addison-Wesley (2012); http://isbn.nu/978-0321856562.

[21] Jackson John David, *Classical Electrodynamics*, Third Edition, (Wiley, New York, 1999); http://isbn.nu/978-0471309321.

[22] Khan Sameen Ahmed, *Introductory Physics Laboratory Manual*, LAP LAMBERT Academic Publishing, Germany (Wednesday the 19 August 2015), 168 pages. http://www.lap-publishing.com/ and http://isbn.nu/9783659771897/.

[23] Khan Sameen Ahmed, *Objective Questions in Introductory Physics*, LAP LAMBERT Academic Publishing, Germany (Friday the 9 October 2015), 408 pages. http://www.lap-publishing.com/ and http://isbn.nu/9783659786198/.

[24] Khan Sameen Ahmed, The Middle East Synchrotron Laboratory and India, *Current Science*, **80**(2), 130-132 (25 January 2001); http://www.currentscience.ac.in/Downloads/article_id_080_02_-0130_0132_0.pdf.

[25] Khan Sameen Ahmed, The World of Synchrotrons, *Resonance Journal of Science Education*, **6**(11), 77-84 (2001); http://dx.doi.org/10.1007/BF02868247.

[26] Khan Sameen Ahmed, *Synchrotron Radiation (in Asia)*, ATIP Report No. **ATIP02.034** (August 2002), The Asian Technology Information Programme, Tokyo, Japan; http://www.atip.org/atip-publications/atip-reports/2002/7305-atip02-034–synchrotron-radiation-in-asia.html.

[27] Khan Sameen A. and Reiss Susan M., Donated Synchrotron will Further Middle East Cooperation; Sharing Synchrotrons, *Optics & Photonics News*, **13**(11), 14-15 (November 2002); https://www.osa-opn.org/home/articles/volume_13/issue_11/departments/global_optics/global_optics/.

[28] Khan Sameen Ahmed, CERN's Early History Revisited, *Physics Today*, **58**(4), 87-89 (April 2005); https://doi.org/10.1063/1.4796963.

[29] Khan Sameen Ahmed, Synchrotron Light in the Middle East, *Europhysics News*, **36**(5), 169 (September/October 2005); https://www.europhysicsnews.org/articles/epn/pdf/2005/05/epn2005-36-5.pdf.

[30] Khan Hajira and Khan Sameen Ahmed, X-Rays, *BaKhabar*, **7**(8), 12 (August 2014); http://bakhabar.biharanjuman.org/.

[31] Riti Sethi, Kumar Pravin, Khan Sameen Ahmed; Anver Aziz and Siddiqui Azher M., Effect of Nitrogen Ion Implantation on the Structural and Optical Properties of Indium Oxide Thin Films, in: Ali Al-Kamli, Nurdogan Can, Galib Omar Souadi, Mohamed Fadhali, Abdelrahman Mahdy and Mahmoud Mahgoub (Eds.), *Proceedings of the Fifth Saudi International Meeting on Frontiers of Physics 2016 (SIMFP 2016)*, 16-18 February 2016, Department of Physics, Jazan University, Gizan, Saudi Arabia, AIP Conference Proceedings, 1742, 030016-1-030016-5 (10 June 2016), (American Institute of Physics); http://dx.doi.org/10.1063/1.4953137.

[32] Khan Sameen Ahmed, Synchrotron Radiation from Prediction to Production, Chapter-4 in: *Horizons in World Physics*, **Volume 294**, Editor: Albert Reimer, (Nova Science Publishers, New York, 2017, http://www.novapublishers.com/), pp. 123-178 (01 November 2017); http://isbn.nu/978-1-53612-515-3.

[33] *Light Sources of the World*, http://www.lightsources.org/.

[34] Jagannathan R., Simon R., Sudarshan E.C.G., Mukunda N., Quantum theory of magnetic electron lenses based on the Dirac equation, *Phys. Lett.* **A 134**, 457-464 (1989); http://dx.doi.org/10.1016/0375-9601(89)90685-3.

[35] Jagannathan R., Quantum theory of electron lenses based on the Dirac equation, *Phys. Rev.*, **A 42**, 6674-6689 (1990); http://dx.doi.org/10.1103/PhysRevA.42.6674.

[36] Khan S.A. and Jagannathan R., Quantum mechanics of charged-particle beam optics: An operator approach, *Presented at the JSPS-KEK International Spring School on High Energy Ion Beams - Novel Beam Techniques and their Applications*, March 1994, Japan, (1994); http://cds.cern.ch/record/263576/files/P00023244.pdf.

[37] Khan S.A., Jagannathan R., Quantum mechanics of charged particle beam transport through magnetic lenses, *Physical Review*, **E 51**, 2510-2515 (1995); https://doi.org/10.1103/PhysRevE.51.2510.

[38] Jagannathan R. and Khan S.A., Wigner functions in charged particle optics. In *Selected Topics in Mathematical Physics* Professor R. Vasudevan Memorial Volume, (R. Sridhar, K. Srinivasa Rao, and V. Lakshmi-

narayanan, Eds.), Allied Publishers, Delhi, India, pp. 308-321. (1995); http://isbn.nu/9788170234883.

[39] Jagannathan R. and Khan S.A., Quantum theory of the optics of charged particles, in: P.W. Hawkes (Ed.), *Advances in Imaging and Electron Physics*, **97**, 257-358 (1996); http://dx.doi.org/10.1016/S1076-5670(08)70096-X.

[40] Conte M., Jagannathan R., Khan S.A., Pusterla M., Beam optics of the Dirac particle with anomalous magnetic moment, *Particle Accelerators*, **56**, 99-126 (1996); http://cds.cern.ch/record/307931/files/p99.pdf.

[41] Khan S.A., Quantum Theory of Charged-Particle Beam Optics, Ph.D Thesis, University of Madras, Chennai, India, 1997. Complete thesis available from *Dspace of IMSc Library*, The Institute of Mathematical Sciences, Chennai, India, where the doctoral research was done, http://www.imsc.res.in/xmlui/handle/123456789/75.

[42] Jagannathan R., The Dirac equation approach to spin-$1/2$ particle beam optics, In *Proceedings of the 15th Advanced ICFA Beam Dynamics Workshop on Quantum Aspects of Beam Physics*, (P. Chen. Ed.) January 4-9, 1998, Monterey, California, World Scientific, Singapore, (1999), pp. 670-681; http://arxiv.org/abs/physics/9803042.

[43] Khan S.A., Quantum theory of magnetic quadrupole lenses for spin-$1/2$ particles, In *Proceedings of the 15th Advanced ICFA Beam Dynamics Workshop on Quantum Aspects of Beam Physics*, (P. Chen. Ed.) January 4-9, 1998, Monterey, California, World Scientific, Singapore, (1999), pp. 682-694; http://arxiv.org/abs/physics/9809032.

[44] Khan S.A., Quantum aspects of accelerator optics, in: A. Luccio, W. MacKay (Eds.), *Proceedings of the 1999 Particle Accelerator Conference (PAC99)*, March 29 - April 02, 1999, New York City, NY, 1999, pp. 2817-2819 (IEEE Catalogue Number: 99CH36366); http://dx.doi.org/10.1109/PAC.1999.792948.

[45] Jagannathan R., Quantum mechanics of Dirac particle beam optics: Single-particle theory, in: P. Chen (Ed.), *Proceedings of the 18th Advanced ICFA Beam Dynamics Workshop on Quantum Aspects of Beam*

Physics, October 15-20, 2000, Capri, Italy, World Scientific, Singapore, (2002), pp. 568-577; http://arxiv.org/abs/physics/0101060.

[46] Khan S.A., Quantum formalism of beam optics, in: P. Chen (Ed.), *Proceedings of the 18th Advanced ICFA Beam Dynamics Workshop on Quantum Aspects of Beam Physics*, October 15-20, 2000, Capri, Italy, World Scientific, Singapore, (2002), pp. 517-526; http://dx.doi.org/10.1142/9789812777447_0042.

[47] Jagannathan R., Quantum mechanics of Dirac particle beam transport through optical elements with straight and curved axes, In *Proceedings of the 28th Advanced ICFA Beam Dynamics Workshop on Quantum Aspects of Beam Physics*, (P. Chen and K. Reil, Eds.), (2003) pp. 13-21, January 2003, Hiroshima, Japan, World Scientific, Singapore; https://doi.org/10.1142/9789812702333_0002.

[48] Khan Sameen Ahmed, The Foldy-Wouthuysen Transformation Technique in Optics, *Optik-International Journal for Light and Electron Optics*, **117**(10), 481-488 (2006); http://dx.doi.org/10.1016/j.ijleo.2005.11.010.

[49] Khan Sameen Ahmed, The Foldy-Wouthuysen Transformation Technique in Optics, in: P.W. Hawkes (Ed.), *Advances in Imaging and Electron Physics*, **152**, 49-78 (2008); Elsevier, http://dx.doi.org/10.1016/S1076-5670(08)00602-2.

[50] Khan Sameen Ahmed, Quantum Aspects of Charged-Particle Beam Optics, in: Ali Al-Kamli, Nurdogan Can, Galib Omar Souadi, Mohamed Fadhali, Abdelrahman Mahdy and Mahmoud Mahgoub (Eds.), *Proceedings of the Fifth Saudi International Meeting on Frontiers of Physics 2016 (SIMFP 2016)*, 16-18 February 2016, Department of Physics, Jazan University, Gizan, Saudi Arabia, AIP Conference Proceedings, 1742, 030008-1-030008-4 (10 June 2016), American Institute of Physics; http://dx.doi.org/10.1063/1.4953129.

[51] Khan Sameen Ahmed, E. C. G. Sudarshan and the quantum mechanics of charged-particle beam optics, *Current Science*, **115** (9), 1813-1814 (10 November 2018); http://www.current science.ac.in/Volumes/115/09/1813.pdf.

[52] Jagannathan Ramaswamy and Khan Sameen Ahmed, *Quantum Mechanics of Charged Particle Beam Optics: Understanding Devices from Electron Microscopes to Particle Accelerators*, 356 pages, CRC Press, Taylor & Francis, (23 May 2019); 356 pages, CRC Press, Taylor & Francis, (23 May 2019); ISBN-10: 1138035920 and ISBN-13: 9781138035928; https://doi.org/10.1201/9781315232515; http://isbn.nu/1138035920 and http://isbn.nu/9781138035928.

[53] Khan Sameen Ahmed and Jagannathan Ramaswamy, Quantum mechanics of bending of a nonrelativistic charged particle beam by a dipole magnet, *Optik-International Journal for Light and Electron Optics*, **202**, (2020); Elsevier, https://doi.org/10.1016/j.ijleo.2019.163626.

[54] Ramaswamy Jagannathan and Sameen Ahmed Khan, On the deformed oscillator and the deformed derivative associated with the Tsallis q-exponential, *International Journal of Theoretical Physics*, **59**(8), 2647-2669 (August 2020); Springer, https://doi.org/10.1007/s10773-020-04534-w.

[55] Khan Sameen Ahmed, Jagannathan Ramaswamy, and Simon Rajiah, Foldy-Wouthuysen transformation and a quasiparaxial approximation scheme for the scalar wave theory of light beams, *E-Print arXiv*: arXiv:physics/0209082 [physics.optics]; http://arXiv.org/abs/physics/0209082/ (2002).

[56] Khan Sameen Ahmed, Wavelength-dependent modifications in Helmholtz Optics, *International Journal of Theoretical Physics*, **44**(1), 95-125 (2005); http://dx.doi.org/10.1007/s10773-005-1488-0.

[57] Khan Sameen Ahmed, An Exact Matrix Representation of Maxwell's Equations, *Physica Scripta*, **71**(5), 440-442 (2005); http://dx.doi.org/10.1238/Physica.Regular.071a00440.

[58] Khan Sameen Ahmed, Wavelength-Dependent Effects in Light Optics, Chapter-6 in: *New Topics in Quantum Physics Research*, Editors: Volodymyr Krasnoholovets and Frank Columbus, (Nova Science Publishers, New York), pp. 163-204 (30 December 2006). (ISBN-10: 1600210287 and ISBN-13: 978-1600210280); http://www.novapublishers.com/, https://isbn.nu//978-1600210280 and https://www.researchgate.net/profile/Sameen_Ahmed_Khan.

[59] Khan Sameen Ahmed, Maxwell Optics of Quasiparaxial Beams, *Optik-International Journal for Light and Electron Optics*, **121**(5), 408-416 (2010); http://dx.doi.org/10.1016/j.ijleo.2008.07.027.

[60] Khan Sameen Ahmed, Aberrations in Maxwell Optics, *Optik-International Journal for Light and Electron Optics*, **125**(3), 968-978 (2014); http://dx.doi.org/10.1016/j.ijleo.2013.07.097.

[61] Khan Sameen Ahmed, Quantum Methodologies in Helmholtz Optics. *Optik-International Journal for Light and Electron Optics*, **127**(20), 9798-9809 (2016); http://dx.doi.org/10.1016/j.ijleo.2016.07.071.

[62] Khan Sameen Ahmed, Passage from scalar to vector optics and the Mukunda-Simon-Sudarshan theory for paraxial systems, *Journal of Modern Optics* **63**(17), 1652-1660 (2016); http://dx.doi.org/10.1080/09500340.2016.1164257.

[63] Khan Sameen Ahmed, Quantum Methods in Light Beam Optics, *Optics & Photonics News* (OPN), **27**(12), 47 (2016), One of the thirty summaries selected under the theme, *Optics in 2016*, highlighting the most exciting peer-reviewed optics research to have emerged over the past 12 months. The summary of the two selected papers [61] and [62] is described in this publication. http://www.osa-opn.org/home/articles/volume_27/december_2016/features/optics_in_2016/.

[64] Khan Sameen Ahmed, Hamilton's Optical-Mechanical Analogy in the Wavelength-dependent Regime, *Optik-International Journal for Light and Electron Optics*, **130**, 714-722 (2017); Elsevier, http://dx.doi.org/10.1016/j.ijleo.2016.07.071.

[65] Khan Sameen Ahmed, Linearization of Wave Equations, *Optik-International Journal for Light and Electron Optics*, **131**(C), 350-363 (2006); Elsevier, http://dx.doi.org/10.1016/j.ijleo.2016.11.073.

[66] Khan Sameen Ahmed, Polarization in Maxwell Optics, *Optik-International Journal for Light and Electron Optics*, **131**, 733-748 (2017); Elsevier, http://dx.doi.org/10.1016/j.ijleo.2016.11.134.

[67] Khan Sameen Ahmed, Quantum Methodologies in Maxwell Optics, in: P.W. Hawkes (Ed.), *Advances in Imaging and Electron Physics*, **201**, 57-135 (2017); Elsevier, http://dx.doi.org/10.1016/bs.aiep.2017.05.003.

[68] Khan Sameen Ahmed, Aberrations in Helmholtz Optics, *Optik-International Journal for Light and Electron Optics*, **153C**, 164-181 (January 2018); Elsevier, https://doi.org/10.1016/j.ijleo.2017.10.006.

[69] Khan Sameen Ahmed, Quantum Mechanical Techniques in Light Optics, in: *Proceedings of the Sixth Saudi International Meeting on Frontiers of Physics 2018*, **SIMFP 2018**, (27 February - 1 March 2018, Department of Physics, Jazan University, Gizan, Saudi Arabia). Editors: Ali Al-Kamli, Galib Omar Souadi, Jabir Hakami, Nurdogan Can, Abdelrahman Mahdy, Mahmoud Mahgoub and Zaka-ul-Islam Mujahid, AIP Conference Proceedings, 1976, 020016 (15 June 2018). American Institute of Physics, ISBN-13: http://isbn.nu/978-0-7354-1685-7, https://doi.org/10.1063/1.5042383.

[70] Khan Sameen Ahmed, Helmholtz mentored many luminaries, *Nature*, **564**(7734), 39 (6 December 2018); http://dx.doi.org/10.1038/d41586-018-07613-5.

[71] Khan Sameen A., and Pusterla Modesto, Quantum mechanical aspects of the halo puzzle, in *Proceedings of the 1999 Particle Accelerator Conference*, Editors: A. Luccio and W. MacKay, (New York City, NY, 1999), Vol. 5, pp. 3280-3281; http://dx.doi.org/10.1109/PAC.1999.792276.

[72] Khan S.A. and Pusterla M., Quantum-like approach to the transversal and longitudinal beam dynamics. The halo problem, *European Physical Journal A*, **7**(4), 583-587 (2000); http://dx.doi.org/10.1007/s100500050430.

[73] Khan Sameen A., and Pusterla Modesto, Quantum-like approaches to the beam halo problem, in *Proceedings of the 6th International Conference on Squeezed States and Uncertainty Relations*, Editors: D. Han, Y.S Kim, and S. Solimeno, (NASA Conference Publication Series, 2000-209899, 2000), pp. 438-441; https://ntrs.nasa.gov/archive/nasa/casi.ntrs.nasa.gov/20000105930.pdf.

[74] Khan S.A. and Pusterla M., Quantum approach to the halo formation in high current beams, *Nuclear Instruments and Methods in Physics Research* Section A, **464**(1-3), 461-464 (2001); http://dx.doi.org/10.1016/S0168-9002(01)00108-5.

[75] Singapore Synchrotron Light Source, http://ssls.nus.edu.sg/.

[76] Websites of the *UNESCO Sultan Qaboos Prize for Environmental Preservation*, http://www.un-qaboos-prize.net/ and http://www.unesco.org/new/en/natural-sciences/environment/ecological-sciences/man-and-biosphere-programme/awards-and-prizes/sultan-qaboos/.

[77] *UNESCO Sultan Qaboos Prize for Environmental Preservation*, Ministry of Education, Sultanate of Oman, (2017); Publication No. 539/2017, ISBN: 978-99969-0-967-2; http://www.un-qaboos-prize.net/.

[78] Khan Sameen Ahmed, 2015 UNESCO Sultan Qaboos Prize for Environmental Preservation, *Current Science*, **110**(1), 15 (10 January 2016); http://www.currentscience.ac.in/Volumes/110/01/0015.pdf.

[79] Khan Sameen Ahmed, 2017 UNESCO Sultan Qaboos Prize for Environmental Preservation, *Current Science*, **114** (02), 252 (25 January 2018); http://dx.doi.org/10.18520/cs/v114/i02/252-252 and http://www.currentscience.ac.in/cs/Volumes/114/02/0252.pdf.

[80] Khan Sameen Ahmed, Singapore Index for climate change, *Nature*, **556**(7700), 174 (12 April 2018); http://dx.doi.org/10.1038/d41586-018-04168-3.

[81] Khan Sameen Ahmed, UNESCO Sultan Qaboos Prize for Environmental Preservation, in *48 Years of Glorious Omani Renaissance* (A tribute to the lasting legacy of His Majesty the Sultan), *A tribute to the Lasting Legacy of His Majesty the Sultan, Success Stories of the CEOs, 48th Glorious Renaissance Day*, Editor: Hassan Kamoonpuri, pp. 30-33 (23 July 2018). Oman Establishment for Press, Publication and Advertising, http://www.omanobserver.om/. The Prizes are awarded every two years http://un-qaboos-prize.net/.

[82] Khan Sameen Ahmed, Legacy of the UNESCO Sultan Qaboos Prize for Environmental Preservation, Chapter-4 in: *A Closer Look at Climate Change*, Editor: Reggie Paredes, Nova Science Publishers, New York, 2018, http://www.novapublishers.com/. pp. 65-94 (October 2018); http://isbn.nu/978-1-53614-601-1.

[83] The *National Parks Board of Singapore*, Singapore, the *2017 Laureate of the UNESCO Sultan Qaboos Prize for Environmental Preservation*, http://un-qaboos-prize.net/2017.html and https://www.nparks.gov.sg/.

[84] The *National Parks Board of Singapore*, https://www.nparks.gov.sg/.

[85] *Convention on Biological Diversity*, https://www.cbd.int/; *User's Manual on the Singapore Index on Cities' Biodiversity*, (also known as the City Biodiversity Index), Convention on Biological Diversity, (2014). https://www.cbd.int/subnational/partners-and-initiatives/city-biodiversity-index.

[86] *Singapore biodiversity: an encyclopedia of the natural environment and sustainable development*, Editors: Peter K.L. Ng, Hugh T.w. Tan and Richard T. Corlett, Editions Didier Millet, Singapore, (2011); http://isbn.nu/978-981-4260-08-4/.

[87] Websites of the *World Science Forum* (WSF), https://worldscienceforum.org/ and http://www.sciforum.hu/.

[88] Khan Sameen Ahmed, Dead Sea Comes Alive with Science, (Report of the World Science Forum (WSF 2017): Science for Peace, 7-11 November 2017, Dead Sea, Jordan), *Radiance Viewsweekly*, **Vol. LV**, No. 44, 26-27 (28 January - 03 February 2018); http://radianceweekly.in/portal/issue/the-great-dissenters-of-indian-judiciary/article/dead-sea-comes-alive-with-science/.

[89] UNESCO World Heritage Centre — *World Heritage List*, https://whc.unesco.org/en/list/.

[90] Khan Hajira and Khan Sameen Ahmed, Date Palm Revisited, *Research Journal of Pharmaceutical, Biological and Chemical Sciences* (RJPBCS), **7**(3), 2010-2019 (May-June 2016); http://www.rjpbcs.com/pdf/2016_7(3)/[244].pdf and http://www.rjpbcs.com/.

[91] Khan Hajira and Khan Sameen Ahmed, Blessed Tree of Olive, *Asian Journal of Pharmaceutical and Clinical Research* (AJPCR), **9**(3), 32-34 (May-June 2016); http://innovareacademics.in/ journals/index.php/ajpcr/article/view/11677.

[92] The *Instituto de Ecología*, Veracruz, Mexico, the *1991 Laureate* of the *UNESCO Sultan Qaboos Prize for Environmental Preservation*, http://un-qaboos-prize.net/Laureates.html, http://www.inecol.edu.mx/ and http://www.ecologia.edu.mx/.

[93] Khan Sameen Ahmed, King Faisal Foundation & its Prizes, *Young Muslim Digest*, **27**(6), 33-35 (August 2005).

[94] Khan Sameen Ahmed, Medieval Arab Understanding of the Rainbow Formation, *Europhysics News*, **37**(3), 10 (May/June 2006); http://www.europhysicsnews.org/articles/epn/pdf/2006/03/epn2006-37-3.pdf.

[95] Khan Sameen Ahmed, Arab Origins of the Discovery of the Refraction of Light; Roshdi Hifni Rashed Awarded the 2007 King Faisal International Prize, *Optics & Photonics News*, **18**(10), 22-23 (October 2007); https://www.osa-opn.org/home/articles/volume_18/issue_10/departments/global_optics/arab_origins_of_the_discovery_of_the_refraction/.

[96] Khan Sameen Ahmed, 2013 King Faisal International Prize for Science and Medicine, *Current Science*, **104**(5), 575 (10 March 2013); http://www.currentscience.ac.in/Volumes/104/05/0575.pdf.

[97] Khan Sameen Ahmed, 2014 King Faisal International Prize for Science and Medicine, *Current Science*, **106**(4), 500 (25 February 2014); http://www.currentscience.ac.in/Volumes/106/04/0500.pdf.

[98] Khan Sameen Ahmed, 2015 King Faisal International Prize for Science and Medicine, *Current Science*, **108**(7), 1202-1203 (10 April 2015); http://www.currentscience.ac.in/Volumes/108/07/1202.pdf.

[99] Khan Sameen Ahmed, 2016 King Faisal International Prize for Science and Medicine, *Current Science*, **110**(7), 1140-1141 (10 April 2016); http://www.currentscience.ac.in/Volumes/110/07/1140.pdf

[100] Khan Sameen Ahmed, Ahmed Hassan Zewail (19462016), *Current Science*, **111**(05), 936-937 (10 September 2016); http://www.currentscience.ac.in/Volumes/111/05/0936.pdf.

[101] Khan Sameen Ahmed, 2017 King Faisal International Prize for Science and Medicine, *Current Science*, **112**(06), 1088-1090 (25 March 2017); http://www.currentscience.ac.in/Volumes/112/06/1088.pdf.

[102] Khan Sameen Ahmed, 2018 King Faisal International Prize for Science and Medicine, *Current Science*, **114** (10), 2014 (25 May 2018); http://dx.doi.org/10.18520/cs/v114/i10/2014-2014 and http://www.currentscience.ac.in/Volumes/114/10/2014.pdf.

[103] Khan Sameen Ahmed, King Faisal prize a Nobel harbinger?, *Nature*, **564**(7736), 345 (20 December 2018); http://dx.doi.org/10.1038/d41586-018-07805-z.

[104] Khan Sameen Ahmed, 2019 King Faisal International Prize for Science and Medicine, *Current Science*, **116** (4), 517 (25 February 2019); https://www.currentscience.ac.in/Volumes/116/04/0517.pdf

[105] Khan Sameen Ahmed, Iran Launches the Mustafa Prize for Sciences, *Current Science*, **110**(6), 961 (25 March 2016); http://www.currentscience.ac.in/Volumes/110/06/0961.pdf.

[106] Khan Sameen Ahmed, Predhiman Krishan Kaw bags the 2015 Subrahmanyan Chandrasekhar Prize of Plasma Physics, *Current Science*, **111** (03), 458 (10 August 2016); http://www. currentscience.ac.in/Volumes/111/03/0458.pdf.

[107] G.B.V.S. Lakshmi, Shumaila, Khan Sameen Ahmed, Azher M. Siddiqui, Thin Films: Polyaniline and Poly(3-methylthiophene), in *Encyclopedia of Plasma Technology* (First Edition), *Editor*: J. Leon Shohet, (Taylor & Francis Encyclopedia Program), pp. 1442-1451, (12 December 2016); http://dx.doi.org/10.1081/E-EPLT-120053953 and https://www.crcpress.com/Encyclopedia-of-Plasma-Technology/Shohet/9781466500594.

[108] Sameen Ahmed Khan, 2019 Subrahmanyan Chandrasekhar Prize of Plasma Physic, *Current Science*, **117** (10), 1561 (25 November 2019); https://www.currentscience.ac.in/Volumes/117/10/1561.pdf.

[109] Barath Harini, Indian initiatives aim to break science's language barrier, *Nature*, **571** (7764), 289-290 (11 July 2019); http://dx.doi.org/10.1038/d41586-019-01815-1.

[110] Khan Sameen Ahmed, Promoting science in minority languages, *Nature*, **573** (7772), 34 (05 September 2019); http://dx.doi.org/10.1038/d41586-019-02626-0.

[111] Khan Sameen Ahmed, Five Years of the National Urdu Science Congress, (communicated).

[112] Khan Sameen Ahmed, Number Theory and Resistor Networks, Chapter-5 in: *Resistors: Theory of Operation, Behavior and Safety Regulations*, Editor: Roy Abi Zeid Daou, Nova Science Publishers, New York, 2013, 99-154 (May 2013); http://www.novapublishers.com/, http://isbn.nu/9781622577880. http://www.scopus.com/authid/detail.url?authorId=8452157800.

[113] Khan Sameen Ahmed, Coordinate Geometric Generalization of the Spherometer and Cylindrometer, Chapter-8 in: *Advances in Engineering Research*, Volume **10**, Editor: Victoria M. Petrova, Nova Science Publishers, New York, 2015, pp. 163-190 (10 July 2015); http://www.novapublishers.com/, https://orcid.org/0000-0003-1264-2302 and http://isbn.nu/978-1-63482-784-3.

[114] Sameen Ahmed Khan, Microsoft EXCEL for Numerical Calculus, Chapter-5 in: *Focus on Calculus*, Editor: Svetlin G. Georgiev, (Nova Science Publishers, New York, 2019, http://www.novapublishers.com/). pp. 177-201 (March 2020). http://isbn.nu/978-1-53617-337-6 and https://novapublishers.com/shop/focus-on-calculus/.

ABOUT THE AUTHOR

Dr. Sameen Ahmed Khan

Dr. Sameen Ahmed Khan is an Associate Professor at the Department of Mathematics and Sciences, College of Arts and Applied Sciences (CAAS), Dhofar University, Salalah, Sultanate of Oman (http://www.du.edu.om/). He did PhD on the *quantum theory of charged-particle beam optics*, from the Institute of Mathematical Sciences (MATSCIENCE/IMSc), Chennai, India, under the supervision of Prof. Ramaswamy Jagannathan. He did Post-Doctoral research at the Istituto Nazionale di Fisica Nucleare (INFN), Padova, Italy and Universidad Nacional Autónoma de México (UNAM), Cuernavaca, México. He has over sixteen years of teaching experience in Oman. He has developed a unified treatment of light beam optics and light polarization using quantum methodologies. This new formalism of optics using quantum methodologies was selected for the *Year in Optics 2016* by the *Optical Society* [of America], highlighting the most exciting peer-reviewed optics research to have emerged in that year (2016). He has presented his work at numerous conferences across the continents. He has authored four books; fifteen book chapters; and over seventy-five technical publications in journals and proceedings of repute. He has over 250 publications on science popularization. Dr. Sameen is one of the Founding Members of the Ibn al Haytham LHiSA Light: History, Science and Applications (LHiSA) International Society (https://www.ibnalhaytham-lhisa.com/) set-up during the International Year of Light and Light-based Technologies (*http://www.light2015.org/*). He is a signatory to six of the Reports on the upcoming International Linear Collider (http://www.linearcollider.org/). Further details at http://orcid.org/0000-0003-1264-2302.

In: Exploring Cities and Countries ...   ISBN: 978-1-53618-514-0
Editor: Kathie Summers   © 2020 Nova Science Publishers, Inc.

Chapter 8

AMPHIBIAN SPECIES DISCOVERY PATTERN IN INDIA: PAST, PRESENT AND FUTURE TRENDS

K. P. Dinesh[1,], C. Radhakrishnan[2] and Nirmal U. Kulkarni[3]*

[1]Zoological Survey of India (ZSI), Western Regional Centre (WRC),
Pune, Maharashtra, India
[2]Chevayur, Calicut, Kerala, India
[3]Mhadei Research Centre, C/o Hiru Naik Building, Dhuler Mapusa,
Goa, India

ABSTRACT

India, a mega diverse country, hosts four biodiversity hotspots harbouring many endemic flora and fauna. Among the fauna, amphibians are the first poikilothermic vertebrates to colonize the land on an evolutionary scale and amphibians are considered as the ecological indicators to define the pristineness of the landscape. To date, India is

* Corresponding Author's Email: kpdinesh.zsi@gmail.com.

known to have within its political boundaries, a distribution of 440 species of amphibians; of these, 372 are described exclusively from the country (4.6% of the global amphibian species). Although amphibian discoveries were initiated in the country as early as 1800's, 128 species were discovered during the colonial period. Between the independence and the new millennium, 51 species were discovered and in the new millennium 193 species were discovered. It is interesting to note that more than 50% of the species have been discovered in the past two decades alone. Here we have attempted to (i) show the chronological pattern of species discovery among the amphibians of India (ii) present accumulation curves to understand the saturation of species discoveries among the amphibians of the country. Analyzing the past and present data, the results suggest that there are more chances for discovery of many more new species from the country.

Keywords: amphibia, cumulative, discovery, India, pattern, species

INTRODUCTION

Amphibians are the first poikilotherm tetrapods (Pough, 1980) to establish on land, being the connecting link between the vertebrate life in water and land (Duellman, and Trueb, 1986). In the era of rapid climate change and vertebrate mass extinctions amphibians are considered to be the 'ecological indicators' (Simon et al., 2011) reflecting the pristinity of a habitat or ecosystem.

Indian land mass accounts for 2.4% of world's land area. Globally around 8000 species of amphibians are documented (Frost, 2019). In India about 440 species (till July 2019) are known to occur and among these around 250 species are from the one of biodiversity hotspot the Western Ghats (Dinesh et al., 2019).

Till the start of the new millennium around 6000 species of amphibians were documented globally and 238 species from India. Since then there has been a 33% of increase in amphibian discoveries globally (Figure 1) which is from 6000 species to around 8000 species. In India, the new millennium witnessed an upsurge of 84% (Figure 2) of documentation from 238 species to 440 species. Among the 440 species of amphibians known from India,

372 species are discovered within its political boundaries and the rest (68 species) from the neighboring countries having their range of distribution in India as well.

With this backdrop we have attempted here to discuss the amphibian species discovery pattern in India (past 220 years) from 1799 (the year of the first amphibian reported from India) to 2019 and to check the species accumulation curve to understand the probability of new species discoveries in the near future. For the current studies we have used the data contained in our amphibian check lists published from 2009 to 2019 (Dinesh et al., 2009 & 2019).

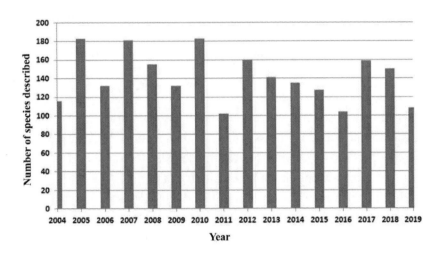

Figure 1. Global pattern of new amphibian species discovery since 2004 (data source https://amphibiaweb.org).

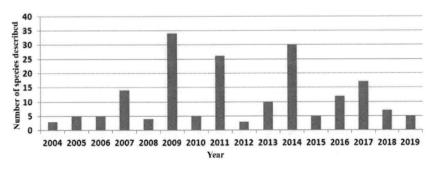

Figure 2. Pattern of new amphibian species discovery in India since 2004.

For the sake of convention amphibian species discovery of the past has been considered under the sections as amphibian species discovery during the rule of East India company; rule of India by the British; India after independence to the year 2000 and amphibian species discovery pattern in India in the new millennium (2001 and thereafter).

AMPHIBIAN SPECIES DISCOVERY DURING THE RULE OF THE EAST INDIA COMPANY (FROM 1757 TO 1858)

The first three species described from India were, *Duttaphrynus melanostictus* (common toad), *Duttaphrynus scaber* (marbled toad) and *Euphlyctis cyanophlyctis* (Indian Skittering Frog) by Schneider in 1799. During the East India Company regime, a total of 28 species were discovered from the country under 8 families and 18 genera. The first leg less amphibian described for the country was a caecilian, *Uraeotyphlus oxyurus*, a species endemic to the Western Ghats. It needs to be mentioned that in those hose days the species descriptions were made based on the morphological characters and body colour alone (qualitative data).

Most of the amphibian studies initiated during this period were by the German and French zoologists like André Marie Constant Duméril (1774-1860) and Gabriel Bibron (1805-1848), Edward Blyth (1810-1873), François Marie Daudin (1776-1803), Johann Jakob von Tschudi (1818-1889), Johann Gottlob Theaenus Schneider (1750-1822), John Edward Gray (1800-1875), René Lesson (1794-1849) and Thomas C Jerdon (1811-1872). Interestingly many of the species described during this period are still unresolved 'species complexes' having wide range of geographical distribution warranting further taxonomic studies (specifically genetic studies). The majority of the species described from India during this period were by single authors and the new species discoveries were restricted to the eastern India (West Bengal, Sikkim and Nagaland) and south India (Karnataka, Kerala and Tamil Nadu).

Type specimens and the reference collections of those periods are still maintained in the Museums of Universitat Humboldt, Zoologisches Museum (ZMB), Invalidenstrasse, Berlin, Germany; Museum National dHistoire Naturelle (MNHNP), Rue Cuvier, Paris, France; Zoological Survey of India (ZSI), Kolkata; British Museum (BMNH), London United Kingdom and Institut Royal des Sciences Naturelles de Belgique, Belgium.

AMPHIBIAN SPECIES DISCOVERY DURING THE RULE OF INDIA BY THE BRITISH FROM 1858 TO 1947

During the British rule of the country, a total of 101 species were discovered under 13 families and 37 genera. During the colonial rule in India, many German, British, Danish, Moravian and American naturalists and zoologists like Albert Günther (1830-1914), Alfred William Alcock (1859-1933), Christian Frederik Lütken (1827-1901), Christoph Gustav Ernst Ahl (1898-1945), Ferdinand Stoliczka (1838-1874), George Albert Boulenger (1838-1937), George S. Myers (1905-1985), John Anderson (1833-1900), Malcolm Arthur Smith (1875-1958), Nelson Annandale (1876-1924), Richard Henry Beddome (1830-1911) and Wilhelm Peters (1815-1883) contributed a lot to the documentation of amphibian fauna of India. Interestingly during this period, two Indian scientists C. R. Narayan Rao (1882-1960) and B. R. Seshachar (1910-1994) were the first to start the 'Batrachology' studies independently, where C. R. Narayan Rao was more involved in the amphibian taxonomy and B. R. Seshachar in the caecilian studies. New species descriptions made from India during the period had species representatives from the foot hills of Himalaya, north eastern India and south India. Due to their usage of colonial locality names for the 'type localities' for the species described during that period, many a described species were not seen/collected/recovered from the field since then. Collections of the period are maintained in the Museums of British Museum (BMNH), London United Kingdom; Bombay Natural History Museum (BNHM), Mumbai, India; Stanford University collections (CAS-SU);

Central College Bangalore (CCB), Karnataka; Museum of Comparative Zoology (MCZ), Harvard University, Cambridge, Massachusetts, USA; Museum National dHistoire Naturelle (MNHNP), Rue Cuvier, Paris, France; Universitat Humboldt, Zoologisches Museum (ZMB), Invalidenstrasse, Berlin, Germany; Universitets Kobenhavn, Zoologisk Museum (ZMUC), Universitetsparken, Denmark and Zoological Survey of India (ZSI), Kolkata.

Among the species described during the period, the genus *Pedostibes* erected in 1876 is still known by only one species *Pedostibes tuberculosus* an tree toad endemic to the Western Ghats having a wide range of distribution. The genus *Melanobatrachus* established in 1878 is still known by only one species *Melanobatrachus indicus* (Figure 3) an Orange Black Tubercled Indian Microhylid frog endemic to the higher elevations of the southern Western Ghats. The other worthwhile mention is the first description of an caecilian *Chikila fulleri* (as *Herpele fulleri*) from Assam with an comment by A. W. Alcock regarding its affinities with the African counter parts during 1904, wherein very recently another three species were added to this group ascertaining the Alcock's findings with molecular studies.

Figure 3. The monotypic Orange Black Tubercled Indian Microhylid frog *Melanobatrachus indicus* from the southern Western Ghats described in 1878.

AMPHIBIAN SPECIES DISCOVERY IN INDIA
AFTER INDEPENDENCE FROM YEAR 1947 TO 2000

Between the end of 19th century and the post Independent Indian regime a total of 50 species were discovered under 11 families and 29 genera. With the end of colonial rule in India in 1947, research on Batrachology was taken over by the Indian scientists S. K. Chanda, Indraneil Das, S. K. Dutta, R. S. Pillai, M. S. Ravichandran, P. Ray, K. Vasudevan, A. K. Sarkar and D. P. Sanyal except for some of the scientists abroad like E. H. Taylor, A. Dubois, R. F. Inger and H. B. Shaffer who worked independently or in collaboration with the Indian scientists. This period started witnessing quantitative data with qualitative data for the species descriptions.

Figure 4. Pig nosed frog *Nasikabatrachus sahyadrensis* endemic to the Western Ghats described in 2003.

From the old collections/unidentified collections deposited in the American Museum of Natural History (AMNH), Division of Vertebrate Zoology (Herpetology), New York, USA; National Museum of Natural History (USNM), Division of Amphibians and Reptiles, Washington, D. C., USA; University of Kansas (KU), Museum of Natural History, Kansas, USA; Museum of Comparative Zoology (MCZ), Harvard University, Cambridge, Massachusetts 02138, USA; California Academy of Sciences

(CAS), Department of Herpetology, San Francisco, California, USA; Museo Civico di Storia Naturale di Genova "Giacomo Doria" (MSNG), Genova, Italy; Museum National dHistoire Naturelle (MNHNP), Rue Cuvier, Paris, France and Museums of British Museum (BMNH), London, United Kingdom new species described were deposited in the respective museums. Fresh collections made during the period were identified and deposited in the Indian National Museum of Natural History (NMNH), New Delhi; Bombay Natural History Museum (BNHM), Mumbai and Zoological Survey of India (ZSI), Kolkata and its other regional centers. Among the 50 species described during the period, 34 species type specimens were deposited in the repositories of ZSI.

AMPHIBIAN SPECIES DISCOVERY IN INDIA IN THE NEW MILLENNIUM (2001 AND THEREAFTER)

In the new millennium, a whopping total of 193 species were discovered under 13 families and 38 genera. With the advent of molecular tools and acoustic data analysis techniques, the Indian scientists described a good number of species independently and jointly with scientists abroad. Among the scientific community, Biju and his team has been involved in the discovery of 88 species of amphibians among the 193 species reported during the period (see Dinesh et al., 2019; Frost, 2019).

Among these, the report of the living fossil frog, the pig nosed frog *Nasikabatrachus sahyadrensis* (Figure 4) by Biju and his team in 2003 and the ancient lineage starry eyed frog *Astrobatrachus kurichiyana* by Vijayakumar and his team in 2019 were once in a century discoveries. Report of the new species *Microhyla kodial* from Mangalore (found adjacent to an abandoned timber yard) by Vineeth and his team in 2018 is speculated to be an unintentional introduction of the species from South east Asia that turns out to be the first 'exotic species' of Amphibia to successfully establish a breeding population in India.

Figure 5. Starry eyed frog *Astrobatrachus kurichiyana* endemic to the central Western Ghats described in 2019.

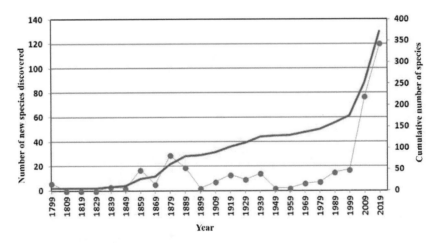

Figure 6. Species accumulation curve (green dots represent the number of new species discoveries and red line represents cumulative new species discovery pattern) for the amphibian species discovered from India between the year 1799 to 2019 (for 220 years).

The amphibian species discovery pattern for the country since the year 1799 clearly suggests that the new species discovery has taken up a good momentum between 1850 and 1940 (119 species in the duration of 90 years) and taken a peaking upsurge in the new millennium (2001 afterwards) (197 species in a span of 19 years) (Figure 6). However, the species accumulation curve has never reached a saturation point in the recent past. Cumulative discovery pattern curve in the last two decades is taking a straight vertical climb without much deflection (Figure 6) suggesting the possibility of many more new species discoveries in India in the coming years ahead.

AMPHIBIAN SPECIES DISCOVERIES WAY FORWARD

India being one of the mega diverse countries holding four biodiversity hotspots in terms of biological diversity, amphibian research is more biased and focused only in the Western Ghats compared to rest of the three biodiversity hotspots. Since the rest of the three biodiversity hotspots share the political boundaries with the adjacent countries, amphibian species discoveries in these regions could be quite challenging as there is exchange of biota across these borders.

Of the known 440 species from the country, 372 species are described from area within the political boundaries of India. Among the remaining 68 species reported from the country, 1 species each are described from Afghanistan, Iran, Laos, Pakistan and Thailand; 2 species each from Malaysia, Philippines, Sri Lanka and Tibet; 7species each from Bangladesh, Indonesia and Nepal; 16 species from Myanmar and 18 species from China.

Hortal et al., (2015), while discussing the importance of seven shortfalls that hampers the understanding of large scale biodiversity, have emphasized the importance and the value of each shortfall individually. In the process of documenting the amphibian diversity of the country scientists have been reporting a good number of new species in the new millennia addressing the 'Linnean Shortfall' (Brown & Lomolino, 1998) and during this process of new species descriptions new geographical records have been documented for many known species (described in the past) addressing the 'Wallacean Shortfall' (Lomolino, 2004). Utilization of molecular tools for addressing the 'Linnean Shortfall' and the 'Wallacean Shortfall' are fulfilling the gaps of 'Darwinian Shortfall' (Diniz-Filho et al., 2013) for the amphibian species of the country.

ACKNOWLEDGMENTS

Authors are grateful to the Director, ZSI, Kolkata and the Officer-in-charge, ZSI, WRC, Pune for the support.

REFERENCES

Brown, J. H. and Lomolino, M. V. (1998). *Biogeography.* 2nd ed. Sinauer Associates, Inc., Sunderland, Massachusetts, xii + 691pp.

Dinesh, K. P., Radhakrishnan, C., Gururaja, K. V. and Bhatta, G. (2009). An annotated checklist of Amphibia of India with some insights into the patterns of species discoveries, distribution and endemism. *Records of Zoological Survey of India, Occasional Paper* No. (302): 1-152pp.

Dinesh, K. P., Radhakrishnan, C., Channakeshavamurthy, B. H., Deepak, P. and Nirmal U. Kulkarni. (2019). *A Checklist of Amphibians of India, updated till January 2019* available at http://zsi.gov.in/Write ReadData/userfiles/file/Checklist/Amphibia_Checklist_2019.pdf (online only).

Diniz-Filho, J. A. F., Loyola, R. D., Raia, P., Mooers, A. O., Bini, L. M. (2013). Darwinian shortfalls in biodiversity conservation. *Trends in Ecology and Evolution*, 28 (12):689-695.

Duellman, W. E., and Trueb, L. (1994). *Biology of amphibians.* Johns Hopkins University Press, Baltimore, Maryland, 670pp.

Frost, D. R. (2019). *Amphibian Species of the World: an Online Reference.* Version 6.0 (date of access 02/08/2019). Electronic Database accessible at http://research.amnh.org/herpetology/amphibia/ index.html. American Museum of Natural History, New York, USA.

Hortal, J., Francesco de Bello., Jos'e Alexandre F. Diniz-Filho., Lewinsohn, T. M., Lobo, J. M. and Ladle, R. J. (2015). Seven Shortfalls that Beset Large-Scale Knowledge of Biodiversity. *Annual Review of Ecology, Evolution, and Systematics*, 46: 523-549.

Lomolino, M. V. (2004). Conservation biogeography. In: *Frontiers of Biogeography: New Directions in the Geography of Nature,* ed. MV Lomolino, L. R. Heaney, pp. 293-96. Sunderland, MA: Sinauer.

Pough, H. F. (1980). The Advantages of Ectothermy for Tetrapods. *The American Naturalist,* 115 (1): 92-112.

Simon, E., Puky, M., Braun, M. and Tóthmérész, B. (2011). Frogs and toads as indicators in environmental assessment. In: *Frogs: Biology, Ecology and Uses* Editor: James L. Murray, pp. Nova Science Publishers, Inc.

INDEX

A

Afghanistan, 2, 10, 196
Africa, 12, 95, 153
agencies, xi, 115, 137, 138, 143, 158
agricultural economics, 74
agricultural sector, 44
agriculture, 20, 34, 45, 52, 69, 76, 95, 109, 110, 129, 138
almonds, 57, 65, 85, 87, 92
amphibia, vi, xi, 187, 188, 189, 190, 191, 193, 194, 195, 196, 197
amphibians, xi, 187, 188, 194, 197
Asia, 18, 91, 120, 134, 148, 153, 155, 160, 166, 167, 168, 172, 174, 194
authenticity, 114, 115, 116, 135
awareness, 15, 70, 73, 97, 110, 117, 155, 159

B

Bangladesh, 7, 27, 196
beneficial effect, 70, 87
benefits, 45, 69, 94, 109
Bhutto, Benazir, 10, 15

biodiversity, xi, 30, 45, 46, 49, 53, 69, 70, 152, 156, 162, 163, 182, 187, 188, 196, 197
biogeography, 198
biotechnology, 161, 168
Brazil, x, 106, 107, 116, 117, 121, 123, 126, 160, 165
Buddhism, 3, 139

C

capital markets, 20, 21
cassata, vii, ix, 79, 80, 83, 84, 87, 89
Central Asia, 3, 12
Central Europe, 98
challenges, viii, 2, 21, 25, 31, 54, 62, 68, 73, 113, 119, 138, 152, 153, 155, 165
cheese, 59, 61, 65, 66, 67, 71, 75, 81, 84, 89, 91
China, 2, 24, 51, 126, 149, 160, 166, 196
Christianity, 13, 139
cities, 4, 17, 31, 32, 43, 44, 46, 50, 51, 53, 54, 58, 59, 70, 125, 126, 127, 129, 133, 135, 163, 164
citizens, 46, 64, 107, 109, 110, 118, 119, 120, 138

city streets, 57

civil society, x, 23, 64, 106, 115, 116, 118

civilization, viii, x, 1, 3, 12, 25, 106, 109

classification, 34, 36, 117, 126, 132

climate, 23, 30, 45, 46, 47, 50, 51, 53, 54, 68, 72, 76, 77, 95, 138, 181, 188

climate change, 23, 30, 45, 46, 47, 48, 49, 50, 51, 53, 54, 68, 72, 76, 77, 95, 101, 137, 138, 151, 181, 188

coffee, 75, 82, 95

colonial rule, 191, 193

commerce, 115, 167

commercial, 10, 37, 42, 44, 76

communication, 5, 138, 169

communities, 5, 13, 107, 108, 109, 119, 165

community, x, 9, 18, 30, 105, 106, 107, 108, 109, 114, 130, 141, 142, 147, 148, 168, 194

competition, 125, 143, 157

conservation, 48, 156, 163, 197

constitutional amendment, 9, 10, 22

construction, 31, 32, 33, 36, 37, 42, 43, 102, 117, 126, 128, 133

consumers, x, 23, 56, 63, 73, 106, 119, 124, 130, 131, 132, 133

consumption, 23, 57, 59, 62, 69, 70, 72, 73, 74, 93, 102, 107, 109

Convention on Biological Diversity, 163, 182

cooking, 56, 67, 82, 91, 132

country of origin, 130

cultivation, 71, 89, 92

cultural heritage, x, 69, 105, 107, 108, 117, 119, 120

cultural values, x, xi, 105, 108, 109, 112, 124, 125, 126, 130

culture, v, vii, viii, 1, 2, 3, 4, 6, 9, 11, 12, 14, 15, 16, 17, 19, 25, 26, 27, 65, 75, 82, 102, 107, 108, 109, 111, 112, 114, 116, 118, 121, 126, 131, 132, 134, 135, 153

cumulative, 188, 195

current account deficit, 21

curriculum, 143, 146, 156

D

destination brand, vii, xi, 120, 124, 125, 126, 127, 128, 132, 133

developing countries, viii, 29, 56, 77

diet, 69, 75, 76, 77, 81, 94, 100, 101, 108

discovery, vi, xii, 98, 141, 163, 183, 187, 188, 189, 190, 191, 193, 194, 195

distribution, xi, 12, 30, 38, 39, 113, 159, 160, 166, 188, 189, 190, 192, 197

diversity, vii, viii, 1, 2, 3, 4, 13, 17, 19, 34, 77, 102, 112, 113, 114, 115, 127, 128, 131, 155, 163, 182, 196

E

East Asia, 149

Easter, 89, 90, 91

Eastern Europe, 86

ecology, 52, 156

economic development, vii, x, 23, 24, 39, 106, 107, 108, 109, 112, 113, 114, 115, 118, 119

economy, vii, viii, 1, 2, 6, 10, 19, 20, 23, 24, 111, 116, 120, 142, 143, 147, 169

ecosystem, 30, 44, 45, 49, 51, 52, 53, 73, 155, 188

education, viii, 2, 11, 15, 22, 24, 25, 69, 138, 140, 143, 144, 145, 152, 156, 162, 168

empowerment, 21, 109, 110, 113, 118, 119

energy, 6, 11, 23, 24, 71, 77, 86, 88, 138, 159, 161, 163

environment(s), 10, 20, 23, 31, 45, 49, 50, 73, 113, 125, 126, 130, 131, 145, 152, 163, 165, 181, 182

Europe, v, vii, viii, 29, 30, 31, 43, 46, 50, 52, 86, 160

European city, 30, 32

European Union, 45, 50, 52, 108, 118, 155

expertise, x, 106, 119, 125, 147, 152, 160, 163, 167, 169

F

families, 16, 31, 56, 108, 190, 191, 193, 194

family system, 15, 16

fish, 57, 63, 65, 73, 74, 81

flour, 63, 66, 71, 73, 81, 84, 87, 90, 91, 92, 100

flowers, 65, 91, 96, 101, 102

folklore, 98, 110

food, vii, viii, ix, 1, 12, 17, 19, 21, 26, 44, 50, 55, 56, 57, 59, 61, 62, 63, 64, 65, 67, 68, 69, 70, 71, 73, 74, 75, 76, 77, 81, 82, 85, 92, 97, 99, 101, 102, 107, 108, 109, 110, 111, 112, 114, 117, 118, 120, 121, 126, 127, 129, 132, 134, 138

food production, 68, 76, 109, 110, 121

food products, 81, 129

food security, 44, 50, 101, 114

foreign exchange, 21

forest ecosystem, 44

forest fire, 46

France, 62, 118, 125, 159, 160, 164, 165, 173, 191, 192, 194, 197

fruits, 56, 57, 61, 72, 81, 82, 84, 87, 89, 92, 93

funding, xi, 137, 138, 141, 144

G

gastronomy, vi, vii, x, 105, 106, 107, 108, 109, 110, 111, 112, 113, 114, 115, 116, 117, 118, 119, 120, 121, 123, 124, 125, 126, 127, 128, 129, 131, 132, 133, 134, 135

gender role, 15

general election, 7, 8, 10, 11

geographical origin, 117

geography, 12

Germany, 125, 160, 166, 172, 174, 191, 192

global warming, 23

globalization, 107, 118, 119, 125, 134

goods and services, 135

governance, 2, 4, 6, 7, 10, 19, 120, 150

Great Britain, 86

Greece, ix, 79, 86, 87

Greeks, 3, 12, 80, 86, 94

greenhouse gas, 73

growth, xi, 16, 20, 21, 32, 35, 43, 48, 49, 72, 112, 137, 138, 147, 168

H

habitat(s), 44, 162, 188

health, ix, 11, 14, 22, 24, 25, 46, 64, 68, 70, 72, 73, 74, 75, 80, 93, 97, 100, 109, 131, 138

health effects, 93

health problems, 73

history, v, vii, viii, x, 1, 2, 3, 10, 11, 12, 19, 21, 25, 26, 27, 56, 67, 68, 70, 76, 89, 98, 99, 101, 102, 105, 107, 108, 109, 111, 118, 132, 139, 153, 155, 156, 171, 172, 174, 191, 193, 197

Hong Kong, 125, 166

hotspots, xi, 187, 196

housing, 31, 44, 138

hub, 142, 167

human, vii, viii, 1, 5, 9, 12, 30, 35, 45, 46, 48, 52, 68, 72, 82, 87, 93, 98, 138, 140, 150

human capital, 150

human health, 87, 93, 98

human right, 9

I

identification, 32, 111, 124, 125, 126, 130, 133, 140

identity, x, 4, 12, 15, 18, 70, 105, 106, 107,
  108, 109, 111, 112, 113, 114, 115, 116,
  118, 119, 123, 124, 125, 126, 127, 129,
  130, 131, 132, 134
illiteracy, 19, 138
income, x, 106, 107, 108, 109, 112
independence, xi, 5, 7, 12, 14, 139, 141,
  143, 169, 188, 190, 193
India, vi, xi, 2, 4, 5, 6, 7, 9, 10, 11, 12, 26,
  27, 72, 125, 138, 149, 160, 166, 169,
  171, 172, 174, 176, 187, 188, 189, 190,
  191, 193, 194, 195, 196, 197
Indonesia, 149, 196
Indus Valley, 3, 12
industrial revolution, 5
industrialization, 118, 138
industries, 8, 109, 140, 144, 152, 155, 168
industry, 20, 73, 115, 134, 140, 141, 142,
  143, 146, 147, 148, 151, 157, 159, 160
infrastructure, 4, 6, 16, 19, 24, 45, 109, 129
ingredients, 56, 62, 63, 65, 68, 70, 73, 80,
  81, 85, 89, 91, 92, 112
insects, 72, 75, 77
institutions, x, xi, 9, 13, 25, 64, 106, 110,
  113, 117, 127, 129, 130, 133, 137, 138,
  145, 155, 166
intangible heritage and Minas Gerais, 106
integration, 4, 13, 15, 110, 128, 131
investment(s), 21, 68, 125
investors, 20, 21, 125, 127, 140
Iran, 2, 126, 160, 165, 168, 184, 196
Islam, 3, 12, 13, 14, 139, 180
Islamabad, 1, 2, 6
Islamic state, 15
issues, viii, 1, 6, 14, 19, 22, 77, 131, 134,
  138, 158, 165
Italy, v, vii, ix, 50, 55, 59, 60, 62, 63, 65,
  67, 69, 71, 75, 77, 79, 80, 81, 82, 84, 88,
  89, 92, 98, 101, 102, 126, 160, 171, 177,
  194

J

Japan, 126, 141, 160, 166, 167, 174, 175,
  177
Jordan, 48, 160, 162, 165, 182
judiciary, 9, 10, 182

K

Korea, 121, 160, 172

L

land use change, 30
Land Use Policy, 47, 53
landscape(s), xi, 2, 30, 34, 50, 110, 125,
  155, 162, 187
languages, 13, 139, 169, 185
Laos, 149, 196
Latin America, 95, 108, 118, 119
legislation, 15, 113, 116, 164
leisure, 36, 37, 40, 43, 45, 109, 124, 125
life expectancy, 139
lifestyle, 56
light, 61, 65, 71, 73, 84, 150, 151, 158, 159,
  160, 162, 169, 171, 178

M

Malaysia, 139, 140, 149, 196
management, 68, 100, 119, 126, 135, 145,
  146, 151, 163, 165
manpower, 140, 141, 144
manufacturing, 20
marine environment, 151
marketing, 110, 116, 124, 126, 132, 133,
  134, 166
meat, 17, 58, 65, 69, 73, 74
medical, 159, 166
medicine, 94, 144, 157, 166

Mediterranean, ix, 27, 33, 46, 47, 49, 53, 55, 57, 65, 69, 75, 76, 81, 85, 99, 101, 102, 108, 164
Mediterranean climate, 33, 164
Mexico, 118, 126, 164, 183
Middle East, 160, 165, 172, 174, 175
migration, 5, 12
military, 6, 7, 8, 9, 10, 25
mission, 141, 142, 147, 149, 163
museums, xi, 137, 138, 194
music, 12, 14, 16, 19, 138, 145
Muslims, 3, 4, 5, 12, 13, 27

N

nanofabrication, 153, 160, 161
nanotechnology, 150
nation brand, viii, 2
National Academy of Sciences, 53
national culture, 12, 15
National Parks Board of Singapore, 137, 162, 163, 182
National Security Council, 10
natural disaster, 46, 164
natural resources, 23, 31, 47, 73, 140, 169
negative consequences, 19
New Zealand, 140, 166
next generation, 151
Norway, 53, 126
nuclear family, 15
nutrient(s), 44, 64, 69, 72, 94
nutrition, 68, 70, 71, 76, 82, 93

O

obesity, 92, 100, 102
oil, ix, 21, 62, 63, 65, 66, 71, 79, 92
olive oil, 63, 66, 76
opportunities, viii, 2, 5, 24, 25, 45, 54, 110, 111, 115, 119, 127, 146, 151, 152, 155, 156

P

Pacific, 120, 134, 148, 155, 166, 167, 168, 172
Pakistan, v, viii, 1, 2, 3, 5, 6, 7, 8, 10, 11, 12, 13, 14, 15, 17, 18, 19, 20, 21, 22, 23, 24, 25, 26, 27, 196
pasta, 59, 61, 65, 67, 68, 90
pastiera, vii, ix, 61, 79, 80, 90
pattern, v, vi, viii, xii, 29, 30, 31, 32, 35, 47, 49, 53, 187, 188, 189, 190, 195
peace, 11, 14, 24, 25
peri-urban, 31, 32
Peru, 108, 118
petroleum, 21, 23
pharmaceutical, 22, 155
Philippines, 149, 196
photographs, 35, 47
physics, 150, 151, 166, 168, 169, 176, 177, 178
pizza, 17, 56, 59, 64, 71, 75, 76
plants, 44, 48, 72, 84, 95, 164
policy, x, xi, 22, 43, 49, 50, 106, 109, 110, 112, 115, 117, 118, 119, 137, 138, 140, 144, 155
population, viii, x, 2, 13, 22, 29, 30, 31, 33, 35, 37, 38, 39, 42, 43, 44, 47, 53, 54, 70, 72, 73, 105, 106, 107, 110, 130, 139, 155, 162, 169, 194
population density, 31, 38, 43, 139
population growth, viii, 30, 35, 39, 42, 53
Portugal, 29, 32, 33, 42, 46, 48, 49, 50, 53
poverty, 12, 19, 138
preservation, x, 45, 81, 84, 106, 109, 113, 114, 115, 165
private sector, 14, 142
probability, viii, 30, 189
professionals, 113, 133, 155, 159
profit, 98, 109
project, 23, 24, 76, 112, 113, 157
prosperity, 24, 91

protection, 16, 111, 116
public administration, 107, 112, 115, 119, 120, 133
public policy, x, 106, 109, 110, 112, 119

Q

quality assurance, 130
quality of life, 24, 25, 31, 46, 47, 69, 106
quantum computing, 151
quantum phenomena, 150
quantum theory, 169, 171

R

radiation, 68, 159, 160, 161, 162, 168, 174, 175
rainfall, 31, 46
recognition, xi, 64, 106, 107, 108, 113, 114, 116, 117, 118, 137, 138, 165
religion, vii, viii, 2, 13, 16
research, vi, vii, xi, 3, 42, 47, 74, 76, 77, 101, 107, 120, 121, 127, 128, 131, 132, 133, 134, 137, 138, 139, 140, 141, 142, 143, 144, 145, 147, 148, 149, 150, 151, 152, 153, 154, 155, 156, 157, 158, 159, 160, 161, 163, 165, 167, 168, 169, 171, 173, 175, 176, 177, 179, 181, 183, 185, 187, 193, 196, 197
researchers, 69, 142, 148, 150, 152, 153, 159
resource management, 22, 33
resources, 6, 19, 26, 30, 31, 68, 73, 95, 129, 138, 150, 152

S

salt substitutes, 70, 75
saturation, xii, 188, 195
Saudi Arabia, 10, 48, 175, 177, 180

scarce resources, 126, 128
school, 143, 145, 147, 148, 157
science, vi, vii, xi, 47, 48, 49, 50, 74, 75, 76, 77, 93, 99, 101, 137, 138, 139, 140, 141, 142, 143, 144, 145, 146, 147, 148, 149, 150, 151, 152, 153, 154, 155, 156, 157, 158, 159, 161, 162, 163, 165, 166, 167, 168, 169, 171, 172, 173, 174, 175, 177, 178, 179, 181, 182, 183, 184, 185, 198
science policy, 137
scope, 147, 160, 167
scripts, 13, 139
seafood, 62, 65, 72, 86, 129
Singapore, vi, vii, xi, 125, 137, 138, 139, 140, 141, 142, 143, 144, 145, 146, 147, 148, 149, 150, 151, 152, 153, 154, 155, 156, 157, 158, 159, 160, 161, 162, 163, 164, 165, 166, 167, 168, 169, 171, 173, 175, 176, 177, 179, 181, 182, 183, 185
social development, 16, 19, 110, 127
society, ix, x, 3, 6, 12, 13, 14, 15, 16, 17, 18, 21, 24, 79, 90, 105, 109, 110, 111, 113, 114, 115, 118, 119, 128, 133, 138, 142, 153
sodium, 64, 70, 94
South Africa, 125
South America, 160
South Asia, 2, 12, 25
South Asian Association for Regional Cooperation, 2
South Europe, 30
South Korea, 125, 126
Southeast Asia, 72
soybeans, 101
Spain, 48, 118, 125, 126, 160
species, vi, xi, 50, 71, 84, 162, 163, 187, 188, 189, 190, 191, 192, 193, 194, 195, 196, 197
Sri Lanka, 10, 149, 196
St. Petersburg, 120, 134
state(s), 2, 5, 6, 10, 12, 24, 45, 50, 81, 111, 112, 116, 133, 139, 141, 162, 163, 168

street food, vii, ix, 55, 56, 57, 59, 61, 62, 63, 64, 65, 69, 70, 71, 73, 74, 76, 77

structure, vii, viii, 2, 6, 15, 16, 35, 43, 112

Sultan Qaboos Prize for Environmental Preservation, 137, 164, 165, 181, 182, 183

sustainability, 69, 73, 74, 109, 116, 119

sustainable development, vii, xi, 30, 47, 74, 137, 138, 182

Sustainable Development, 48, 173

Sweden, 126, 141, 160

sweet products, 80, 88

Switzerland, 48, 141, 160, 166

synchrotron, 153, 159, 160, 161, 162, 168, 174, 175, 181

T

Taiwan, 125, 160, 166

technologies, 150, 151, 158

technology, xi, 24, 137, 138, 140, 141, 142, 146, 148, 149, 154, 155, 157, 159, 160

temperature, 31, 33, 48

territorial, 33, 39, 52

territory, ix, x, 2, 5, 32, 44, 55, 63, 70, 80, 105, 109, 114, 127, 128, 130, 131

terrorism, viii, 1, 11, 19, 25

Thailand, 125, 126, 149, 160, 196

theoretical approach(es), xi, 124, 128, 129

tics, 172, 174, 176, 177, 180

tourism, vii, x, 105, 108, 109, 110, 111, 113, 115, 116, 117, 120, 121, 123, 124, 125, 126, 127, 128, 129, 130, 133, 134, 135, 167

tourism and Minas Gerais, 124

traditions, ix, 19, 65, 79, 112, 114, 126, 129, 131, 138

training, 7, 16, 112, 140, 144, 146, 148, 149, 151, 152, 159, 163, 169

transcription factors, 93

transformation, 36, 41, 169, 178

transformations, 52, 59, 73

transport, 167, 176, 177

transportation, 48, 167

Turkey, 125, 126

Turks, 12

type 2 diabetes, 101

U

UNESCO, 64, 69, 75, 108, 112, 119, 121, 126, 135, 137, 158, 159, 162, 163, 164, 165, 168, 173, 181, 182, 183

United Kingdom, 51, 160, 191, 194

United Nations, 2, 54, 75, 119, 158, 163, 164

United States, 10, 53, 113, 155

universities, 15, 144, 146, 147, 160, 167, 168

urban, vii, viii, 8, 15, 17, 29, 30, 31, 32, 33, 34, 35, 37, 38, 42, 43, 44, 45, 46, 47, 48, 49, 51, 52, 53, 54, 56, 71, 126

urban areas, viii, 15, 29, 30, 31, 32, 49, 51, 53, 56

urban population, 17, 43

urban settlement, viii, 29, 35

urban sprawl, viii, 30, 31, 32, 43, 44, 46, 47, 48, 49, 50, 53

urbanisation, 30, 32, 39, 44, 46, 54

urbanization, 51, 53, 54

USA, 37, 51, 125, 160, 166, 192, 193, 197

USDA, 88

V

variations, x, 71, 90, 123, 124

vegetables, 17, 56, 57, 65, 69, 70, 81, 88, 93

vegetation, 37, 44

Vietnam, 149

violence, 5, 12

vision, 46, 76, 125, 163

vitamins, 61, 67, 72, 94

W

war, 5, 7, 9, 11
waste, 57, 68, 138, 163
water, 24, 45, 60, 62, 63, 66, 69, 82, 90, 94, 100, 138, 163, 188
water quality, 45
water resources, 45

wealth, 12, 19, 98
well-being, 45, 47, 48, 52, 73, 94, 97, 131
wetlands, 36, 37, 40
woodland, 37, 45
World Bank, 19
World Health Organization (WHO), 70, 92, 103
World Trade Organization (WTO), 2
worldwide, 5, 56, 74, 90, 118, 158, 166